T0383002

The Liberal Arts and Management Education

Calling for the transformation of undergraduate education, Harney and Thomas argue that the liberal arts should be integrated into the traditional management curriculum to blend technical and analytic acumen with creativity, critical thinking and ethical intelligence. In describing their vision for a new Liberal Management Education, the authors demonstrate how a holistic pedagogy that does not sacrifice one wealth of learning for another instead encourages participation and integration to the benefit of students and society. Global in sweep, the book provides case studies of successfully implemented experimental courses in Asia and Britain, as well as a speculative chapter on how an African Liberal Management Education could take shape, based on African-centred principles and histories. Finally, the book argues that the stakes of this agenda go beyond mere curricular reform and pedagogical innovation and speak directly to the environmental, business, political and social challenges we face today.

Stefano Harney is Honorary Professor in the Institute of Gender, Race, Sexuality, and Social Justice at the University of British Columbia. He is also a Visiting Critic at Yale University Art School and Professor at the Theory Tutor, Dutch Art Institute. He is coauthor of *The Undercommons: Fugitive Planning and Black Study* (with Fred Moten, 2013). He runs the reading camp and art project Ground Provisions with Tonika Sealy Thompson. He co-founded School for Study a nomadic collective of university teachers experimenting with co-teaching.

Howard Thomas is Professor Emeritus of Strategic Management and Management Education at Singapore Management University and the Ahmass Fakahany Distinguished Visiting Professor of Global Leadership at the Questrom School of Business, Boston University, USA. He is a highly cited scholar, with fellowship awards from the US Academy of Management, the British Academy of Management, the Strategic Management Society, the Academy of Social Sciences and the Institute of Directors. He was also awarded the Richard Whipp Lifetime Achievement Award of the British Academy of Management in 2013 and the Strategic Leadership Award from the Association of Collegiate Schools of Business International (AACSB) in 2014.

The Liberal Arts and Management Education

A Global Agenda for Change

Stefano Harney

University of British Columbia

Howard Thomas

Questrom School of Business Boston University, Singapore Management University

CAMBRIDGE
UNIVERSITY PRESS

CAMBRIDGE
UNIVERSITY PRESS

University Printing House, Cambridge CB2 8BS, United Kingdom

One Liberty Plaza, 20th Floor, New York, NY 10006, USA

477 Williamstown Road, Port Melbourne, VIC 3207, Australia

314–321, 3rd Floor, Plot 3, Splendor Forum, Jasola District Centre,
New Delhi – 110025, India

79 Anson Road, #06-04/06, Singapore 079906

Cambridge University Press is part of the University of Cambridge.

It furthers the University's mission by disseminating knowledge in the
pursuit of education, learning, and research at the highest international
levels of excellence.

www.cambridge.org
Information on this title: www.cambridge.org/9781108473156
DOI: 10.1017/9781108561839

First published 2020

Printed in the United Kingdom by TJ International Ltd, Padstow Cornwall

A catalogue record for this publication is available from the British Library.

Library of Congress Cataloging-in-Publication Data
Names: Harney, Stefano, 1962- author. | Thomas, Howard, 1943- author.
Title: The liberal arts and management education : a global agenda for
change / Stefano Harney, Howard Thomas.
Description: Cambridge, United Kingdom ; New York, NY : Cambridge
University Press, 2019 | Includes bibliographical references and index.
Identifiers: LCCN 2019036048 | ISBN 9781108473156 (hardback) | ISBN
9781108561839 (ebook)
Subjects: LCSH: Business education--Curricula. | Management--Study and
teaching (Higher) | Humanities--Study and teaching (Higher)
Classification: LCC HF1106 .T56 2019 | DDC 650.071/1--dc23
LC record available at https://lccn.loc.gov/2019036048

ISBN 978-1-108-47315-6 Hardback

Oh my body, make me always a man who questions!

Frantz Fanon

A good traveller has no fixed plans
and is not intent upon arriving.
A good artist lets his intuition
lead him wherever it wants.
A good scientist has freed himself of concepts
and keeps his mind open to what is.

Lao Tze

Contents

Preface

By most standards, and despite many criticisms, business and management schools have been one of the major success stories of global higher education, particularly over the last fifty years. The AACSB (Association for the Advancement of Collegiate Schools of Business) estimates that there are around 13,000 institutions globally offering business degrees (Peters, Smith & Thomas, 2018). This is probably a lower estimate of the true number.

As a consequence, it is important at the outset to track the evolution of business schools from a historical perspective. The phases in the evolution of management education can be clearly identified and mapped (see Peters, Smith & Thomas, 2018; Thomas, Lorange & Sheth, 2013).

First, in the 1800s to early 1900s, often called the 'trade school' era, early management educators sought to develop a responsible, reflective and insightful managerial cadre acting as professional stewards of an organisation's resources; this was envisaged by Joseph Wharton, in his founding of the Wharton School in the University of Pennsylvania in 1881.

Second, the period until the 1950s was one in which there were clearly defined national schools, mainly in the United States, and the AACSB was founded in 1916. Nobel laureate Herbert Simon called this period the 'wasteland of vocationalism'. Khurana (2007) adds that in the United States in the mid-1950s only 150 universities offered business degrees, representing the majority of such degrees worldwide.

Third, path-breaking foundation studies occurred from 1960 to 1990, namely the Gordon and Howell reports, which promoted the development of a golden age of US business schools. The schools were encouraged through grants from the Ford Foundation and Carnegie Foundation to professionalise and strengthen management education; hire faculty with doctorates; produce high-quality publications; adopt a research philosophy of logical positivism; study quantitative methods and behavioural science; and, although not directly stated, have an anti-communist, pro-capitalist style. These reports, in turn, promoted extraordinary growth in business education degrees globally.

Fourth, there was the advent and storm of the rankings from around 1990, which heralded the dawn of a new era that saw business schools as businesses. The rules of their metrics game were framed by the foundation studies and enshrined in paradigms and models such as the MBA, which had already been widely developed. The rankings era also emboldened European business schools to develop their own identity and their own business models, and schools like LBS, INSEAD and IMD became globally recognised as leading European role models (Fragueiro & Thomas, 2011).

Fifth, since about 2005, we witnessed the emergence of business education models from developing economies such as China, India and other Asian/Latin American economies, reflecting their geographical, contextual and cultural identities. Further, following the global financial crisis, we have seen a period of significant adaptation of business school models, reflecting the impact of the financial crisis and the resulting increasingly complex and volatile political, social and global economic environments.

Yet, in the face of the undoubted success of business schools, we recognise, as Khurana clearly argues, that business schools have become hired hands' of business and have abandoned goals of developing professional managers. We believe that many of the criticisms exemplified in Parker's book (2018), written from a UK perspective, link closely to the dominant paradigms adopted in the early 1990s following the advent of the rankings era. When business schools became 'businesses', the argument is that they taught market managerialism as the 'only game in town and paid lip-service' to issues of sustainability, social justice and inclusion. In those criticisms Parker would be joined by others such as J. C. Spender (2008) and Chris Grey (2005), who described the business school as no more than a finishing school; Richard Whitley, who characterised business schools as educating managerial elites; and Starkey and Tiratsoo (2007) and others, who framed a business school's motivation as indoctrinating students with a fixation on markets and individualism, thus emphasising the primacy and efficiency of markets and the resulting measurement of shareholder value.

Indeed, Sumantra Ghoshal (2005) argued most persuasively that the business schools, in their desire to become serious academic players and be perceived as legitimate in academia, had been guilty of perpetuating and teaching 'amoral theories' that destroyed sound managerial practices and produced managers who were advocates of shareholder value and profit-maximisation rather than responsible professionals.

In so doing, they may have contributed to ethical failures such as Enron and the global financial crisis through, among other factors, a lack of intellectual understanding of both the history of capitalism (e.g. the crash of 1929) and the nature of business cycles.

A key consequence of this amoral focus has been that the self-interest of relevant parties has replaced a proper ethical and moral scope and that the principle of trust, central to the operation of market capitalism, has been either eroded or abandoned.

It is our assertion that the global financial crisis was a watershed in the strategic thinking of many parties in the management education field as the core business models had remained relatively static over time. Deans and management education associations have now increasingly focussed on the need for change, innovation and adaptation of existing models of management education. As Pettigrew and Starkey (2016) clearly noted, this raised critical questions and comments from many observers about the legitimacy and impact of business schools in the fast-paced and uncertain global context.

Indeed, the many studies in management education that Howard Thomas (Thomas et al., 2013b, 2014, 2016a, 2017) and his colleagues have conducted over the last decade have confirmed that there is no 'one-size fits all' model of a business school. Schools vary in factors such as their country of origin, their political and social context and their culture and values.

Some business schools have turned the mirror on themselves and have stressed that they have been too slow to take disruption seriously. Nevertheless, it is clear to us that there has been significant change in business schools worldwide, particularly in adapting to technology, digitisation and inclusive growth. Further, and much more significantly, there is important and encouraging evidence from students in both Europe and the United States that business school students have moved on from behaving like customers and acting like greedy profit-maximisers to focussing on purposeful work such as tackling issues of sustainability, inequality and social and financial inclusion; they also aim to achieve a more balanced, holistic view of management education, encompassing all of the key sectors of the economy, namely business, government and civil society.

Consequently, we believe strongly that we need more holistic, balanced management education models and have some sympathy for Martin Parker's proposition that we devise 'schools for organising', which focus on sustainability, social justice and inclusion. Indeed, this is a valuable suggestion. It is clear from World Bank research that the US model of a public corporation exists primarily in more mature countries such as the United States and Canada, Australia, Japan, etc. As a consequence, we should be researching other forms of organisation and corporate life such as mutuals, co-ops and social enterprises, which occur in many emerging markets. These forms of organisation focus on creating good outcomes for a broad range of stakeholders rather than just wealth creation for shareholders.

The challenge for business schools is clearly to redefine their purpose (Thomas, 2017). Typically, in many current programmes students are taught that the purpose of management is to promote the value of markets and maximise their returns at the expense of others.

We therefore need a wider set of perspectives to improve narrow Western models of capitalism. In terms of inclusive growth and capitalism, it is clear that in the ten years since the global financial crisis, growth has stalled, productivity is largely static, innovation rates are falling and new business formation is moderate at best. There is a growing sense that the current model of market capitalism has failed to deliver better living standards for significant sectors of society while creating much greater corporate power. It requires significant modification and change. It appears also that we are at an inflection point in the organisation of capitalism, and the direction that we may take in the future is perhaps towards a more balanced mix of capitalism and democratic socialism.

We note that significant effort is clearly being directed to develop more responsible schools for business and management, which we believe should be anchored around objectives of liberal management education and inclusive growth. Indeed, liberal education models advocate that instead of focussing narrowly on specific management and analytic skills, the humanities and social sciences should be the anchors in broadening the curriculum and learning objectives of a management education alongside courses in specific management topics.

In our view, management education is an important component of first-rate universities and higher education. As long as business is at the heart of a global society, it should be at the heart of a global university. However, as stated earlier, rather than focussing solely on the technical management skills, management education should also endorse the humanities and the breadth of social sciences as foundations of the curriculum.

Therefore, our collaborative work in this volume has arisen from our deep involvement in enhancing the liberal management education model, which is the basis of the core curriculum of all undergraduate programmes at SMU. Indeed, our prior experience has been mainly in undergraduate (UG) business education. However, it should be noted that UG business education provides the largest UG major in both the United Kingdom and the United States. UG business education also dwarfs traditional postgraduate management education. UG business education is therefore arguably a much more significant place to intervene in the education of future managers than postgraduate programmes.

Our collaboration arises from our experience of the adoption of liberal management education models not only in Singapore but also in the United States, particularly during Howard's deanship at the University of Illinois at Urbana-Champaign. We have been inspired in our study by the work of Anne Colby and her colleagues (2011) in an important report of undergraduate business education in the United States sponsored by the Carnegie Foundation and the Aspen Institute. One of the main conclusions of her study is that the liberal arts tradition is in danger of being lost and usurped by a business school curriculum that has become too narrow and technical.

We believe strongly in the role of liberal management education in enhancing responsible, holistic and balanced education at all levels of the business school. Hence, we have spent the last four years explaining the logic of liberal management education. In developing this book we argue that students (whether undergraduate or postgraduate) exposed to the humanities (such as arts, culture, history, literature and philosophy) are much better prepared to develop their capabilities in areas such as moral and ethical reasoning and critical thinking, which are growing in importance to society. In essence, they become much more rounded, responsible and flexible global citizens.

We have enjoyed collaborating on this book and hope that you find our ideas and arguments interesting and insightful.

Acknowledgements

This book has arisen primarily from our broad set of experiences as academics in management education and our continued interaction with students, individuals and professional organisations in the field.

Howard Thomas would like to acknowledge the many colleagues and organisations who have supported his work and research over the course of a lifelong career in management education. In particular, during his tenure as a 'serial' Dean across several continents (including Asia, Europe and North America), he has received support from funding provided by EFMD (the European Foundation for Management Development), GMAC (the Graduate Management Admissions Council) and AACSB (the Association for Collegiate Schools of Business International). In that context he would like to recognise the wise counsel, foresight, generosity and warmth of outstanding professional leaders such as Eric Cornuel, Director General and CEO of EFMD, and Matthew Wood, Operations Director of EFMD; David Wilson (the former CEO of GMAC) and Sangeet Chowfla (the current CEO of GMAC); and John Fernandes (the former CEO of AACSB) and Dan LeClair (the former COO of AACSB and now CEO of GBSN, the Global Business School Network).

There are also many individuals and collaborators who have influenced Howard's thinking and insight about management education. Charlies Handy, Peter Moore and Jim Ball at London Business School; the late Howard Raiffa and Paul Vatter at Harvard Business School; Ken MacCrimmon and Danny Kahneman at UBC, Vancouver; Venkat Venkatraman at BU and MIT; Sumantra Ghoshal at MIT, INSEAD and LBS; Dipak Jain and the late Dan Jacobs at the Kellogg School at Northwestern; Bob Berdahl, Larry Faulkner, Fred Neumann, Joe Porac and Jagdish Sheth at the University of Illinois at Urbana-Champaign; and Mike Shattock, Andrew Pettigrew, Robin Wensley, John McGee, David Wilson, Amanda Goodall, Lucio Sarno and David VandeLinde at Warwick University. Of course, he would also like to thank his colleagues at Singapore Management University, whom he will acknowledge further shortly.

It is also important to recognise the value and openness of the dialogue and debate that takes place between deans and also journalists in the management education community. In the latter category, Della Bradshaw, recently retired from the *Financial Times*, stands out as a wonderful and warm commentator on our field. Among deans to acknowledge, there are far too many individuals to note. However, Howard is extremely grateful for the support and counsel of Michael Page (Bentley), Michel Patry (HEC Montréal), John Kraft (Florida), Andy Policano (UCI, Irvine), David Schmittlein (MIT Sloan) and Ken Freeman and Susan Fournier (Questrom School, Boston University) in North America; George Benwell (former dean at Otago, NZ), Lin Zhao (Shanghai Jiao Tong, China), Ryuji Konishi (Tokyo, Japan) and Hiro Kono (Japan) in Asia; Peter Lorange (CEIBS, Europe), Santiago Iñiguez de Onzoño (IE, Madrid, Spain), Alfons Saquet (ESADE, Spain), Jordi Canals and Carlos Cavallé (IESE, Spain) and Johan Roos (Hult, Sweden) in Europe; Kai Peters (Ashridge and Coventry), Heather McLaughlin (Coventry), Simon Collinson (Birmingham) and Sharon Mavin (Newcastle) in the United Kingdom; Nicola Kleyn (GIBS, South Africa), Nick Binedell (GIBS, South Africa), Daneel van Lill (University of Johannesburg, South Africa), Enase Okonedo (Lagos, Nigeria), Ali Elquammah (AABS, Morocco) and Thami Ghorfi (ESCA, Morocco) in Africa; and finally Gabriela Alvarado (ITAM, Mexico) and Fernando D'Alessio (Centrum) in Latin America deserve special thanks and gratitude. Howard would also like to thank former doctoral students such as Alex Wilson (Loughborough) and Julie Davies (Huddersfield) for their continued help and collaboration.

However, it is extremely important to recognise the considerable personal and institutional support provided by Singapore Management University (SMU). Howard, after his deanship in SMU's business school from 2010 to 2015, became director of the ASMEU (the Academic Strategy and Management Education Unit), which has provided research support through research assistance to this and other projects in the management education field. In addition, the early wise counsel from 'KP' Ho, chairman of the board of trustees; Janice Bellace, the founding president of SMU; Chin Tiong, the founding provost of SMU; Raj Srivastava, now dean at ISB India and the second provost at SMU; and David Montgomery, Stanford and former SMU dean, provided him with the ability to transition to, and clearly understand, Asian cultures as he took his first steps as a dean in Asia. They also stressed the importance of a balanced, holistic management education model embracing general education and particularly the liberal arts. Beyond that Professor Arnoud de Meyer, previous president of SMU, has mentored and given advice in his inimitable quiet but incredibly effective leadership style. His continuing long-term friendship is much valued and appreciated by Howard. Further, it is also important to recognise the support and warmth of the current president, Lily Kong, who is a strident advocate of the principles of liberal management education.

Howard Thomas would like to thank many other SMU colleagues, particularly those in the Lee Kong Chian School of Business (LKCSB), who have supported this endeavour. They include Dean Gerard George, Deputy Dean Rick Smith, Brian Rodrigues, Gregor Halff (now at CBS), Annie Koh, Ong Siow Heng, Francis Koh, Melvyn Teo and Benedict Koh. In particular, Howard would like to single out the contributions of Tom Estad and Michelle Lee, associate deans of undergraduate education at LKCSB, who also are strong supporters of liberal management education.

Associate Dean Michelle Lee is also a coauthor of many of Howard's papers and books about the evolution of global management education. Tom Estad, who is now at the University of Rochester in the United States, collaborated with us on an earlier version of Chapter 2.

Howard would also like to single out the continued contributions of his wife, his very best friend and coauthor of several recent articles and books. Not only is he grateful for her writing and organisational ability but also, more important, for being the strength and anchor for the Thomas family.

Stefano Harney would like to thank his undergraduate students at SMU and at Queen Mary University of London who encouraged and inspired him in his attempts to blend liberal arts and management education. Stefano would also like to thank his friends at School for Study, a collective of university teachers trying to teach differently by exiting the individuation machine. Stefano would also like to extend deep thanks to Jacqueline Khor. Jacqueline was much more than a copy editor. She was a stimulating interlocutor on this project. Stefano would also like to express his gratitude to all of the heads of school who made room for him to think about the liberal arts and management studies over the last fifteen years of his long march through the business schools, beginning with Gibson Burrell at the University of Leicester School of Management, Michael Rowlinson at Queen Mary School of Business and Management, and of course Howard Thomas at Singapore Management University. Gerald Hanlon also at Queen Mary was a visionary head as well as a stout friend.

During the writing of this book, Stefano's mentor and friend, the poet and teacher William Corbett passed. His example of meeting every enthusiasm with a call for more inspired Stefano's teaching for two decades. Stefano emulates him every day.

Stefano's contribution to this book is dedicated with love and gratitude to Her Excellency Tonika Sealy Thompson, Barbados' Ambassador to Brazil, who gave him the gift of two consecutive fall semesters in San Francisco with her, where he wrote his part of the book.

Finally, the quality and readability of our work and written arguments has been considerably improved by the persistence of Julia Greenslade, Howard's P.A., and the wisdom and excellence of our freelance editor, George Bickerstaffe. We thank them and also our current editors at Cambridge University Press, Valerie Appleby, Tobias Ginsberg and our original commissioning editor, Paula Parish. None of them, however, are responsible for the final end product, which we hope you enjoy.

Part I

Liberal Management Education Today

1   Towards a Liberal Management Education: Arguing the Case

This book argues that the road to reforming global higher education runs directly through management education. In this first chapter we set out the case for a liberal management education that is appropriate to the conditions of the contemporary university and the global political economy. Our address is multiple.

First, we speak to our colleagues in business schools. We speak to them with the confidence that, like us, they wish to offer the best possible education to students, and we speak to them in the hope that they will see both the wisdom and the practicality of experimenting with a new management curriculum that is blended and intermixed with vital knowledge from other social sciences and the humanities.[1]

Second, we speak to all those committed to the global expansion of higher education, especially to leaders in higher education because without their vision and support, such necessary but sweeping reforms will not be possible. We interviewed leaders in two case studies who demonstrated that in the contemporary university, such direction from above is crucial, and conversely, experiments from below eventually become exposed.

Third, we speak to our students. In many ways the book is an improvisational performance of what their education might look like, an attempt to inspire and convince them to take a leap into unfamiliar but deeply welcoming waters. But first let us open our defence of liberal management education.

Much has been written on the future of the university, diagnosing management education either as a symptom of the decline of higher education values or as a tonic for those already decayed values. For those who see the disenchantment of the university's mission in its use of a profane managerialist language – most famously Bill Readings's *The University in Ruins* (1997) but also more recently in Stefan Collini's

---

[1] We will be addressing management education's current relationship to science and maths and its possible relationship, including the way a liberal management education might disturb and recombine the 'two cultures' thesis of E. P. Snow.

influential writing about the UK system (2012) – business education and business schools are a pitch invasion by hooligans who do not respect the traditional separation of the university from the mundane world. On the other hand, for those who see the university tradition (and the traditional university) as an archaic and elitist remnant – most notoriously in Clayton Christensen and Henry Eyring's *The Innovative University* (2012) – business knowledge and practices derived from the business world can revive and repurpose the global university. We take a third approach.

Management education is here to stay, and it will remain at the heart of the university today just as the study of religion was at the heart of the medieval university and the study of science of the modern university. As long as business is at the heart of global society, the study of business will be at the heart of the global university. This is neither an indication of ill health nor a cause for celebration. It is a fact. The question is what one does with this education today. The answer to that question will do much to determine the character of the global university and its capacity to confront the pressing problems of the day. We try to answer that question in this book by considering the reform of management education around the globe.

Our starting point is the Carnegie Foundation for the Advancement of Teaching's 2011 report, *Rethinking Undergraduate Management Education: Liberal Learning for the Profession*, a milestone in higher education policy reformulation. The report called for nothing less than a rethinking of management education in its entirety. Rather than focussing solely on technical business skills, management education would welcome the humanities as the foundation of its curriculum, and the two forms of education professional and liberal, would be melded into a holistic curriculum. Thus planted at the heart of management education, the liberal arts would by implication also face a very different future. As we will argue, such a blending would not so much be the combining of two polar opposites as the uncovering and nurturing of the origins of management education in the humanities and social sciences. Even more important, this blend would give management students access to the vast trove of Enlightenment thinking on ethics at the heart of the humanities and to the benefits of holistic approaches to history and society at the heart of the social sciences. Management students would consequently be prepared as leaders of society and not just business, and they would be committed to an ethical planet not just an ethical business. Business schools have long espoused these goals, of course, but the curriculum to encourage this kind of thinking has often been marginalised in favour of curricula focussed on narrower and more momentary business concerns. What we are calling in this book a liberal management education would ground the study of the business world within an understanding of the wider world more generally as is implied in the Carnegie Foundation report.

Yet the Carnegie report, admirable as it is, is far from complete and far from adequate. The most obvious deficiency is its focus on the United States alone. At a time when management education is already global, and growing exponentially in many parts of the world, a focus on the United States not only leaves out the rest of the world but also leaves unanswered many important questions that arise when one attempts to apply this analysis and prescription globally.

For example, how does one begin to talk about and develop a management education based in the humanities and the social sciences in areas of the world that do not have a broadly established tradition of teaching the liberal arts in higher education? Or how would one incorporate the traditions of science and engineering into liberal management education in parts of the world where the study of business has been tied to technical universities? Or how would one convince societies where higher education resources are scarce to invest in a curriculum that is heavily inflected with 'academic' and not just practical learning? Such questions are not within the national remit of the Carnegie report, but they are raised in this book.

Indeed, this book is centrally concerned with the global challenge of liberal management education. Moreover, it argues that the challenge of liberal management education is in many ways the challenge of the global university more generally. It becomes hard to avoid the more general conclusion that the challenge of global higher education is nothing less than to produce global citizens who can live ethically and sustainably while providing material, spiritual, cultural and social wealth for all of the planet. If the stakes appear high, it should be remembered that the humanities and the social sciences themselves emerged amid global ambitions.

The humanities marked the triumph of the Enlightenment over European tyrannies of church and state; their works, still studied today, consist of themes adequate to this search for a new world. The social sciences emerged at the end of the nineteenth century, as Auguste Comte said, 'to predict and control' the progress of this new world amid the challenges of mass society. Management studies was to be the field that would inherit this social scientific impulse in the transition from mass society to global society. But, as the Carnegie report makes clear, by forgetting its roots in the humanities and social sciences and by trying to go it alone, management education has failed to meet these challenges.

Our argument is that a liberal management education, grounded in its own living heritage of the social sciences and humanities, may finally be up to the task.

In this book, we will be primarily concerned with undergraduate management education globally. The Carnegie report distinguishes itself not just in its proposal to integrate the liberal arts and management education but also by its focus on undergraduate education, albeit in the United States alone. Most previous critiques of management education, including the most famous, such as those by Henry Mintzberg (2005), have focussed on postgraduate education, and especially on the MBA. Or such critiques have focussed on the rise of the business school and business scholarship, such as Rakesh Khurana's (2007) history of the field in the United States.

We will neglect neither scholarship nor postgraduate education – they cannot be fully separated without dividing the bodies of teachers and scholars working in business schools. But we aim to concentrate attention on the global phenomenon of undergraduate business education. Business education is changing the nature of the university around the globe, reconfiguring its student body, its faculty, its scholarship, libraries and resources and, perhaps most profoundly, its relationship to business and society.

For instance, the very idea of a university having stakeholders owes much to the rise of business education, especially at the undergraduate level. Previous professional education might have been in dialogue with professional bodies, and universities might have had relationships with local communities (sometimes fraught ones), alumni and government funders. But the idea that universities could calibrate their education to the needs of businesses would be unthinkable without the university's capacity for delivering business education.

In the postwar expansion of higher education in the United States, technical, agricultural and scientific education expanded, but the liberal arts maintained their centrality, reflecting the uneven rise of liberal democratic ideals in that period. Though liberal arts operated on a general principle of preparing citizens and literate and numerate employees, they could not concern themselves with the vicissitudes of national or global economies.

And yet this new relationship has also been problematic, not only because it is difficult – if not impossible – to harmonise the cycles of business or its innovations with the rhythms of study but also because the preparation of citizens risks being eclipsed in the effort. Now that higher education is embarked on a global expansion, such difficulties are thrown into even sharper relief.

The advent of the business stakeholder is just one change marked by the rise of management education globally. In this book we look also at the emergence of 'ethics' as a subject. Previously embedded in the curriculum of the humanities or rendered as rules and regulations in legal and medical education, ethics today floats free and causes some perplexity and anxiety as it drifts through curricula.

Pedagogy, too, is changing under the influence of management education, with the rise of case teaching, a method very different from textual analysis in both its procedures and assumptions.

So too are new subjects introduced in undergraduate education through increasingly influential management programmes. Leadership studies, for example, as well as entrepreneurship and team-building, are now widely required of all undergraduates, or at least available and popular with students regardless of concentration.

The power of management education is also altering existing subjects, from communication, literature and language to information technology, engineering and biotechnology. In many instances, universities are creating special provisions for business students in these already established fields just as scholarship in those fields arcs towards business and management studies.

These are among the important changes we cover in the book. With each of these changes comes the emergence of new educational and institutional dilemmas as well as new perspectives and angles on existing and historical dilemmas. Most crucially, the global rise of management education offers the best opportunity we have to match higher education to globalisation, an ambition begun with the humanities, continued with the social sciences – including its dialogue with the natural sciences – and culminating, we argue, in the need for liberal management education.

The book includes chapter-length cases from Singapore and London and prospects for liberal management education across the African continent and in the traditional centres of business school teaching such as the United States. At the heart of the book are three historical chapters demonstrating the interdisciplinary origins of management studies and the decades of intercourse between management studies and the social sciences and humanities. The point of these chapters is twofold:

> First, they prove the point that management studies are genetically interdisciplinary and thus, we argue, ought to be taught that way.
>
> But, second, it provides resources for doing so and for making the case to students for the true interdisciplinary makeup of management studies.

The research in this book comes from historical research, firsthand interviews conducted by the authors and from our experience lecturing, teaching and presenting research on management education around the globe over the last two decades. The book also offers reasons why ethics education fails – not because it is overwhelmed by other kinds of reasoning and values but because it has insufficient depth.

It also examines the specific institutional considerations in scholarship and pedagogy in implementing a liberal management education.

'A Way Out'

The term *liberal management education* sounds a strange note. Does it refer to some form of alchemy in which the properties of the liberal arts are mixed with the properties of a management education? Does it signal a political position of liberalism inside business studies? Does it perhaps mean a loosening of the management canon, an invitation to learn without having to follow a structure?

Of course, the word *liberal* has all of these connotations in different contexts and more besides. But in what follows we will use this term to diagnose a problem in management education and to offer a way out of this problem for management education, a way out for the university, and a way out for society itself.

The phrase 'a way out' was chosen by Immanuel Kant in his short essay, *What Is Enlightenment?* (1784) (Kant, 1992, pp. 2–4). For Kant, enlightenment meant first and foremost 'a way out' of what he called the 'self-imposed tutelage' or the 'immaturity' of mankind. Enlightenment was a way out because it offered an alternative to accepting dogma, arbitrary authority or received wisdom by, as he famously put it, 'daring to know'.

To dare to know was to think for oneself, to use reason, to seek truth. This audacity to know was what Kant believed characterised the thinking of his time, what came to be known as the philosophy of the Enlightenment. And in a lesser-known text, *The Conflict of the Faculties*, published in 1798, Kant also explained how this might be done in the university and how this maturity of mankind might be achieved but also what obstacles stood in the way of students and faculty achieving this enlightened state of thinking.

For Kant, philosophy, and especially a philosophy that constantly questioned its own premises and existence, was the key system of thinking for achieving the freedom of enlightenment. Kant saw enlightenment also as an achievement of human freedom. He called philosophy in the university 'the lower faculty'. He called what today we would call the professional schools 'the higher faculties'. By this he meant they had to answer to the outside world, whereas philosophy had to answer, indeed must only answer, to itself. Thus the conflict in any education. Students and members of these faculties needed to find some way to reconcile a pursuit of education for itself, for enlightenment, with a pursuit of worldly vocation, which in Kant's day meant medicine, law, or, ironically, because of the politics of church and state in his time, theology.

One will certainly recognise that this predicament of reconciling the lower and higher faculties in the university is still our modern predicament. In today's university the liberal arts have replaced – or in some traditions augmented – philosophy as the lower faculty. From advice by and for university leaders to critiques of the failure of the liberal arts and to Jacques Derrida's famous campaigns for philosophy in France, many have taken up the challenge first presented by Kant (Derrida et al., 1996; Menand, 2010; Miller, 2012; Readings, 1997). But few have examined this predicament where it is most sharp and perhaps most consequential in today's global university, in management education.

What Is at Stake

Management education is the higher faculty *par excellence* today. Business schools, it may be argued, are the most worldly, the most subject to outside pressure and the most involved with life beyond the university. They are also among the most powerful faculties inside universities. Not surprisingly, even a brief look at management education suggests it is the higher faculty most at odds with the lower faculty. But this is far from a matter of mere academic politics or institutional imbalances.

Kant was concerned in both of works mentioned earlier not just with philosophical enlightenment for its own sake. He was convinced that reconciling the lower and higher faculties would produce enlightened individuals who would produce an enlightened society. He saw the way out for students as an ongoing, never-completed project of reaching maturity, as indeed he saw the project of enlightenment in society.

The stakes for Kant were clear. The lower faculty had to be preserved and developed, not only for all students but also for all humankind. These are the same stakes we see in liberal management education.

Many have called for the renewal of the lower faculty in the university and the taming of the higher faculties. We ask whether the most powerful of the higher faculties must only be the enemy of this project or whether, as we suggest, a liberal management education might be the ally of such a project and a passageway between the lower and higher faculties.

We therefore begin with a look at management education and its predicaments, particularly focussing on the way it comes to externalise the project of maturity for students that is at the heart of Kant's project and the conditions and justification that produce this externalisation. We then look at the way management education might take its place in the university community and contribute to Kant's project, and we conclude with a case study in which we are trying to pursue just such a reconciliation of the faculties.

What Is Management Education Today?

What is a management education today? Are we so sure of the answer to this question that we are only disturbed by the introduction of the word *liberal*? Or does this unusual pairing remind us that the content, form and purpose of management education is itself an unsettled matter? Does the introduction of the word *liberal* reveal a certain lack of confidence or even faith in our definition of management education itself? A quick look at the literature on management education will yield an equally quick answer to these doubts.

It is far from settled, far from confident, far from certain. From Mintzberg to Drucker to Khurana, the careers of both the business school and business education have come under persistent and high-profile scrutiny. Any number of uncertainties about this education haunt the literature, even if they do not directly address the underlying conflict of the faculties as inaugurated by Kant.

Mintzberg (2005) notes that management is not a science: 'management certainly applies science; managers have to use all the knowledge they can get from the sciences and elsewhere. But management is more art, based on "insight", "vision", "intuition"' (p. 10). He summarises the practical role of the manager as follows: 'Put together a good deal of craft with a certain amount of art and some science, and you end up with a job that is above all a practice' (p. 10).

In an insightful article on the content of management education, Livingston (1971) wrote the following comments, also quoted in Mintzberg

(2005, p. 38): 'Formal management education programmes typically emphasise the development of problem-solving and decision-making skills ... but give little attention to the development of skills required to find the problems that need to be solved, to plan for the attainment of desired results or to carry out operating plans once they are made.'

Livingston's clear viewpoint is that management education should have a broad perspective, including the skills of problem search and framing, strategising and implementing change. Above all it should not be characterised by narrow, functional specialisation. As Schoemaker (2008) notes, management is surrounded by paradox and ambiguity and, hence, requires holistic thinking and important skills of synthesis as well as insights into analysis and analytic thinking (Schoemaker, 2008; Thomas et al., 2013).

But one does not have to be familiar with the debates among management scholars to develop doubts about management education. One simply has to try to teach management in a university and especially to teach the burgeoning cohorts of undergraduate business students in universities around the globe. Here in these undergraduate programmes, one encounters many of the uncertainties and instabilities of management education amid the pressing conditions of its global growth as the pre-eminent higher faculty.

That expansion has been spectacular, and management education could be forgiven for suffering some growing pains. The pioneering programmes in the United States and Europe were undergraduate programmes: Wharton at the University of Pennsylvania, Tuck at Dartmouth College (1900), and the Harvard Business School itself (1908). In Europe, undergraduate schools of commerce such as Birmingham, UK (1902), Vienna (1856), Cologne (1891), St Gallen (1898) and the French *Grande Ecoles* appeared around the same time.

But business and management studies in the United States subsequently expanded as a postgraduate pursuit, where its split personality as a practitioner and research subject has long been noted (Thomas & Wilson, 2011). These postgraduate programmes assumed a maturity of the student and a previous university degree in another field. However, in the last thirty years there has been a veritable explosion of undergraduate management education with, for example, virtually every higher-education institution in the United Kingdom sporting a business school.

The *Guardian* league table lists 118 such programmes in the United Kingdom in 2016. And today in the United States there are more students enrolled in for-profit business programmes alone than are enrolled in the entire University of California system.

Maturity in Management Education?

Yet while all this expansion inevitably leads to teething problems, it also makes the urgent question in undergraduate management education all the more consequential and all the starker. Is a nineteen-year-old undergraduate student really ready to start thinking as a manager? And even more to the point, will a twenty-two- or twenty-three-year-old graduate of a management education undergraduate programme be ready to start acting like a manager?

Should we be teaching someone of this age and development about leadership theory or human resource management or mergers and acquisitions or the financial management and auditing of other people's money?

With what level of ethical, spiritual, social, cultural and political maturity are we working here? Do we think so little of the skills of management that we believe they can be taught regardless of the maturity, experience and worldliness of the student? Or do we think so much of management education that we regard it as complete and self-sufficient and capable of encouraging 'the audacity to know' as Kant would say?

Or, as we will argue, is it the case that this question of the way out of immaturity, in Kant's sense an education for enlightenment, has yet to be fully posed or answered in management education? There can be little doubt that management education welcomes this engagement of its students with the real world and trains them for action. The question lies in whether we can expect this action to be mature and enlightened or whether instead undergraduate management education leaves students in what Kant called 'a self-imposed tutelage'.

It is worth recalling that management education has long sought to distinguish itself from the liberal arts (and indeed the basic sciences and social sciences) by pointing to its connection to the business world, its applicability, its relevance and its tangible effect. Even if this is sometimes exaggerated and often the source of anxiety for business schools themselves trying to live up to this distinction, there is nonetheless an element of truth to it. We in the business schools do teach very consequential skills. We teach leaders and managers to make decisions about other people. We teach financial analysts and accountants to make decisions about other people's money. And in marketing we teach students to use the words that will inform what others consume and the images that will form the background of daily life for many.

By contrast, teaching Shakespeare to English majors or Herodotus to history majors or migratory bird patterns to ornithology majors does not place upon the student either the expectation or the burden that decisions made upon graduation will affect the lives of others with such immediacy.

Now it may be argued that graduates of business programmes enter into organisations that continue to guide their maturation and offer checks and balances against the dangers of inexperience. But nonetheless, students leaving one of the globally leading undergraduate programmes can expect very quickly to find themselves supervising others, offering advice on investments or making decisions about sourcing and supply chains. At this point, not only will these students be only twenty-three or twenty-four on average, but they will also have relied on a management education to give them the ethical, spiritual, social, cultural and political maturity that this education in many ways may simply have assumed from the outset.

Not only do we put a responsibility upon students in business and management undergraduate programmes in excess of what is asked of a humanities or social science or basic science student, but we also appear to assume that this 'relevant, practical and applicable' business and management curriculum will supply students with the maturity to handle this concomitant responsibility.

Leaving aside for the moment whether anyone of that age should have so much responsibility thrust upon them by universities or by society, we are still left with the question of whether management education is itself behaving responsibly and maturely in the way it turns out these new leaders of men. Does it hold to its responsibility to society by preparing students who will manage others, make investment and fiscal decisions, source products and extract resources?

Or we could go further and ask whether management education as it is currently taught offers not just a curriculum that is responsible but also an enlightened educational experience that allows its students to develop a maturity in matters of ethics, spirit, society, culture and politics or that allows students to 'dare to know'. We would argue that the answer is that in both practice and in often unarticulated theory, the maturity of the student is commonly treated as an externality by management education.

Whatever the unspoken theory behind this externalisation – and later we explore several sources of this theory – in practice, the maturity of the student is treated by undergraduate management education as something to be developed by the students themselves on their own time and to be cultivated through whatever elective course or core courses a particular university has in place in addition to the management major. Or, at least with matters of regulation and legality, they may be delegated to some external policing function or governance mechanism.

Certainly a look at the undergraduate curriculum of leading business schools in the United States, Europe and Asia suggests no systematic integration of the traditions of the lower faculty (what for Kant was philosophy) and what today would be placed under the liberal arts, especially those liberal arts courses that are taught precisely to encourage enlightenment and a way out of immaturity.

One can find stand-alone ethics courses in many undergraduate programmes and courses on sustainability or business and society in others. But such courses are not only separated from core courses on accounting, finance, marketing, strategy, etc., they are also vastly outnumbered by them and rarely, if ever, form a consistent pathway or theme throughout such programmes that would allow for consistent attention to the maturity of students throughout the three or four years of their undergraduate education. If there is a conflict of the faculties today in management education, then the higher faculty has largely relegated the lower faculty to the margins.

There is, of course, some variation in undergraduate management education. It is true that some US undergraduate programmes must coexist with a liberal arts core curriculum. But it is equally the case that unlike in the liberal arts, where a growing maturity is the very purpose of the education, business and management education has tended to see the teaching of business knowledge and business skills as its primary function, and as it takes over in the third and fourth years it merely defers the question of whether a pedagogy based around business knowledge and business skills could itself contain sufficient curricular material for the (continuing) maturation of the students.

In other words, it merely postpones the externalisation. This externalisation has its own causes and justifications. They must be examined, if anything like a liberal management education and reconciliation of the faculties is to be achieved.

Causes and Justifications of Externalisation

Kant defined higher faculties by their worldliness, the pressures they are subjected to and, in his time, the way they had to obey the authority of the professions. In a curious way, though it is a powerful higher faculty, business does not have the same worldly conditions as other professional faculties, with the possible exception of accounting. Parents may be regarded as stakeholders in the education of all students no matter what the major, particularly given the rapidly increasing costs of tuition. But the presence of employers and professional associations is selectively distributed in higher education. Both are prominent in business education, including in undergraduate management education. But while professional associations tend to know their members and their regulatory environment and to offer advice on this basis, the advice of employers is not always as coordinated or coherent.

On the one hand, employers often want someone trained in the technical operations current to the sector, but on the other hand, when the sector changes, they want that same employee to be flexible, creative and adaptable. They will say one minute that they want students with advanced financial and accounting skills but the next minute demand a student who can learn, who has had exposure to traditions of critical thought and who can offer new solutions, a student with maturity.

This is a tall order, and common sense tells us that someone drilled in technical operations does not simply become 'creative' at the flick of a switch, any more than someone encouraged to offer new ideas can be contented with, or even good at, highly routinised, complex, technical work.

Employers can be forgiven for this. Shifts and twists in the economy today are generally more rapid and less predictable than changes in the law or in medicine. But as many have noted, business schools risk looking desperate as they shift and twist to catch these changes in the economy and employer sentiment.

Justification of Convenience

More consequentially for our argument, this has also led to what we might call a justification of convenience in management education. Because business schools sometimes feel condemned to this dance with economic change, they encounter what we are calling the convenient argument that management education encourages maturity by confronting students with real-life situations and dilemmas of exercising power in the real world.

Some of this argument rests on the conceit that sitting in a classroom using artificially constructed cases really does simulate real business situations in a way that stimulates maturity. But another part of this argument rests on the assumption that maturity develops in action rather than reflection, in problem solving rather than problem posing, in seeking answers rather than more questions, in competition and pressure rather than the suspension of these conditions.

At first it might appear that philosophy lines up clearly against management education on this count. But a separation of philosophy from some of its stereotypes quickly reveals a number of branches from phenomenology to praxis philosophy, which are strongly oriented to action, as are a number of specifically moral philosophies.

It is also the case, however, that even action-oriented philosophies reflect on the role of action in thought. They do not imagine that experience without specifically philosophical reflection will be the best teacher. It is unclear where such philosophical reflection on real-world experience would be found today in management education. Indeed, it is difficult to find anyone in management education who makes a philosophical argument for maturity through action without reflection, and aside from a few popular platitudes about the school of life, this argument appears a convenient one for a higher faculty feeling the winds of constant change.

Nonetheless, this justification of convenience does have similarities to one of the three justifications for externalisation we did identify, the justification of ethical sufficiency, which states that nothing more than business knowledge and experience is necessary.

Justification of Ethical Sufficiency

We use the term *ethics* rather than *enlightenment thinking* or *daring to know*, or for that matter *critical* or *critique* because if there is any potential for translation between management education and the liberal arts, it would appear to lie in this term, accepted by both as a key value of education and, by extension, a key value within the maturity of humankind, even if these challenges will raise different understandings of the term. Ethical sufficiency describes what was certainly the traditional attitude but also the pedagogical and the political position in most business schools, though it has been shaken in recent years, particularly after the series of accounting scandals of the 1990s and 2000s and the financial scandals of 2007 and 2008.

Ethical sufficiency is encapsulated in the famous quip from Milton Friedman that the 'business of business is business'. Although this was more of an ideological assertion than a reasoned argument, the idea that business does best by making wealth for employees, managers, shareholders and ultimately society is deeply entrenched in business and management thinking (Meltzer, 2012; Zingales, 2012). It follows from this view that an ethical education means teaching management students to make productive decisions that lead to wealth maximisation in business. This has gone further, especially in recent years, to embrace entrepreneurial activities as being even more wealth generating and in that sense even more valuable to society.

This last point is the key to ethical sufficiency, the background belief that business, above all other pursuits, is in a sense the most ethical pursuit because it produces the wealth that makes every other pursuit possible. Therefore an education that stressed other values would not only be unnecessary but also in a sense unethical for not allowing the value of wealth making to take precedence.

Obviously, advocates of liberal management education might argue that a stronger sense of history or ethics or aesthetics might also lead to a greater capacity for wealth making. But when they argue beyond this point by saying that liberal management education may also lead to a more mature capacity to handle that wealth, this is often received and rejected as a criticism of the ethical sufficiency of making wealth its own good.

Although this most orthodox of positions on business ethics and therefore on management education has suffered some setbacks, it still predominates, as anyone who examines research journals or business schools' teaching programmes will discover. Ethical questions, to say nothing of social, environmental and political questions, are not entirely absent nor is the attitude to such questions dismissive. They are simply not regarded as directly relevant to much of the research and teaching that maintain their ethical sufficiency by focussing on wealth making (Dunne & Harney, 2013).

Justification of Ethical Superficiality

This justification sees ethics as superfluous to management education and is thus the justification that comes closest to articulating the externalisation that happens in the practise of management education. This position asserts that matters of ethics, morality and social policy are best handled elsewhere, or indeed sometimes, with a troubling complacency, that they are already sufficiently handled elsewhere.

Most obviously, the law must be followed and government regulation adhered to in the process of the ethical sufficiency of wealth making. Less obviously, following the law and adhering to government regulation will lead to an ethical society. But if following the law is not enough – and in jurisdictions such as Singapore but not Singapore alone, such behaviour is indeed often considered sufficient – then nonetheless, the issues are best dealt with beyond business and therefore outside the management education curriculum. Government policy or civil society or religious institutions or private philanthropy or family life must address the gaps.

Similarly, criticism of society belongs in a sociology department, and debates about history or science or art belong in the relevant parts of the university but outside the business school.

As with ethical sufficiency, this argument is less often articulated fully than implied in the way management education is set up and taught. And like ethical sufficiency, it has suffered its setbacks and contradictions as a position, regulatory failure being the most glaring example. But most of all, both of these positions have been undermined by the growth of real-world business thinking that is engaged with processes far beyond wealth making and is not content to leave this to someone else. The practitioner journals in particular, such as *California Management Review*, *Sloan Management Review* or *Fast Company*, are full of stories of businesses that do well by doing good, but also with stories of the integration of every aspect of thinking, criticising, creating, judging and enjoying that might once have been thought to be someone else's business. Some MBA and specialist master's programmes to which such journals are most closely allied have begun to incorporate aspects of a liberal management education as a result of this eruption among practitioners. Undergraduate management education has been very much less affected.

Justification of Ethical Suspicion

Why is this? It may be that today undergraduate management education is the most conservative part of the business school in the traditional sense of the word. It may be that this part of the higher faculty is the most insulated from worldliness by the mere duration of its education and its programme integration with the rest of the university. Moreover, MBA and specialty master's programmes need to be attentive to changes in the business world to remain attractive to those with business experience.

But neither parents nor students can put the same just-in-time demands on undergraduate programmes. This is probably a good thing for our interest in reconciling the lower and higher faculties in undergraduate management education, but it is not without its own problems.

Research-oriented faculty members clustered in undergraduate programmes are today more specialised in discipline-based 'silos' than ever and more focussed on succeeding inside that specialty, feeling the pressure to publish or perish. This too probably produces an organisational culture of caution and, more precisely, of remaining within a discipline and even sub-disciplines. This caution and conservatism may insulate the undergraduate curriculum to some extent from fashions and fads but can also lead to what we might call ethical suspicion.

This term signals a wariness that introducing ethics or liberal management education will dilute the expertise, focus and ultimately career chances of research-oriented faculty who will see a growing division between their teaching and their research in leading journals, which, alas, do not share a concern for the lower faculty. Faculty may even begin to feel threatened, afraid they are in some way being judged as insufficiently trained in other disciplines, schools of thought or ways of teaching that accompany liberal management education. This leads to a politics of disciplinary suspicion, but it can also bleed into politics proper, accusing liberal management education of sneaking a political agenda, a liberal agenda, in through the curriculum and undermining the professional status and integrity of the business scholar.

Of course, it is rarely articulated so bluntly, nor does it have to spill into overt political positioning. But liberal management education does face a misreading on the basis of ethical suspicion – that it is trying to smuggle something foreign into the business school, whether it is just sociology or the bogeyman of socialism itself.

The price of indulging these justifications is high, as many have recognised. But so too are the opportunity costs. What is largely forsaken is what makes an undergraduate management education different from one offered by a for-profit educational company or from professional training inside a firm, namely, the university.

Management education is aware of the branding and marketing advantage of an established university as part of its own prestige; less often does it ask from where the prestige of the university, rather than its own particular university, emanates. It is precisely as Kant understood: in the relation of the faculties, the university became a special place, and it is from this relation of the faculties that undergraduate management education draws its reputation but not, sadly, its education.

But what if undergraduate management education stopped externalising ethics and the maturation of its students and with that stopped externalising the university itself? Could management education contribute to the historic mission of the university as what one might call 'a community in the world but not entirely of it' at a time when that mission is profoundly challenged by many of the real-world forces the business school embraces? And could the embrace of that historic mission be a way out to maturity for management education?

A long tradition would argue that the higher faculties, and business schools in particular, cannot contribute to this mission. Even Kant can be read this way, though he never sought to define the university without them. But as subsequent critics sought to preserve and extend the university's autonomy from both state and economy, the view of the higher faculties and particularly the business school became harsher.

Cardinal Newman (1852) himself proposed that professional education should not belong in any university. Newman's principles of education and his idea of the university should be seen as guiding principles in examining the present and future positioning of management education. Newman, who believed in both a moral authority and freedom of thought, argued that simply acquiring knowledge without simultaneously cultivating liberal, intellectual skills would result in a poor and inadequate education. The purpose of a liberal education is to develop those critically important intellectual skills of analysis, criticism and synthesis and to use them to leverage knowledge acquisition wisely and effectively.

Consequently, Newman felt that the university context and the relentless pursuit of liberal education was probably not the place for training and learning professional knowledge. He advocated the separation of professional schools from universities (and included law and medicine as professional schools).

Thorsten Veblen (1918) also argued against the presence of business schools in the university context, noting that they do not serve the needs of society relative to medical schools. He believed that business schools focussed too heavily on teaching the methods and techniques for students to achieve personal, private gain (Gabor 2002).

The contemporary philosopher Simon Blackburn expresses the view of not a few in the humanities. Writing of the Athenian envoys cited by Thrasymachus in Plato's *Republic*, Blackburn characterised them as 'the Machiavellian men of realpolitik, knowing they live in a dog-eat-dog world and adapting themselves'. Blackburn concludes that they were 'the direct ancestors of *blitzkrieg*, terrorism, the worship of the free market and the ethics of the business school' (Blackburn, 2007, p. 34).

It would certainly seem that few are looking to the business school to shore up the mission of the university or restore its status in but not entirely of the world. But if we can now recall the term *liberal management education* not just to mark a problem of immaturity in management education but also as a way out then perhaps, against the odds, not only can management education begin to dare to know, but liberal management education may also even come to prove the critics wrong. It may even come to the rescue of the university itself.

The University as an Idea

Kant's *Conflict of the Faculties* is also sometimes credited with inaugurating the idea of the modern university. He hoped that the autonomy of reason and the pursuit of truth could be protected in the university. In this hope he initiated a discourse on the idea and the purpose of the university as a unique modern institution that would be developed and expanded by Alexander von Humboldt and Cardinal Newman, among others.

This discourse would entwine university education with the pursuit of enlightenment and maturity of the student and, through the student, promote the development of freedom of thought for society generally. This action on society at a distance is still what makes the university different from other institutions.

As Kant made clear, it was never the case that the modern university was to be, in the minds of its greatest advocates, 'an ivory tower' in its pejorative sense. For Kant, von Humboldt and Newman, the university was always to have a relationship to society but one that was effective because of its difference from the rest of society. It was to be a special community, at its best, which protected people from the real world long enough for them to do what is so difficult to do in the real world: study together, reflect together and reconsider together.

It is no accident that such institutions were founded not just in Europe but also in India and China by religions with a history of retreats, silent contemplation and collective prayer. Though most universities have become secular, they retain this aspect of retreat, community and reflection. Of course, the modern university maintains itself as a place of retreat from the real world, of reflection on the real world and even of unworldly community amid the worldly community. It must be responsive, connected and attuned to this real world, its changes, demands and challenges, even if simply to retain its distinction from this world.

Ideally its engagement with the worldly community serves to show the world that the value of the university is its very difference. The reaffirmation of this difference from the real world serves to strengthen the mission of the university as a place for reflection, retreat and community.

But the difference the university makes, and makes of itself, is far from secure.

Writers such as Kirp (2003, 2009), Angus (2009), Menand (2010) and Cole (2010) note that modern universities have abandoned their fundamental beliefs in liberal education and their role as institutions of thinking and learning. Instead, they argue that universities have become increasingly commercialised and have financial goals (performance indicators) as guiding principles in their vision. Consequently, they want university leaders to affirm the basic values of the modern university and more clearly to specify the role that professional schools such as business schools should play in its evolution.

Other writers have noted the way the university's worldly role as workplace or policy shop for governments has also put at risk its special community. For instance, Marc Bousquet (2008) argues persuasively that the contemporary US university relies on a cheap labour force of its own postgraduate students; Rebecca Lowen (1997) earlier charted the transformation of universities in the Cold War.

Kant himself understood that universities and governments could not be entirely disentangled, and he took care to offer a contract in which worldliness would coexist with retreat and the higher faculties with the lower. In this contract he sought an autonomy from the authority of the state for enlightened thinking even as he also seemed to believe that the state itself could come to exhibit an enlightened authority under the influence of such thought.

Whether it chooses to believe that real-world engagement is the only path to maturity or justifies externalisation in some other way, management education does little to take advantage of the resources available to it to complete this maturity with moments of reflection, retreat and common study. Indeed, business schools have sometimes been labelled the enemies of this tradition.

We think this is not necessarily accurate. The obliviousness of management education to the vital resource of the university is more the by-product of its externalisation of their students' rise to maturity than it is any hostility to enlightened thinking or rejection of the motto, 'dare to know'.

However, the profound distance between management education and the liberal arts institutionally and intellectually should not be denied.

The Mission of the University and the Core Curriculum

As we have said and as would be generally accepted, the liberal arts are the modern embodiment of these unworldly communities, though some would argue that Anglo-American philosophy has forfeited such a role.

At their best the liberal arts have both remained separate and been profoundly changed by the world around them, especially in the last forty years, with the rise of new humanities subjects such as women's studies, cultural studies and postcolonial studies, all of which owe their otherworldly study to very worldly social movements and social change.

The longer history of liberal arts education is a complex one. In some ways they are the descendants not just of Kant's lower faculty but also of von Humboldt's organisation of the modern university into disciplines. They also have traces of Cardinal Newman's shift to national literatures as the embodiment of what Kant sought in philosophy and even what he sought in his contract with the state.

More recently the liberal arts have taken on the responsibility of anchoring the mass expansion of the 'multiversities' in the United States while also continuing to serve as a mark of social distinction in private US universities, a function they have had to share with qualitative social science and economy in elite universities in the United Kingdom and even to some extent with law and medicine in colonial contexts.

But whether as an inheritance of Kant's lower faculty or Newman's national literatures or subsequent variations, what persists most uniquely is what might best be described as a way of reading. Whether reading Aristotle or John Donne, the student of the classic liberal arts education was taught to appreciate the loftiness or aesthetics of the text, to place that text in its proper place in the tradition of enlightenment thinking or later of 'Western Civilisation', and to distinguish intellectually between such texts and the more vulgar texts of the contemporary and popular world.

We can, of course, be wary of much of this for what now appears to be its eurocentrism and classicism, if not its formalism.

What is most intriguing, and enduring, about this form of reading is its pedagogical assumption. Because by reading these texts students were understood to be inheriting an ethics, a sense of judgement, an aesthetic ability and a sociocultural sophistication that would later serve them as the leaders in politics and commerce as well as in the arts and culture. In other words, the texts, through close readings, were understood to provoke in the student the development of what today we would call criticality, creativity and analytical ability as well as an ethical, social and cultural ordering of the world.

Such an idea – that great texts contain a 'civilisational' treasure trove of ethics, aesthetics and social or political wisdom – remains central to the liberal arts. Even the so-called canon wars in English departments in the 1980s ended up substituting other canonical texts and imbuing them with a similar power.

Shorn of much of its elitist and mystical trappings, this idea of texts containing secrets revealed by close reading remains at the heart of the most influential form of liberal arts education today, the core curriculum.

The core curriculum is the place most students in US multiversities as well as in large private comprehensive universities encounter the liberal arts. Only a small percentage of US students take the liberal arts, and fewer still attend liberal arts colleges. But millions encounter the liberal arts in core curricula. And as American ideas of the university have spread and become more influential with globalisation, a liberal arts core curriculum, often admixed with general education, has spread too.

Indeed, the idea of the core is intimately bound up with expansion and with the problems that expansion has posed to that idea of the university as a place apart, of retreat, reflection and community. Universities took in new disciplines, new students and new mandates, especially around local economic development and internationalisation, which meant they had more and more secular, some would say profane, connections with the real world. The demands of these connections diluted, narrowed and sometimes threatened the liberal arts as the embodiment of the unworldly community.

The core curriculum, once the province of elite universities such as Chicago and Columbia seeking to mediate between their liberal arts and professional schools, became a mass higher-education phenomenon. Through a core curriculum, what the University of Chicago refers to as a common conversation among all students and faculty about the great traditions of thought and expression, the liberal arts continue to exercise their influence. Conversely, universities continue to assert their special place in the world.

And yet, if management education were to see this core curriculum not as a matter of outsourcing maturity but as part of what makes management education a university education, there are still pedagogical obstacles that must be overcome.

Conflict between the Core and Management Education

As was suggested already in the discussion on reading classic texts, there is a style of pedagogy that accompanies the liberal arts and is retained in core curricula. Part of this style is a close reading of texts. Other aspects of the style include discussion, debate and the Socratic method, none of which is unfamiliar to management pedagogy at its best. This practice of close reading and interpretation of texts does, however, clash with two other features of management education that require our attention.

The first of these is the technical heritage of management teaching. Cardinal Newman's university is not the only evolutionary root of the global university. There is another tradition extending from the French engineering schools of the nineteenth century to the land grant universities in the United States set up under the Morrill Act, to the Soviet academies of engineering that in turn spurred on the National Defense Act in the United States in 1957. This history of technical education was not confined to engineering, though many technical and scientific areas were subsumed under these early engineering schools.

In colonised nations, for instance, another version of this technical education was to be found in the agricultural colleges and medical schools set up from Trinidad to Singapore to Senegal as part of the colonial projects of 'commerce and civilisation'.

In many cases, in both Europe and the colonised world, business schools emerged from within these institutions. In other cases, as with the French Chambers of Commerce, business schools were set up by employers' associations with practical and technical training in mind. The history of book-keeping education is even older, but it too emerged outside the classical university.

The teaching style of technical education was industrial, in the sense that it was designed to be immediately practical to commerce and industry and that it was a 'mass' education prior to the wider massification of higher education. It was understood that the world needed accountants and engineers in large numbers (as well as nurses, plantation managers and a host of related technical professionals).

To provide this workforce, not only was it necessary to concentrate on passing on technical knowledge and skills; ensuring the standards of the training and dealing with the scale of the teaching were often paramount. This led to a style of teaching and testing far different from what evolved in the German, British and US elite universities housing the liberal arts. These schools did little or no research and were seen by Herbert Simon as 'wasteland[s] of vocationalism' (Simon, 1991, p. 138).

This industrial style is also an inheritance of the business school today. Whereas other professions such as medicine and law control the market and therefore the absolute numbers of their industry – and this feeds back to their professional education – business schools remain vulnerable to the temptation of unlimited numbers and industrial teaching on an ever-increasing scale.

The few professional bodies in business are insufficient to control the labour force, and the idea holds that a society can never have enough entrepreneurs or managers with obvious implications for business programmes. Nonetheless, this industrial style developed for good reasons historically, and new technologies are transforming the delivery of this kind of teaching. The point is not to pass judgement on the style but to note its difference from the other traditions feeding universities.

Pedagogical Innovation in Management Education

Nor have business schools ignored the challenges that arise from industrial teaching and other professional schools. Indeed, business schools – especially Harvard – have contributed a major innovation in university pedagogy, especially professional education: the case approach.

Whether the case in business or the case study in law or the casebook in medicine, the case approach has constituted a massive and largely successful reform of industrial pedagogy.

But does this approach represent a bridge to the liberal arts method of close reading and interpretation? The answer must be yes and no. To the extent that the case approach introduces dialogue, discussion and opinions, it offers a point of integration with the liberal arts method. But as some business scholars have acknowledged, the case is not designed to be read too closely. When it is, heroic narratives, or what liberal arts would call master narratives, begin to surface while inconsistencies, ideologies and histories all lurk beneath.

Such texts are designed to be clear in order to set the terms of the discussion. But close readings look not for clarity but ambiguity, contradiction and interpretations that vary according to historical and social position, to say nothing of issues of culture, gender and race. The case approach is not against exploring these issues, but does not seek to find them in the wording, symbolism and implicit positioning of the text of the case itself.

For example, Harvard business cases can be read in just this way, against their intention but suggesting other pedagogical lessons could be learned from them. And this is the most important point: that in the encounter between the liberal arts, or core curriculum, and management education, new pedagogies can emerge. Moreover, it is worth repeating that this close reading method is not the only one in the liberal arts, just as methods in the business school are mixed.

Other liberal arts pedagogical methods include historicising materials, comparative analysis and ethnographic approaches, all of which would be familiar in some form to management educators.

Finally, to invite management education to retreat into that unworldly space to reflect together with the liberal arts is not to invite a silent guest but one who will talk back about the real world and about pedagogy.

To give management education the time to reflect is also to give our students access to this tradition and an experience of retreat and contemplation that is simultaneously a powerful and enlightened intervention in society. In the next chapter we deepen our analysis of liberal management education as a conceptualisation.

> To approach the Other in conversation is to welcome his expression, in which at each instant he overflows the idea a thought would carry away from it. It is therefore to receive from the Other beyond the capacity of the I, which means exactly: to have the idea of infinity. But this also means: to be taught. The relation with the Other, or Conversation, is a non-allergic relation, an ethical relation; but inasmuch as it is welcomed this conversation is a teaching. Teaching is not reducible to maieutics; it comes from the exterior and brings me more than I contain.
>
> Emmanuel Levinas, *Totality and Infinity* (1969)

The central argument of the Carnegie Foundation (2011) for the Advancement of Teaching's 2011 report is that students are best served when they are taught that today's society has different 'spheres', each with potentially different values that may be other than those of the business sphere. Only such an insight will ensure that students have what the report calls 'the critical distance' to become global citizens.

The authors point out that the values of family may differ from the values of government, which may differ from the values of civil society, which in turn may differ from the values of business. Carnegie argues that a global citizen must learn to recognise these differences and develop ethical strategies to deal with them. But, the report authors assert, the problem with management education is that, in general, it does a poor job of teaching students to understand and respect different value spheres. Indeed, the authors' field investigations revealed that many students tend to apply the values of business to all spheres of life. By implication, current business students will make poor ethical leaders as they are unable to recognise other spheres of value.

The report proposes, therefore, to integrate the liberal arts with management education more thoroughly in undergraduate business education, and the authors do find a few hopeful examples of this strategy in their field research, although not many. According to Ann Colby and her colleagues, who wrote the report, the liberal arts can teach students to recognise different value spheres, and they insist that making connections between the liberal arts and management education will assist business students in identifying and respecting these differing values.

In this chapter, we are going to take issue with some of the assumptions in the Carnegie Foundation report. We do this to argue for a liberal management education for undergraduates that is reflective and critical, both aspects being vital. Such an approach can be found in our case study on Singapore Management University's liberal management curriculum in the next chapter.

We also acknowledge the report's insights and importance in extending the conversation on management education beyond its usual borders, particularly into undergraduate education (Arenella et al., 2009; Chew & McInnis-Bowers, 2004). We also note with appreciation the depth of analysis of the history of management education undertaken by the authors and the diligence of their field research and interviews, the latter all too rare among those opining on management pedagogy and curriculum (Thomas, Thomas & Wilson, 2013).

Nonetheless, despite sharing the Carnegie authors' goals, we will take issue with their analysis and prescription. In particular, their comparison of the business profession to the other professions seems to us to contain a crucial flaw.

Unlike the other professions, there are no equivalent disciplines or sub-disciplines that take business as a sociological and historical object of study. Or, to use the language of the report, there are no independent disciplines that look at the sphere of business values *from a critical distance*. Medicine and engineering have the autonomous disciplines of the history of science and the philosophy of science. Law has political theory, including legal theorists housed in politics departments. But business has no such independent inquiry outside the discipline proper.

Several consequences derive from this difference in other professions for which the report does not account. Without a critical lens to put the subject of business in perspective and to place its values within a specific sphere, not only are the liberal arts weakened by the impression that business values can adapt to all spheres, but also the liberal arts themselves appear merely reflective rather than critical.

Without the lens of a liberal discipline studying business from a critical distance as a specific phenomenon of society and history, the liberal arts appear to have more to say about their own spheres than they do about the sphere of business.

In our view, a true liberal management education (Harney & Howard, 2013) must reflect both sides of the liberal arts – reflective and critical – and both sides of the management student – one able to operate ethically within the sphere of business values and one able to step back from that sphere – and using a multilectic perspective, place it in context to the other spheres enumerated by the Carnegie authors. This requires something that is absent from the report's prescription and largely absent from academia itself.

What is required is a lens trained on business *from the outside*, allowing business students to see themselves through the lens of their specific ethical sphere and thus allowing them to recognise the different ethical spheres of others. As the ethics philosopher Emmanuel Levinas (1985) might say, only through such an encounter – through the lens of the Other as Other – will the management student be able to build a properly ethical capacity.

To support our criticism of these shortcomings, we will use the example of our own curriculum at Singapore Management University (SMU), where we are trying to produce what we want to call a liberal management education. These efforts are still in progress, and there is still work to be done. But we will argue that a different kind of ethics emerges under a liberal management education.

When the liberal arts produce both a reflective and critical pedagogy, business students can see themselves through a different lens, embracing a theoretical and practical pluralism. But to put this kind of pedagogy in place requires taking the Carnegie Foundation report one step further.

The Carnegie Report

We begin with a review of the Carnegie report, a truly important document. We can only hope it reaches a wide audience among university educators and especially among business school leaders. The report treats business education with respect, aligning it with legal, medical and engineering educations as part of the core professional education mission of the contemporary university. It thus both supports and draws upon the line of thinking made visible most recently by Rakesh Khurana's well-known book, *From Higher Aims to Hired Hands* (Khurana, 2007).

Carnegie grants business education this elusive professional status alongside its peers, but provisionally. The authors see a difference in business education – one might even say a deficit. In comparing previously undertaken studies in other areas of professional education, also funded by the Carnegie Foundation, they found that the curriculum in those professions made room for what they call a 'plural' worldview. Whether law, medicine or engineering, these professional curricula did not teach their sphere of values as the only sphere nor as the rightly dominant one. The authors found the attitude in the curricula of business schools and among business professors and business students to be more monolithic.

Rather than acknowledging that the values of business were but one set of values among others, these values were deployed to extend to every area of life. Thus the values of efficiency, productivity, profit- and utility-maximising and competition were understood by many in the business school to be universal values, not values specific to their profession. Or, in the vernacular, the report found many business students believed 'you could put a price on everything'.

Other spheres of life, and other contexts, whether family, religion, environment, social life, play and leisure, were viewed through the lens of market values according to the Carnegie field research. However, one of the shortcomings of this otherwise thorough investigation by the Carnegie Foundation is that it proffers no explanation as to why this ethical pluralism did not exist for business students, a shortcoming we would attribute to the lack of an autonomous discipline investigating business. We will return to this topic later.

It should be stressed that Carnegie is not in the least hostile to business education as legitimate education nor to the business world nor even to the values of the business sphere, in their proper place. Indeed, the Carnegie report's criticisms are not unlike some that have been uttered from within the field itself, as the authors acknowledge.

When, for instance, the authors write eloquently about the way the cultivation of judgement is sacrificed to the reassurance of scientific method, they could easily be mistaken for Mintzberg (2005), Bennis and O'Toole (2005) or any number of other critics from within the discipline of management studies (Augier & March, 2011; Pfeffer & Fong, 2002). However, one crucial difference ought to be emphasised. The Carnegie authors apply these criticisms to the vastly expanding undergraduate business degree. They also make the astute point that although it is regrettable that these 'scientific' models dominate both academic scholarship and, in retail form, the textbooks studied by students, this scientific approach does serve a purpose. It provides the 'rigour' that legitimises business as an academic subject on the one hand, while providing, on the other hand, the concrete technical skills, or the appearance of them, to students worried about competing in a complex technical job market dominated by the financial sector.

Judgement as a skill that sees degrees of truth and constant variation in condition is not a skill susceptible to being taught or tested through the verifiable, falsifiable, controllable proofs of quantitative models.

The authors proclaim with a note of discovery that judgement is called 'leadership' in business education, and they are right that it certainly should be. But those on the inside of the profession know too well that there is no part of business knowledge that does not soon become captive to modelling, including leadership studies. Judgement persists as a value in some leadership studies, albeit often crowded out by modelling, prediction and aspirations to scientific accuracy in human affairs.

The authors also write a lot about ethics, beginning by recounting a familiar history of the business school rooted in Wharton and other schools at the time committed to education as a social trusteeship, producing a class of responsible gentlemen, and a few gentlewomen, who would rule with a sense of the overall social good from within the professional sphere in which they trained, whether as clergy, civil servants, lawyers or, in the case of Wharton in the 1880s, business. Carnegie reports the results of field site visits with different programmes; interviews with professors, students and university leaders; and observations of classes at several American campuses. They study how management education currently teaches ethics and social responsibility. They also advocate structural changes to curricula that would facilitate integration between the liberal arts and management education.

Finally, after a defence of the liberal arts, especially its reflective character, the authors attempt to apply the 'lessons' of the liberal arts to two management subjects, entrepreneurship and globalisation, drawing examples where they can find them from among their field site visits.

Rethinking the Report

The central argument of the Carnegie report – that students should learn to recognise a pluralism of value spheres – is also the singular *theoretical* contribution the authors make to debates on management education and particularly to theoretical discussions in the sub-field of business ethics. Business ethics claims a diversity of philosophical or theoretical positions but rarely speaks positively of an existing sphere of values in business, a sphere comprising values such as efficiency, competition and wealth production.

If this specific value sphere of business is acknowledged at all in business ethics literature, it is regarded as incomplete and requiring augmentation rather than consisting of fully formed values in their own right, forming their own sphere. Indeed, even if business ethicists do, rarely, acknowledge different spheres of values, they do so without including business values as a bounded and legitimate sphere, regarding business values as either ubiquitous or not worthy of the term *value*.

This in turn has serious consequences. It means that business ethics cannot posit a *pluralism* of value spheres because it does not regard itself as a distinct, limited and valid value sphere. Its values are invisible or they are negative. Thus, business ethics scholars tend instead to apply one ethical standard at the outset to all situations or to judge one ethical outcome after an action in any number of situations or to cultivate an individual ethics in each student.

In other words, rather than thinking in terms of spheres or using a theoretical lens that is truly plural, they think either of one overall ethic, or an infinite number of situational or individual ethical possibilities.

But the idea of plural spheres of value suggests that there may be values that are not easily reconciled. In this case, ethics is not about holding values or discovering values but figuring out ways to live in a world where others might have values different from yours and respecting the boundaries of these different spheres, including when they are incommensurate. There is, in fact, a philosophy of ethics that supports this notion of plural spheres, though it is rarely invoked in business ethics, despite being derived from the twentieth century's most important ethical philosopher, Emmanuel Levinas. We will return to Levinas when we explore the curriculum at SMU.

Without invoking Levinas, the Carnegie report nonetheless points towards this different approach to ethics and is, therefore, an important departure from the standard business ethics literature. We thus want to re-emphasise its landmark contribution to debates in business education through its conception of plural spheres of values.

However, the Carnegie report proposes to help students learn about and negotiate these different spheres by exposing them to the liberal arts and in particular bringing the liberal arts closer to management education. The report complains of what it calls the 'barbell' effect in the programmes on which it reports. The authors note that field visits found weighty liberal arts courses at one end of the curriculum and weighty business subjects at the other end. In many instances there was only 'a thin bar' connecting them, suggesting it was difficult for students to connect a stand-alone course on entrepreneurship on the one hand and one on world literature on the other.

The authors advocate more exposure to the liberal arts, which will in turn expose students to these different spheres of values, whether religion, family or nation. The authors also advocate bringing the liberal arts into closer contact with the management curriculum. But it is this latter move we find problematic for its unexamined assumptions. It assumes that the liberal arts can be easily reconciled with management education as it is currently taught. We question this because in this encounter some of the central strengths of the liberal arts – classical and reflexive qualities – can appear as weaknesses or at the very least sit uneasily with the more mercurial and worldly qualities of management education.

These power dynamics undermine the Carnegie report's strategy. To explain further, it is necessary to look more discerningly at the liberal arts and at what the report hoped to gain from advocating the teaching and blending of these topics alongside business subjects.

Which Liberal Arts?

The liberal arts are, of course, many things in many places. In his recent polemical book *Blow Up the Humanities*, the well-known cultural studies scholar Toby Miller (2012) argues that there are today in the United States two humanities: one an elite pursuit; the other a form of job training. The first (Humanities One) is concentrated in private universities and flagship public universities in the United States as well as represented in more narrow programmes at elite universities in Europe. The other (Humanities Two) is composed around majors in communications, training for teachers and criminology, among other more vocational uses of the liberal arts.

In Miller's view both share a search for meaning but are otherwise divided by class and institution to say nothing of the students' life prospects. The search for meaning is suppressed in Humanities Two while it floats free of material conditions in Humanities One.

Just as the Carnegie authors wish to bring the liberal arts and management education together, Miller advises bringing the two Humanities together to form what he calls Humanities Three. But unlike the Carnegie authors, this critic sees Humanities Three (or what we would call liberal management education) as bringing the question of meaning to the way all subjects are taught.

A Humanities Three curriculum should therefore raise the question of meaning in every class, in every subject, and it should tie this question of meaning to real, material conditions faced by the students. These real, material conditions are what business education might call relevance or real-world application. In other words, just as with Miller's proposed Humanities Three, liberal management education would raise questions of meaning in management education, asking about meaning in the business world.

By asking about meaning and tying these questions to real-life business situations, liberal management education would give students the lens to see their sphere of study as having its own set of values, thus allowing them to compare and contrast these values, producing a proper pluralism.

In suggesting that Humanities Three should aim its question of meaning at all subjects, not just its own, Miller anticipates one of our arguments: that the liberal arts remain weak when they focus only on themselves, no matter how integrated they are with management education, and no matter how often they are invoked to reveal other spheres of values. They must be used to turn business into a distinct sphere of values, too, not just point to their own spheres. Otherwise the liberal arts will be brushed aside.

As Miller's argument makes clear, the liberal arts' 'weakness' in the face of management education goes beyond the divisions and differences in form and is a material one, bound to the condition of contemporary society. The very occasion of this Carnegie report is the rise of management education not just absolutely but at the expense of the liberal arts. Students are choosing to study business not English literature.

This shift, we would argue, is attributable in part to certain qualities in the liberal arts that, while not weakness in general, have proved disadvantageous under the circumstances. The growth of management education is rarely connected to the growth of business, and the latter is rarely understood as a phenomenon of a different scope and scale than the spread of law or medicine.

Perhaps for this reason the Carnegie report underestimates the vulnerability of the liberal arts to the powerful logics of business and to the full force of management education, especially when unchecked by the critical side of the liberal arts.

How the Liberal Arts Work

What we treasure about the liberal arts is the propensity for self-reflection, interpretation and respect for a tradition of study. These qualities are undoubtedly what the Carnegie authors had in mind when they recommended the liberal arts as the right pedagogy for a pluralism of value spheres. But these qualities, or indeed values, are also at odds with much of contemporary life where productivity, innovation and the management of risk try to minimise uncertainties of interpretation, overcome the weight of tradition and short-circuit the slowness of self-reflection; we might say that the sphere of business is precisely full of such values.

On this question we could do worse than quote the most famous critic of business, Karl Marx, who nonetheless appreciated this aspect of capitalism more fully than most capitalists of his day: 'All fixed, fast-frozen relations, with their train of ancient and venerable prejudices and opinions, are swept away, all new formed ones become antiquated before they can ossify. All that is solid melts into air, all that is holy is profaned and man is at last compelled to face with sober senses his real conditions of life and his relations with his kind' (Marx, 1848, p. 3).

Next to this value sphere, what chance do the values of self-reflection, respect for tradition or open interpretation really have? It may be forgotten that Marx is writing appreciatively of business as a revolutionising force here. But this is also the origin of the split character of the liberal arts. It will be an education for the few, and when it becomes an education on an industrial scale, it will bow to this powerful value sphere described by Marx.

As Christopher Newfield documents in his two-volume history of the liberal arts in the twentieth century (Newfield, 2011), the romantic view of higher education in which the liberal arts protect other spheres of values and produce the social trusteeship coveted by the nineteenth century is a dangerous illusion.

The massification of the liberal arts was very much bound up with the rise of white-collar employment and not otherworldly knowledge. The power of the values in the sphere of business identified by Marx in the nineteenth century grew in the twentieth century and exploded with globalisation.

Though the liberal arts responded to globalisation by introducing world literature or the recovery of Asian philosophy or ramping up language study abroad, such a curriculum was never going to compete with the globalising value sphere of business.

But because management education represents this powerful economic discourse on globalisation, it has often eclipsed any global approach to the liberal arts.

The overwhelming discourse of globalisation as a business phenomenon meant that to study globalisation was to study business and often to study its values without fully acknowledging them or asking about their meaning. Globalisation is said to be about free trade, competition, new products, new services and renewed entrepreneurship. Other kinds of globalisation – globalisation of environmental concerns, for example, or human rights concepts or spiritual revivals in the search for meaning – put forward through the liberal arts were often overpowered by this economic globalisation.

The Reflective and the Critical

The authors are not wrong therefore to desire liberal arts that foster a quest for meaning in a globalised world, even if such reflection sits uncomfortably under the pressures of the business sphere, where many would acknowledge the importance of judgement but few would take the time to study it.

The liberal arts are indeed the right pedagogy for such reflection. For example, one of the very first lessons one learns in art history is the relationship between art and artifice, particularly through perspectival critique in Renaissance painting but also from the study of the Impressionists or Modernism or indeed Conceptual Art. The visual arts draw our attention to what is artificial about them, to the way they pretend to be what they are not and cannot be. 'The scene is not real.' It is a picture. It is therefore a form of self-reflection, of turning inward, of placing the subject and object, and creating distance between subject and object, representation and represented. To study art is to enter into a sphere of human endeavour that always foregrounds reflection, from the portrait through to the abstraction, where something or someone looks back. This is also the case with literature – when it talks back.

And, of course, what separates literature from business case writing is not that one is a story and the other is not. Both are stories, and it is not that one is true and the other is not. Some of the greatest works in modern literature, from George Orwell to James Baldwin, are nonfiction. Rather, what separates literature and business case writing is not how they are written but how they are read. Literature is written to be open to interpretation in its very language, not just in the facts it presents. It turns us inward to the way it is made, to ask what is this knowledge made only of words when words do not hold their meaning?

This question is not an ethical one, at least in the first instance; much less is it about any responsibility to the literary or teaching professions. It is a question of meaning and reflection on meaning.

Why study something that is not true? Or if it is true, it so quickly descends into different interpretations that it might as well not be true. So what does it mean to encounter a world so unstable in meaning, so full of different and seemingly undecidable views? The liberal arts at their best have built the moral maturity of students with this vertiginous moment of meaning that Jean-Paul Sartre named simply 'nausea'.

But this is not the whole story of the liberal arts, although unfortunately it is close to the whole story for the authors of Carnegie, who fall into the trap Newfield warns us about – romanticising the liberal arts nostalgically.

If the authors of the report cannot see another side to the liberal arts and place unrealistic faith in their reflective side, this is because of the basic shortcoming in their comparison of management education to the other professions.

Management education differs from law, medicine or engineering not because its sphere crowds out other spheres of values but because it lacks any disciplines about itself.

What Is Really Different about Management Education?

Looking more closely at the reports Colby and her colleagues produced on legal, medical and engineering education, we soon discover that there is a subtle but important difference in the relations of power between the value spheres.

Liberal arts maintain their reflective qualities when integrated in these professional spheres but also assert a more powerful quality, a critical quality that focusses not just on re-evaluating their own knowledge and their own object, as is common in the arts and literature. Some of these liberal arts disciplines are aimed squarely at re-assessing and judging the spheres of law, medicine and engineering. For medicine and engineering the development of the disciplines of the history of science, the philosophy of science and the sociology of science (or science studies) means that independent, liberal arts disciplines look at the same object as medical or engineering education but maintain a critical distance.

After Critical Legal Studies failed to maintain this internal disciplinary distance, legal education had only political theory to contribute (at arm's length) to its concerns. Yet, as the recent return of Schmittian legal theory in Europe (Mouffe, 1999) and Arendtian legal theory in the United States attests (Young-Bruehl, 2009), legal political theory continues to contribute to viewing the law as an artificial, man-made object in historical and sociological contexts, not just a body of professional practices and precedents.

But business has no such disciplinary 'other', no liberal arts discipline devoted to scrutinising it. Certainly individual business scholars might investigate philosophy, history or sociology as a way to view the knowledge object of business. But one could not say that any such discipline exists.

Business history is certainly not the same as the history of business knowledge, and it is rare to find a text interested in placing such history in the context of the societal or intellectual history of the moment rather than simply in the history of business thought or life spans of companies.

The Critical Management Studies (CMS) movement may offer some useful insights, but it remains firmly inside the discipline of management and functions very differently from the liberal arts of philosophy, history or even sociology (French & Grey, 1996). It is perhaps most surprising that there is no sociology of business knowledge similar to the study of laboratories in science studies, certainly not as a consistent discipline or sub-discipline.

There is little history of business that is not simply business history, and there is little philosophy of business knowledge interested in placing this knowledge in a philosophical context or in a history of social, political and economic thought rather than trying to place more philosophy in business. In other words, the liberal arts do not play that powerful critical function reinforced by distinct and autonomous disciplines and sub-disciplines that they are able to play in other professional education.

There is no one studying the way business has 'produced its own object', to use Michel Foucault's (2002) famous formulation. As a result, the liberal arts cannot make business 'strange' by viewing it from a distance, and consequently it fails to show itself as a specific sphere with specific values to be negotiated, not assumed or ignored.

If the liberal arts cannot turn business into an object, they cannot provide the lens for business to see itself as a specific sphere nor therefore can they help to constitute that pluralism of spheres that the Carnegie report advocates. To use another of Foucault's concepts, without critical scrutiny from the liberal arts, business is 'normalised'; its sphere remains invisible, and its values become either non-values or everyone's values. What is blocked is the possibility of a different ethics, where ethics is not the values you hold but your ability to recognise the values of others.

Ethics of Difference

The reason we focus on the ethical philosophy of Emmanuel Levinas is that his philosophy addresses very directly one of the main complaints of the Carnegie Foundation's report. His philosophy also best describes the way we are attempting to teach our students ethics at SMU.

Levinas approaches ethics differently from much of the Western philosophical tradition. Although his work potentially has much in common with Eastern philosophy, Levinas, unlike Martin Heidegger, one of his most important predecessors, shows little interest in or knowledge of Eastern philosophy and sadly little respect for it. Nonetheless, his conception of ethics has as much to do with Eastern philosophy as with the ethical tradition of thought in Europe from which he was attempting to break.

In particular, Levinas did not believe in the notion, going back to St Augustine, that we have an interiority waiting to be discovered, and as we discover this interiority we develop an ethical view of the world or indeed seek one out to give us an explanation of what we have found in ourselves.

Levinas believed that our interiority was undeveloped and only became developed when we encountered – that is, recognised – the other person, as other from us, as different, as not just a version of us or a reflection of us. We then have to figure out how to deal with someone who might have different interests, desires and goals. And the rules we constantly develop and revise for this purpose are what Levinas calls ethics. In other words, ethics develops between two people, not inside ourselves. And it never finishes developing and must be revised in every new encounter with the other, with someone else.

Seeing someone and not recognising him or her as other, as having his or her own being not reducible to oneself is not just unethical; it also prevents one from developing an ethics. Seeing someone and recognising that he or she is different from oneself, and that his or her values are potentially different, too, forces one to develop a way to live with the other. This process of learning to live with the other who is truly different and not just a version of oneself to be assimilated or translated into one's own values is the beginning of ethics for Levinas. There is, of course, more to Levinas, and we have had to summarise his position somewhat brutally. But we will argue that this model of ethics not only suits business education. It is also at work in the example of SMU.

A Unique Institution

Like the universities visited and studied by the Carnegie team, SMU has in recent years had to contend with what that team calls the 'bar-bell' effect, two weighty areas with only the thinnest connection – core curriculum at one end and a majors curriculum at the other, at least in the minds of the students and probably a few professors too. But there is also something different about the core curriculum at SMU from those universities in the United States visited by Carnegie.

SMU has no liberal arts faculty; it is a university composed primarily of professional schools – law, business, accounting, information systems and economics. The social science school focusses increasingly on policy and quantitative research, moving it close to the methods of the professions.

One might jump to the conclusion that trying to run a core curriculum without a liberal arts faculty would be a disadvantage. One might say too that the problem of the barbell is compounded by the heavy weights of professional education at one end and light weights of piece-meal liberal arts courses at the other end of the long thin bar, making this education unbalanced and unwieldy for the students, as well as only thinly connected.

However, as we practise it as SMU, we have tried to turn a potential weakness into a new strength. We do this by addressing the difference between business as a professional education and the other professions, a difference neglected by Carnegie.

Our liberal management education attempts to keep both sides of the liberal arts in focus, raising questions of meaning in the liberal arts and in management education. We promote a form of learning that helps students understand different spheres of value, including the sphere of value based in management education. Students thus encounter other values as other, rather than simply as more aspects of the world to be incorporated into the business world. As useful as they might be as part of the business sphere of values, social enterprise, corporate social responsibility or ethical leadership are not what we teach in liberal management education. They are part of the management education curriculum precisely because they can indeed be incorporated into that sphere of business values, precisely because they use the same lens. Liberal management education is concerned with developing this lens, but also with respecting other lenses, other spheres. We believe the resulting ethical pluralism helps our students grow to maturity.

But how do we keep the liberal arts from being absorbed by business, from becoming overwhelmed by business values in a curriculum that after all faces all the pressures the Carnegie Foundation report rightly enumerates after studying the business schools it visited? We direct the critical faculty of the liberal arts towards the sphere of business. For students to grasp their values as specific, they must also comprehend through critical thinking the way the business sphere is sometimes 'other' to those they encounter beyond the business sphere. Only then will the encounter be one that generates a new ethics.

3 Singapore Management University: A Case Study

Singapore Management University (SMU), at eighteen years old, is a relatively young institution, and its founding represents a considerable investment in resources and hopes by the government of Singapore. Set up as a specialty university, it features a cluster of university disciplines: social sciences, management studies, accounting, economics, information systems and law. It was set up without any dedicated departments in the humanities, arts and performing arts or sciences and engineering. Its progress has been little short of astonishing, and many of its programmes and schools are now ranked among the best in Asia and in some cases the world.

Nonetheless, its youth as an institution and the colonial educational legacy of rote learning make it equally remarkable that it should be the site of a bold ongoing experiment towards what we are calling liberal management education. SMU incorporated the idea of a liberal arts–inspired university core at its inception when it was working with a top business school in the United States, Wharton school of business, on the design of its initial curriculum. This university core curriculum was designed to offer a breadth of learning to complement the more in-depth learning of each major. The core forms the base on which SMU continues to build a liberal management education. At the time of this writing, a recent blue-ribbon commission is set to add to this goal.

The existing core courses are not outsourced but instead are taught within the business school and other higher faculties. Moreover, they are designed to set the tone for undergraduate management education by challenging students to dare to know. These courses strive for the combination of reflection and criticism that we argue is vital if this curriculum is to fit today's purposes.

Included in this core curriculum is a history of science course – 'Technology and World Change' – incorporating elements of science in society and an examination of the rise of scientific thought. The course allows students to critically address the dominance of technological and scientific modes of thinking. The core curriculum also requires a course called 'Business, Government and Society', which together with a course on ethics and social responsibility, provides students with the opportunity to attend to and examine their level of ethical maturity.

The trick with such courses at SMU is to link them to disciplinary knowledge, whether business or law, without teaching them as disciplinary courses. However, it is not just a matter of their interdisciplinary composition, but something more profound. It is about teaching students 'to know knowledge', as Michel Foucault (2007) put it.

In discussing Immanuel Kant's essay on enlightenment, Foucault suggested that not only was this search for maturity through enlightenment still our vital task today but also that enlightened thinking helps us in this task. We should not just know the world but also know our knowledge of the world and subject this knowledge to scrutiny, criticism and revision to ensure it leads to more human freedom.

These courses must help students learn why they learn, how they learn and how to question that learning itself. Disciplinary knowledge is too often concerned with building knowledge, not raising these deeper questions about whether the knowledge we have is fit for the purpose. SMU's core curriculum aspires to the latter as a pedagogy of maturation for its students.

Leadership at SMU

If we are to explain the success of this experiment at SMU, and indeed the staying power of this curriculum and its evolution and periodic rebirth, we must begin with leadership. Though we can draw many parallels between the liberal management education efforts at SMU and those at Queen Mary University of London, covered in the next case study, we can also mark the difference.

Persistent, multiple leadership at all levels of the university marks the SMU model. In contrast, leadership at Queen Mary was not consistent in vision, and with a few very notable exceptions, it meant that rather than a top-down model, Queen Mary represented a bottom-up model. We will see that this model proves less sustainable in today's university, no matter the locale.

SMU's leadership in the period of this case study (roughly 2012 to the present day) spoke consistently and publicly about the need for a management education that was 'both broad and deep'. The presidents, provosts and deans were aligned throughout these six years (and indeed back to the university's founding) in supporting the liberal arts curriculum requirements and the key courses such as Technology and World Change and Business, Government and Society.

However, the arrival of a new provost in 2015, who was subsequently appointed president in 2018, marked a further commitment and elaboration of the project.

Dr. Lily Kong had been a social science scholar and provost at the more traditionally structured National University of Singapore. But she had also been a motivator in the creation of the Yale-NUS campus, a high-profile experiment in bringing an undergraduate liberal arts education to Singapore, inside NUS campus but set apart in its special mission. In an article penned on her appointment as provost, she signalled her commitment and vision. In an op-ed for *The Business Times*, a Singaporean newspaper, Professor Kong wrote: 'I would like to believe that a management university with a curriculum that combines specialisation with the holistic and broad-based approach of the liberal arts may well best serve the future needs of Singapore. In this, SMU takes a lead. My wish is to add to the SMU curriculum more humanities modules in the years ahead' (Kong, 2015, p. 17).

When interviewed for this book, the then provost, now president, elaborated on her vision for a blended professional and liberal arts education for undergraduates at SMU. She stressed the integration key to this education:

Often we have students saying, 'I do a double major' and what they mean is 'I sit in a class on economics and I sit in a class on OBHR',[1] and we expect them to make those connections, somehow. A good liberal arts education, I think, demonstrates and models the way in making those connections and helps the students connect the dots. So, to the extent that the breadth of education and the connections, and making those connections across disciplines work, I think, the liberal arts prepares students for a much more complex, interconnected world.

In addition to stressing the importance of connecting disciplinary knowledge for an 'interconnected world', the president also stressed another form of integration: duration. Rather than only taking a liberal arts course as part of a first-year 'foundation', as in some professional undergraduate education, the president suggested this more robust approach:

I also think that some of the value of liberal arts can come later. I use a geographical metaphor to make this point ... If we want to irrigate land, [we] need to dig deep into the artesian well to reach the water table for the water to come up and irrigate. And in a certain sense, the interdisciplinary or multidisciplinary perspective is enriched when you have a deep disciplinary perspective. So, I actually do think that some broad foundation, some deep domain and then returning to making those connections would be an interesting difference and more than interesting – maybe, in my view, more valuable.

---

[1] Organisational behaviour and human resources.

The value propositions of such an integrated education – in pedagogical approach and in duration – is spelled out when she adds:

More generally, I would like to think and I believe that there would be business schools that do help students to deal with the VUCA[2] world, which includes the ambiguous nature of the world that we have and the ambiguous nature of fact. All that about fake news, etcetera is about being able to tease out and to be able to deal with ambiguity, nuance, reality fiction. And I actually think that the liberal arts combined with a professional education, a good professional education say in business and management, will reinforce one another.

In the interview the president was well aware of the challenges but firm in her vision and leadership. For example, when asked about the possible reluctance of Singaporean parents to embrace what might look like a less instrumental approach, and the ability of some students taught in the traditional way to adapt to this integrated, blended education, she responded by noting:

I think that the journey to getting students to understand that answers to questions are not just binary [then] that journey I think has started. How well the journey has been travelled is a different story but the journey has started … So if you take the humanities programme in some of the junior colleges, or if you take the theory of knowledge course in the IB[3] programme in the school, in the IB schools. I think some of those programmes really work at trying to get students to understand ambiguity and that answers are not just binary, correct or incorrect. SOTA[4] is another case in point, having looked at some of what they do in the school. I don't say that it's true for the entire education system, pre-university, but the journey has started.

Near the conclusion of the interview the president made clear that SMU's experiment had been, and would continue to be, a special one, dedicated to finding a particularly Asian liberal management education:

'Management is not management in the abstract and in the theoretical, it needs to be contextualised in time and place. Likewise, liberal education, liberal arts education as we know it typically, has had European roots and American presence today, and are therefore taught within those contexts and therefore extremely Western, in terms of Western civilizations and understanding Western cultures, etc.

But liberal arts education as it is devised and delivered in Asia, needs, needs desperately to recognise the Asian context and to deliver that. And the

---

[2] Volatility, uncertainty, complexity and ambiguity, a phrase used to describe business conditions.
[3] International Baccalaureate, a high school curriculum.
[4] Singapore's School of the Arts, an arts-oriented independent high school.

Yale-NUS College, which I was involved in earlier, attempted some marriage of the two, the East-West perspectives. So I do think that in delivering liberal management education in Asia, it must be contextualised to Asia ...

What emerges clearly in this interview is the vital role of leadership in aiding faculty members, students and parents, as well as the wider university community, in glimpsing a full and confident vision of liberal management education. The other half, of course, is implementation. We turn now to an example of such work on the ground.

The Capstone

In her op-ed piece Professor Kong also offered the following remarks:

Integrating humanities (and social sciences) into business education is not a new endeavour at SMU. For example, all business students in their graduating year take a Capstone course, with an option to take a 'great books course' where they study a selection of literary classics and works of philosophy. The course gives students a chance to examine how the great thinkers, writers and artists have tackled societal issues and asks them to draw lessons for their own societal leadership to come. This is a recognition that the best literary and artistic works offer insights and opportunities for self-reflection.

This Capstone option had, at the time of Kong's op-ed, been taught for two years. It was conceived, developed and taught by the authors of this book. But it is not self-congratulatory to say it was and remains the most ambitious attempt at SMU to realise a true liberal management education. It also remains highly popular among fourth-year undergraduate business students.

Up to eight sections of forty students are taught each academic year. This is a remarkable enrolment given the syllabus to which students have access before making a choice. Many of these students have never voluntarily taken a course in literature, philosophy, history or sociology. For the preceding two years of their academic career they have likely taken only business classes. Yet when they review a syllabus promising to engage them with Sigmund Freud, Karl Marx, Frantz Fanon, Simone de Beauvoir, Friedrich Nietzsche, Lao Tze, Zen Buddhism and Mayan philosophy among other topics, large numbers repeatedly, year on year, sign up. So much so that without the able and enthusiastic participation of former dean Professor Pang Eng Fong, demand could not be met.

Thus we might take this as circumstantial evidence that students may be much less resistant to such blending and more open to expanding their education than might have been assumed. Given that student evaluations have also been consistently above the school norm, we could even conclude that the students knew what they were doing when they took this opportunity.

It remains to be explored why other faculty in the school have not shown similar enthusiasm for the course. The reasons may be professional pressure to teach more recognisable courses or perhaps professional training that leads towards specialisation rather than an interdisciplinary breadth of approach (remembering 'interdisciplinary' in business schools often refers to combining insight from marketing and accounting, not marketing and literary theory or accounting and anthropology).

It may even be that faculty members believe, incorrectly in our view, that the humanities and social sciences are either inconsequential to the pursuit of management studies or at cross-purposes with it.

In any case, this book, as we have said, is written in part to convince colleagues otherwise, and the Capstone course at SMU remains one of our prime pieces of evidence for the prosecution. In the first weeks of the Capstone, students begin to encounter the great books of both the Western and Asian traditions.

The course description in the syllabus runs as follows:

We need to put philosophy and the humanities back into the core of our business education. Our future corporate leaders need to have the thinking skills necessary to appreciate the complexities of what it means to be human, as well as business's role in sustaining an inhabitable, healthy planet. The scientific management emphasis on efficiency and profit at all costs can no longer take precedence over human values. These are the words of Dean Johan Roos writing in the *Harvard Business Review* in 2015. In this course we will indeed be putting the core philosophy and humanities back where it belongs, at the heart of your business education, in the Capstone – the summation of your business education. We will examine the meaning of our lives as a way to develop an understanding of our own place in the world, our role as business leaders and our harmony with the earth.

We begin with classic texts concerned with the emergence of modern life and the questioning of the modern subject, reading the three great European theorists of modernity: Marx, Freud and Nietzsche. We will then expand our search for meaning globally, studying the works of Frantz Fanon in Algeria, Lao Zsi in China and Chimamanda Ngozi Adichie in Nigeria. We then move on to contemporary philosophical and literary thinkers including Shunryu Suzuki from Japan and Arundhati Roy from India. We pursue the search for meaning in modern life through a number of philosophical approaches, including the search for purpose, for happiness, for solidarity, for peace, for illumination, for justice and for accomplishment.

We have included the full course description to reinforce the point that students know what they are 'getting into'. Moreover, the course offers objectives that go much beyond many of their other courses:

By the end of this course, students will be able to

- Utilise concepts from philosophy and the humanities to illuminate their lives and see more deeply into their world.
- Examine the meaning of their lives and explore their futures based on prominent theories of modernity and counter-modernity and the self, the subject and the world as found in great works of literature and social theory.
- Think reflexively about their educational, work and social experience as business students, using classic texts from the course.
- Formulate collective and self-determined strategies for living a harmonious, happy and responsible life on the planet.

Can such goals be met, in one semester, even with the foundation students received in the first year or two of their undergraduate education? Final projects suggest such goals are at least within reach. Of special note here are the volumes produced by Professor Pang Eng Fong of final reflection essays written for his sections. Many of the essays glow with self-discovery and demonstrate the keen new eyes through which many students view the world.

In Professor Stefano Harney's class, students confront the classic texts of Karl Marx in the first two weeks, reading selections from the *Economic and Philosophical Manuscripts* and from *Capital*. In the first week, students examine alienation at work. In the second they consider the issue of commodity fetishism. Comparisons are drawn to the way management studies handle topics of meaning at work and in consumption.

Students then turn to selections from Sigmund Freud and are asked to consider that they may not know their own wants and desires as much as they think. The classes also consider the uncanny in popular culture, films, video games and cable television, where zombies, artificial intelligence and new species abound. Later classes will feature Zen Buddhist meditation exercises, feminist psychology and postcolonial theory. For example, using the work of Frantz Fanon, we map Singapore to see the vestiges and persistence of what Fanon called the settler town and the native town.

The course moves quickly and is not without its bumps for the students. Textbooks in management studies strive to make issues clear, to achieve transparent prose and to resolve issues into correct and incorrect answers. Reading Nietzsche, even short passages projected on the board with the professor's help, can be a challenge – not because of what he says but because of the way he says it. In fact, Nietzsche's sense of overcoming rings true with many business school students. But helping the students to understand that form and content are connected – a point to which we will return in our chapter on Africa – requires encouraging them to peer into a world much more nuanced, contradictory, conflicted and emergent than they had perhaps assumed.

Similarly, asking students to look inside themselves risks certain disturbances not normally associated with an OBHR or an e-marketing course. When we read some of Carol Gilligan's *In a Different Voice* and watch several interviews with her, gender relations in the classroom are shifted, and predictably, new voices emerge. Such moments must be carefully curated by the instructor. Nonetheless, both students and professors in the Capstone reported high levels of enrichment and satisfaction overall.

Other Considerations and Challenges at SMU

Inspired and indeed constructed in part by Wharton at the University of Pennsylvania, the SMU core curriculum was based on an institution that was drawing on some of the best liberal arts courses and best professors in the United States if not the world. SMU took on this curriculum structure without that resource. But what the university did have was a commitment to a broad education for students and a tradition of leadership that continues with President Kong.

SMU's educational philosophy has from the outset been to provide an education that was both deep in its concentration on professional knowledge and broad in its exploration of knowledge areas that raised questions of meaning and context to balance this professional training. However, in order to ensure that there was balance and not a lopsided or awkward barbell curriculum, the university had to invent a core curriculum approach that would balance the reflective and critical qualities of the liberal arts.

This approach compensated for the lack of an autonomous discipline dedicated to observing business knowledge by building this critical function inside each course to create the 'multilectic' view the university sought for its students, while promoting the ethical encounter it believed would result. Hence core courses on Technology, or Government and Society or Leadership, Creativity or Ethics and Social Responsibility could not simply draw from the disciplines of business, law, accounting or economics. Nor could the social science department be expected to take on such a massive curriculum alone.

In order to teach technology, for example, as something other than an in-depth subject about the application of technological innovation to business, business plans and adoption patterns, SMU had to conceive of the course Technology and World Change much more broadly.

Using philosophy, history and sociology SMU helps students step back from the impulse merely to learn how to apply technology, a skill they will learn at any rate in SMU's depth subjects. Mirroring the way the history and philosophy of science gives medical or engineering students the perspective to see their field as just that, a specific field or sphere with its own values, SMU helps their students step back from technology and consider the larger question of 'man versus machine', of the mastery of the environment by technology and of the technological imagination replacing a humanistic imagination.

Students begin to see their first impulse – to apply technology to innovation – as a specific desire emanating from within a specific value sphere. But challenges remain. Some of our colleagues teach 'Technology and World Change' precisely through the specific desire of this specific sphere, without offering students the lens to position that desire within a pluralism of spheres.

A similar approach can be taken in our Leadership and Team Building core course. Of course, such a subject could be taught as a depth subject or as merely an introduction to a depth subject. Or if we were to follow the formula of the Carnegie report, we might have students read Shakespeare's *Julius Caesar*. But instead we call on the liberal arts critically, situating the rise of leadership studies in business within wider changes in the business world and society, from the rise of the imperial presidency in the United States to the role of mass media and social media in proclaiming new leaders.

Students see their urge to be leaders in a historical and sociological perspective and view leadership from a distance, perhaps even asking what it means when all 800 students in a business programme want to be leaders. Again, this approach is not yet uniform, with some faculty believing this course is best kept within a discipline, but we encourage others and lend institutional credibility to those who see the value of a reflective and critical liberal arts raising questions about meaning in the discipline.

SMU's course on Business, Government and Society is perhaps the most logical place to help students encounter the Other and 'be taught', as Levinas suggests. An encounter with a sphere of values that is different, and not just a version of one's own values already latently contained within one's sphere, but something genuinely other, provides something from which one may learn. Thus we go beyond the standard stakeholder theories that assume all the values of all the spheres can be organised around the business sphere. It asks students to consider a strategic lens from within the experience of other spheres of value, whether it be the public sector or civil society. The idea is to disorient the central role of business in stakeholder theory and reorganise a properly plural set of spheres, an idea that does not always come to the fore in every class.

Finally, with our Ethics and Social Responsibility course, we intend to give students the chance to go beyond business ethics as it is currently taught. By introducing a pluralism of spheres, a Levinasian understanding of ethics, we come full circle in our curriculum, using the critical side of the liberal arts to question even business ethics itself. Instead of asking students to find within themselves their ethics – typical of the maieutics of business ethics (its Socratic method) – we ask them instead to experience their ethics from a critical distance when it comes in contact with other value spheres and other ethics. Needless to say, this also means that students can learn to concentrate on improving ethics within their sphere – for instance, where it is desperately needed in the financial sector, including Singapore's – rather than imagining their ethics are appropriate for all spheres of society.

Indeed, liberal management education promises to place management students themselves in two spheres – one looking out from the sphere of business ethics and one looking into this specific sphere – and recognising through critical distance that it is one sphere, however important, among many.

Moving beyond the formulations of the Carnegie Foundation's report, liberal management education at SMU recognises both sides of the liberal arts – the reflective and the critical – and both sides of the management student – able to operate ethically inside the sphere of business values and able to step back from that sphere and place it in context with a pluralism of spheres that respect each other.

What are the results of this experiment at SMU, and will we escape some of the challenges faced by the programmes studied by the Carnegie Report authors?

Certainly SMU has something to teach, but also to learn, from the best of what Carnegie has discovered. However, the university's national focus is certainly a limit here. It turns out that the notion of plural spheres of values, as we suggested at the outset, and despite Levinas himself, resonates with many philosophies outside Europe. The Taoist understanding of nature as a sphere of values, Buddhist ideas of seeing one's own value sphere as a device for holding on to the self, and African concepts such as *Ubuntu* (among others) are all examples of a pluralism that goes beyond the European interiority of maieutics.

As we build our liberal management education, we also build a model suitable for the global business school. Such a global business school can strengthen itself by incorporating Asian ethical philosophies that stress humility and harmony with other spheres.

Then, too, in other courses such as Analytic Thought, Creativity, Communication and Aspects of Leadership, our core curriculum departs from the method of the liberal arts while nonetheless aiming at broader forms of thinking based on the principles of a university as a place of retreat, reflection and community. It departs precisely around methods, and insofar as it devolves into textbook learning, it may not be entirely satisfactory.

In the liberal arts, students learn skills: not directly by naming them or studying them, but through the close study of great texts which are thought to embody and impart all these skills and more. Indeed, to extract the liberal arts from their context would be to instrumentalise them and lose the richness of their meaning. On the other hand, management education that names skills it wants to teach could be seen from the opposite perspective as a talking back to the liberal arts, precisely that which management education does when it enters the university of retreat, reflection and community. In fact, that kind of blending – one might say the 'real' blended learning – of liberal arts and management education might be just the formula of a liberal management education.

At SMU, the core curriculum operates mostly as a foundation prior to the majors, engaging students in the first year before they turn solidly to the study of their major. While the core has some definite advantages over an orthodox management education, it is not yet a liberal management education except perhaps in the hybrid points inside the university core, blending elements of management education with the liberal arts tradition.

For a full liberal management education to emerge, SMU must persist with courses like the Capstone. The university must ask: how can core courses include elements of critical, ethical, spiritual, social, cultural and political reflection, retreat and community among their industrial, practical and relevant lessons? How could an accounting student pause to reflect on the tools he or she has just learned and investigate not just the usefulness of these tools but also instances of their abuse? Such a lesson would, of course, be both from the real world, given the surfeit of examples of accounting abuse, and a reflection on how a technical tool becomes an ethical problem and under what historical and social conditions it becomes so.

Or, how could a human resource management course incorporate attention to some of its roots in theories of psychology and psychoanalysis? And in what ways would the differences between brain science and symbolic therapies help students understand human organisations today? How could a strategy course on narratives and storytelling among leaders incorporate history and historiography as discussions of the context of such narratives? How could a finance class integrate rather than separate financial analysis and the analysis of financial crises globally and historically? How could a course on innovation include reflection on the very concept of the new in modern and contemporary art as a way to illuminate innovation in business?

The list of possibilities is as powerful as the combined force of the traditions of the liberal arts and management education.

It ought to be clear that it is in the interest of every university to facilitate the joining up that SMU is pioneering. The more parts of the university enrich its uniqueness as a place 'in the world but not entirely of the world', a place where retreat, reflection and community give the university its special value, the better for the university and its sometimes-fragile liberal arts tradition. Equally the unsolved challenges of rapidly expanding undergraduate management education can be met by this joining up too, a joining up that at the ontological level mixes reflective and critical outlooks.

As this book goes to press, SMU has begun to share its philosophy on the new core curriculum and implement the courses and pedagogical approaches designed to see that vision realised. This vision is driven very much by President Kong, but also drew on a wide range of input. It is also perhaps fair to say that it builds, in part at least, on the concept of a liberal management education. This new core draws on three interrelated pillars of knowledge: capabilities, communities and civilisations. Under capabilities are grouped key academic skills like numeracy and reasoning. Under communities one finds such courses as Economy and Society, and Technology and World Change, all taught with an attention to the Asian 'continental' context. Civilisations houses the most exciting course from the perspective of this book, Big Questions, together with the Ethics and Social Responsibility course cast in global context. One of the innovative aspects of this core curriculum is the integration of international experience and community service such that both are not isolated requirements or resume-builders, but practical extensions and experiments in the three pillars themselves. This new core is yet to be taught but looks poised to transform undergraduate learning and take another step towards realising a liberal management education in Asia, placing SMU in turn at the global forefront of innovation in professional education.

In the next chapter we will suggest that a liberal management education can draw on a rich interdisciplinary, blended history of research in management studies and social sciences. Though the liberal management education of the future will be something new, it must draw on this rich historical foundation to stand strong.

4   The School of Business and Management, Queen Mary, University of London: A Case Study

In 2010 when first-year undergraduate students arrived to take up their studies in the School of Business and Management at Queen Mary, University of London, the inaugural reading they encountered was a lecture by Theodor Adorno.

Adorno, the great German sociologist, was, along with Herbert Marcuse, a member of the renowned Frankfurt School. Like Marcuse, he worked in parallel with management studies and management education in enlightening ways. The students read a lecture he had delivered to sociology students in Germany in the late 1960s.

Adorno opened his lesson to the students with the following proposition: I can either teach you sociology or I can teach you to get a job, but I cannot do both.

The Queen Mary students were asked to consider the contradiction Adorno proposed. Why, for example, would an education in sociology prevent a student in Germany at the time from getting a position in social work or as a government researcher into social problems? Adorno goes on to explain his position. He claims that his critical stance against the way that professions like social work function or indeed against the way society functions would doom students to be either unfit for such positions, according to their supervisors, or unwilling to take them up, according to their conscience.

Needless to say, the Queen Mary students were puzzled. Had they stepped into the wrong classroom? Some of them may have checked to see if they were really in Academic Skills for Business, a first-year, first-semester course. But there was no mistake. They were about to get their first lesson in liberal management education and experience their first taste of a management curriculum completely blended with key elements from the humanities and social sciences.

In this course alone, students would go on to read Simone de Beauvoir, Karl Polanyi, Max Weber and C. L. R. James, to name but a few. Discussions would cover world history, economic history, women's rights and feminism, colonialism and racism, and industrial struggles. All the while, diaries, presentations, in-class writing, and practice in sourcing and referencing imparted academic skills were completed – not in the abstract, through canned case studies, but in the context of actually existing societies past and present. Not least was the skill of learning to read prose that went beyond the simplicity of textbooks – which artificially cut up time, space, knowledge and student life itself, as Gerard Hanlon, the head of school, would argue in an inspirational piece for the *Financial Times* during this period.

Up to this point, we have been discussing liberal management education as an imagined task of the individual professor in the individual classroom (although recent moves are now afoot to alter this individualist approach at SMU). But as many of our examples from the interdisciplinary history of management studies make clear, curriculum is not an individual matter, any more than research is. These are collective endeavours.

In this chapter we are going to focus on one full-scale experiment in liberal management education: the recent case study of the School of Business and Management at Queen Mary, University of London. We will focus especially on the collective practice of making the curriculum. But what makes Queen Mary such an important case study is the integration of this innovative liberal management education with the liberal management scholarship, research and public profile of the institutions, supported by symbiotic recruitment, hiring and retention policies.

In other words, Queen Mary offers us the chance to look at the necessarily holistic approach to creating and implementing a liberal management education. In order to create the curriculum, one must recruit and empower faculty who have the abilities and the interests to work collaboratively on such a curriculum.

In order to retain and promote that faculty, a school must prioritise and value scholarship and a public research profile in keeping with curricular goals. This means taking the liberal management scholarship and public programming as seriously as the liberal management curriculum. In what follows, we will evaluate the success of this case study and the challenges and barriers the experiment faced.

Typical and Untypical Success

Success in the first instance can be measured in the standard way, using the metrics that any business school might employ. During the period in which this curriculum was taught and implemented, and during the period in which the public research profile and publications came to reflect liberal management education ambitions, the School of Business and Management scored historic highs. Though a relatively new and small business school, it tied with the much more established and much larger Cass Business School at City University in London in the UK government's Research Assessment Exercise, a ranking that remains to this day Queen Mary's high-water mark. Indeed, a return to more traditional scholarship strategy saw the school slip badly in the rankings at the next assessment exercise.

Three years after those first students sat down with Theodor Adorno, the Queen Mary also received the highest ratings on the National Student Survey, again the highest ranking either before or since in the history of the school.

But these traditional measures do not capture the full value of the project for students, for faculty or for the university.

Students were exposed to a breadth of learning and skills that went well beyond professional training. They had access to other faculties and schools, to community projects and to public programmes. They developed a sense of being global citizens, the use of critique and dissent to innovate and a commitment to common means and destinies. Faculty had the chance to bring the best of their research together with new influences in business and in the humanities to create something truly unique, true of their singular characters and yet at the same time part of something larger – a coherent and holistic approach to student education across an entire curriculum and an entire undergraduate career.

The university gained not only cosmopolitan, sophisticated, independent-minded students but also a flurry of public programming, scholarship, journalism, public lectures, community seminars and new grants that put Queen Mary on the map in business studies and beyond.

There was a buzz about the school all over London and in much of Europe. People knew something was happening there. One look at the public programme featuring everyone from the French feminist philosopher Luce Irigaray to the great American sociologist Stanley Aronowitz to the more important black studies scholars of the day, Fred Moten and Denise Ferreira da Silva, was enough to tell you: something was always going on in this business school. It might be a residency by a community cartography collective from North Carolina in the United States, or a new student publication on the fees debate, or it might be a community media lab. The sense was that the school had become a hive of intellectual activity well beyond the borders of management studies – or perhaps by reimagining those borders radically.

Curriculum

The basis of all this exciting programming and emerging reputation remained the curriculum. The entire faculty was involved in its redesign, with a core of a dozen faculty members volunteering to revise courses and share the results for discussion, feedback and further revision.

Queen Mary began with a standard three-year UK undergraduate curriculum, one that had essentially been functioning as a service curriculum to other more established programmes in the university that wished to include business skills, as these courses were understood to impart, as part of their students' portfolios of courses.

After gaining broad consensus to revise the curriculum, the dozen faculty members together with some doctoral students keen to be involved in the changes produced a number of core modules: Academic Skills, Business and Society, Introduction to Strategy, Markets and Society, Research Methods, New Media and Marketing and Ethics and Politics. Later Global Commodity Chains would be added to this group and upper-level specialty courses taught by faculty.

Each of these modules integrated humanities, social science and management studies. Some modules were developed by an individual faculty member, some by a team and some by a faculty member and a doctoral student.

Let us take a close look at some of the innovations, starting with first-year courses such as Business and Society and moving on to second-year core modules such as Introduction to Strategy. Business and Society functioned as an introduction to the entire revised curriculum, together with Academic Skills for Business. Business and Society organised its weeks around the major issues facing society and the role of business therein. It was a mostly contemporary curriculum because students would study the history and emergence of these relationships in Markets and Society in the second year.

From the outset it was made very clear that this was neither an ethics course nor a course on social responsibility. Rather, it posed the question of boundaries; where was it appropriate for business to operate and to take a lead and where for society to take precedent? This deceptively simple question soon led to robust debates each week in the accompanying seminars.

Weekly lecture topics ranged from education to health, family, war, the environment, gender and race. Often discussion revolved around identifying how mutually imbricated business and society are, moving on to judgements about the wisdom of this entanglement.

But this was only one element of the course. From this perspective it is clear that management studies blends with sociology, as indeed was reflected in some of the readings and much of the discussion. However, the module also took a different approach to teaching methods. Seminar leaders with backgrounds in theatre, performance and the visual arts mixed and remixed theatre exercises, film and sound, as well as performance studies from their own backgrounds.

The key figure in the course was Tim Edkins, at the time a joint doctoral student with the progressive and number-one Research Assessment Exercise-ranked Drama Department at Queen Mary. The resultant 'mixtape' seminar room drew on both the social sciences and humanities and also formal innovation in the way learning took place. Management students experienced the arts as an immersive experience, reorienting their views on the societal issues of our day and on the weight of different methods of gaining knowledge and interpreting and acting on these issues.

Whether studying contemporary popular music and film or visiting art exhibits in the East End of London, all came closer to students' daily lives than sociology or management articles might. But there was also a challenge to see all of these sources and influences as a whole, as relatable and as germane to the issues.

Introduction to Strategy is perhaps a course not thought to be conducive to liberal management education, except perhaps to include some military or 'great man' political history. But at Queen Mary students experienced an immediate reversal in perspective when they entered the lecture hall. They had arrived with expectations that they would learn to be strategists and perhaps thereby a leader; they would learn to be like the business leaders they admired.

The first lecture inverts these expectations by posing the following question to the students: how are you strategised? This lesson is drawn, of course, from the work of Michel Foucault (1979), the French historian and social theorist so influential in the humanities. Students are asked to consider how they might be the object of someone, or something, else's strategy. The question is both unfamiliar and uncomfortable for the students. But soon they begin to see the point and take up the challenge. How do they know whether their desires, their goals and indeed their sense of who they are is drawn from within them and not the product of different discourses and knowledge areas that produce them?

Of course, at first they focus on more obvious ideological examples such as the way the media creates images and stereotypes of people or the way advertising manipulates our wants. But soon, with the encouragement of the lecturer and seminar leaders, they reach the Foucauldian plane.

A number of deeper observations tend to emerge: to study a subject like business is to accept it as a category and therefore to accept its categorisation of you; to be normal or successful requires defining others as abnormal or failures; and to accept responsibility for your career is first to accept the idea that individuals, rather than society or institutions, should be the first level or the unit of analysis, to give a few examples of what typically emerged during the term. The introduction of the work of Michel Foucault into a strategy module was also the opportunity to place strategy in the context of the human sciences that Foucault studied and about which he revised so much of our thinking.

This course was rendered by Dr Matteo Mandarini, who also subverted the expectations of the students around the usual cast of leaders by suggesting that the first modern thinker of strategy was Lenin and then arguing his case forcefully and convincingly. Some years later when Columbia University Press published the *Factory of Strategy* by Toni Negri (2015), translated by Mandarini's colleague, Dr Arianna Bove, Mandarini's unorthodox argument seemed vindicated.

Dr Bove's influence was everywhere at Queen Mary, not least in the powerful resource she produced with her partner, Dr Erik Empson, called *Generation Online* (Bove, n.d.). It featured translations of and essays on major contemporary European philosophers, especially those studying work and finance in new ways. The site became a kind of sourcebook for the school. Franco 'Bifo' Berardi's (2009) *Soul at Work* would also resonate with the whole project at Queen Mary in uncanny ways, and it was again Dr Bove who brought him to the campus to speak. We will return to public programming later, but Dr Bove also offered the undergraduate Research Methods course. It is unlikely any business school student before or since has been exposed to the range of philosophical issues and the ways Dr Bove instructed the students.

She convinced them of the priority of thinking through these issues before one sat down to imagine how the human world could be investigated, much less investigated using traditional scientific methods. Her intellectual seriousness and commitment to students steadied us throughout those years.

The upper-level course Organisational Change and Development was revised and taught by Dr Emma Dowling, a political theorist with a doctorate from University College London. She was a specialist in the theory and practices of social movements and a veteran of the antiglobalisation movements at the turn of the twenty-first century. Dr Dowling turned the course upside down. To start with, she asked students to submit one sentence about organisational change.

The next week she presented a number of quotations about organisational change. She read them aloud, considered them with the class and then asked if anyone could tell her the names of the organisational theorists they had just discussed. There was silence. She then told them the sentences were those they had written. They were the organisational change experts.

It was a point she would continue to make as she blended standard management theory and social movement theory.

Change in organisations, she taught, comes from below, indeed from the students. It should not go unremarked that her course, indeed a whole year of the Queen Mary project, coincided with the biggest student movement the United Kingdom had ever seen, protesting fees and cuts and calling for student voices in higher education.

Dr Dowling also brought to our attention the kindred work of journalist Paul Mason, and his book *Live Working or Die Fighting* – leaping back and forth between contemporary labour conditions in the developing nations and the history of employment relations in the United Kingdom, mainland Europe and the United States – became another foundational text of the school.

Innovations of style and substance were inseparable in this new curriculum, as with Dr Dowling's course.

We return again to Business and Society to provide another example of true blended learning in method and content. It was not simply merging the content of the humanities and social sciences with management studies but methods too: here, a method from the humanities and the arts.

The course began with the thought of the great literary and postcolonial theorist Gayatri Chakravorty Spivak (2005). She defines the goal of humanities education as 'the non-coercive rearrangement of desire' (p. 148).

Teaching on the module, Dr Gavin Grindon, Dr Erik Empson and Dr Tim Edkins, who was a doctoral student integral to the reform, together with Stefano Harney, devised a curriculum where students would encounter business and management through its expression in art, literature, essays and performance. But in an effort to enact this noncoercive approach, students would also be encouraged to understand this encounter through the methods of the arts, through interpretation, expression, elaboration, creation and performance.

The course sought and found exhibits and performances around London that incorporated economic, business and management subject matter in different guises and emanations. Students were to attend and review the works. Students were also to make films and to watch films as film, or at least humanities, students. When students were shown the films *Life & Debt* or *Examined Life*, they did so with the following questions posed to them:

- What is the connection between the message of the film and the visual style of the film?
- What is the connection between the message and the sound? Why is this important?
- In what ways could it be said to enhance the message and in what ways detract from the message?
- Is there more than one message, and do they contradict each other at any point? Is this bad or good?
- When did you stop paying attention? When were you trying to pay attention while others were not? Why?
- Could you sense any changes in your own emotions or even in your body during the film? Did you tense up? Get restless? Get angry or sad?
- What about those around you? Could you feel any emotions in the room?
- If no one sees the film, is it still there?

Leaders built the seminars around how the students answered these questions about the viewings, prompting work that would happen elsewhere. Seminar leaders urged students to look at art, film etc. not for how they could be put to work but for how they worked on the students and how the students could come to work on, and for, each other through these works. Seminar leaders like Dr Empson suggested readings that could bring out aspects of leadership, competition, management and organisational behaviour, including works of science fiction such as Philip K. Dick's (1969) *Ubik* and works of journalism such as Norman Mailer's (1997) *The Fight*, about the Muhammed Ali versus George Forman boxing match in what was then Zaire.

One later addition to this blended curriculum is worth noting. Both international business and supply chain management received enrichment and enlargement in the hands of Dr Liam Campling and later Dr Elena Baglioni. Both came with recent doctorates from the School of Oriental and African Studies (SOAS) at the University of London. With backgrounds in the interdisciplinary field of development studies, both were eager to extend this principle of cross-disciplinary pedagogy and urgent engagement with the challenges of field sites.

Supply chain management was integrated with a Global Commodity Chains course, placing more emphasis on who controls resources, the sustainability of chains and key questions on whether improved supply chains automatically elevate poverty, improve the lives of women or lead to national development.

International business was combined with international politics to ask similar questions about whether foreign direct investment, out-sourcing and offshoring, and export zones are effective forces for equity and democracy. Questions of leadership in international business were tied to effective local problem solving and the politics of the 'glocal'.

Faculty Recruitment and Hiring

The recruitment, hiring and retention of faculty members able to design such a curriculum and to invent styles of pedagogy appropri-ate to it began under one dean of the school and continued and inten-sified under the next. The first dean, Professor Michael Rowlinson, came from the area of Critical Management Studies (CMS). This open-minded and accomplished historian of business was imaginative and confident in his appointment of new faculty members. Though the eventual project of a liberal management education – or a humanities-based management studies as it was called at Queen Mary – was not a CMS project, CMS was a tributary source and therefore worth a brief overview in this context.

CMS enjoyed an emergence and flowering in the 1990s particularly in the United Kingdom, with later shoots emerging in Scandinavia, Australia and New Zealand. As the story goes, attacks in the 1980s by UK Prime Minister Margaret Thatcher on university sociology pro-grammes and her government's promotion of private enterprise and unfettered markets together combined to produce, ironically, CMS. Universities saw a demand for more business programmes inspired by this ideological climate. Sociology Departments (together with the perennial punching bag, media studies) experienced increasing hostil-ity and even ridicule from tabloid newspapers and university adminis-trators alike. They came to be seen as the disloyal opposition, though they were hardly alone in opposition during the Thatcher era or its aftermath of free market–devoted UK governments from John Major to Tony Blair.

However, many industrial relations experts and sociologists of work ironically found new employment in the burgeoning business schools as well as respite from embattled and squeezed Sociology Departments.

Attuned to the new realities of neoliberal Britain and its workplaces, they soon developed an internal critique of management techniques drawing more from Foucault and Lacan than from Fabian or Marx. They joined an already vibrant community of critical accounting scholars – the key figure here was Professor Tony Tinker – who were already producing oppositional literature that was rarely heeded even as the accounting profession went through repeated upheavals.

At Queen Mary, a next-generation innovator of such accounting scholarship, Dr Ishani Chandrasekara, would be adored by students and faculty alike for her blend of accounting, colonial history and post-colonial futures.

However, CMS scholars generally had an implicit deal with the business schools that employed them. They were free to conduct their research according to their conscience (at least until the net of national research assessment tightened around them in more recent years) but in return were to teach their courses in line with business school ortho-doxy. The first dean at Queen Mary hired boldly, bringing in young scholars with expertise in postcolonial theory, contemporary phi-losophy and politics, many with European and global experience and research sites.

But the dean did so within this implicit concordat, encouraging them to take up standard core courses and teach them according to busi-ness school standards. This proved an unexpected boon for the project at Queen Mary. It meant that these interdisciplinary scholars, many holding degrees from outside business schools, learned their trade. When it came time for curricular experiments, these scholars were well acquainted with the foundations and premises of the management sub-jects they would seek to blend with humanities and social sciences.

The next dean was a sociologist, Professor Gerard Hanlon, and he subsequently appointed a humanities scholar, Stefano Harney, as asso-ciate dean. Professor Hanlon's research was in the area of the soci-ology of professions. Later, perhaps with the experience of Queen Mary's experiment in mind, he wrote a highly original and damning book on some of the founders of management theory, *The Dark Side of Management* (Hanlon, 2016). In any case, with his bold leadership, the curricular project really took shape alongside the interdisciplinary scholarship and burgeoning public programming.

Hanlon and Harney continued to seek out scholars from the social sciences and humanities to complement existing management and CMS scholars, creating a blend of expertise fit for purpose. Three recruit-ments came to complement the philosophers and social and political theorists only recently recruited.

Dr Dowling, with experience of social movements, was joined by a media theorist, Dr Amit Rai, working at the intersection of the cinematic theory of Gilles Deleuze and postcolonial theory, and philosopher and sociologist Professor Denise Ferreira da Silva, working on the critique of the Enlightenment from a black radical perspective in a senior position.

The recruitment of this notable faculty had its challenges, of course. Scholars from other fields had to be convinced that being appointed by, and teaching in, a business school would be consonant with their interests. The proposed collective curriculum reform was therefore very important in recruitment just as the faculty members were to be very important in curriculum reform. Business school colleagues and university administrators also had to be convinced of the merit of hiring outside the discipline.

The Queen Mary project benefitted from an enlightened vice-provost in this regard. He was a respected historian of the sixteenth and seventeenth centuries, who also carried sympathy for the Republics in the Spanish Civil War and for the crusading Spanish judges prosecuting contemporary fascist leaders. He understood the logical case for a humanities-based management studies curriculum. In lighter moments he referred to the school as his Sociology Department.

Recruitment was only part of the challenge; retention and promotion also presented obstacles. Although the project emerged at a time when the research assessments conducted nationally still offered some room for innovation – for instance, the Association of Business Schools' publications list included social science journals – newly recruited scholars were to be judged by a discipline not their own. It was a testament to these young scholars that all eventually attained permanent appointments and survived this challenge. But it required considerable support, explanation, preparation and in some cases faith from colleagues and the university.

Most important, new and established faculty members who shared interdisciplinary interests and a desire for reform began to form a loose collective through conversation, socialising, sharing work and laying out visions for what they hoped to accomplish in teaching. As a group they took considerable and very serious interest in the conditions and circumstances of the students and their shared workplace, the university.

A more established figure, Professor Peter Fleming, already adept at navigating business schools (while writing a string of highly critical and literate books on the ideology of business and management), proved a valuable friend in these conversations. Fleming has gone on to become

the finest critic in management studies, with the rare gift of communi-
cating this critique to a wider audience (Fleming, 2009, 2015a, 2015b,
2017, 2018). To this day, his books are often the go-to guides to business
and management for humanities scholars around the world. Collective
conversations were rich, warm and genuine among this band of faculty,
in sharp contrast to the barely concealed jealousies, neuroses and petti-
ness that (stereo-)typically attended faculty relations. Keynes's famous
statement – that university battles are so vicious because the stakes are
so low – could finally be reversed; camaraderie emerged because of the
shared sense that the stakes were so high.

Queen Mary at this time was a university that truly served its neigh-
bourhood, enrolling large numbers of students from the East End of
London. This produced a welcome diversity in the class, with the majority of the students coming from families of Asian descent, mixed with
many other new arrivals from Africa and Eastern Europe especially
(Human Resources, n.d.). The faculty preparing curriculum reform
began by analysing these students, their histories, abilities and desires as
best as could be discerned in the classroom and on the campus. Clearly
these were students who brought a worldly prospect, often having international families and international life histories, and they continued to
live a multicultural, multinational life in their London neighbourhoods.

On the other hand, they were often the first from their families to go
to university. Many had chosen to study business because they did not
feel confident, or perhaps were not made to feel confident, in humanities
and social science subjects. Many chose to study business because they
had a keen sense of wanting to find employment and provide for their
families. And some chose the discipline because they came from families that had micro, small and occasionally medium-sized businesses.

The question arose of how to reform a curriculum given these student profiles. The question never arose of whether such students could
support a reformed curriculum. All the faculty members remained
united in believing that the students at Queen Mary would benefit, perhaps even benefit more than similarly prepared and established student
populations. This confidence in students may have influenced other
faculty members, a mix of more orthodox CMS scholars teaching in an
established way and some faculty members specialising in equality and
diversity issues.

In any case, the full faculty membership supported the call for reform.
And several beyond the core group participated by reforming courses
or teaching on the refashioned Academic Skills course. However, it was
not the more established faculty alone who joined the new recruits in

this reform. A vital and vibrant component of the curriculum revision and the teaching experiments was newly arriving PhD students and new adjunct seminar leaders attracted specifically to the project.

The Doctoral Programme

Viewed from other departments, business schools are often thought to face no financial pressures. Viewed from the administrative offices of the university, business schools are often thought to be the solution to financial pressures. If a business school can get the balance right, sharing resources while also retaining resources, it can make allies and accomplices of both other departments and the administration.

The business school at Queen Mary did just this, and one reward was a generously funded doctoral programme that included doctoral students registered across departments; again Drama and Geography in particular participated in the collaboration, though Politics too would soon join in.

Moreover the symbiosis of the project boosted the quality and energy of the candidates who began to apply to the doctoral programme. Many could see that something was happening at Queen Mary, but many also played key roles once they arrived in elaborating what was happening in both public programming and teaching. Along the way, the school completely revised its teaching programme for the PhD and innovated joint preparation with other departments.

We have discussed some of the teaching innovation from both doctoral students and adjunct seminar leaders. But here, one public programme that announced the innovations of the school's public research programme across Europe and in the United States must be mentioned. That was the Art of Rent Series (n.d.; Matteo, n.d.), produced jointly by two highly talented young PhD students, Matteo Pasquinelli and Paolo Do. It brought economists, sociologists, cultural studies and management studies scholars to campus on a semester-long programme of public talks and discussions. The very interdisciplinarity of the programme and its geographic reach was previously unknown at any business school in London. The title came from an article by the geographer David Harvey (2002) in a discussion of gentrification in Barcelona. This programme, like many others at the school, also benefitted and learned from the pioneering site Generation Online, mentioned earlier.

Art of Rent featured four public events over the spring semester in 2008. The first session was entitled 'The Art of Rent, Profit, and

Intellectual Property' (Harvey, 2002) and featured Matteo Pasquinelli together with the Paris-based economist Carlo Vercellone. This was Vercellone's first appearance in the United Kingdom. The next month, 'Rent, Crisis, Financialisation' (Harvey, 2002) featured the late dance scholar and social theorist Randy Martin in his first UK visit from his base at New York University. It also featured the economists Christian Marazzi from Switzerland and Costas Lapavitsas from SOAS. Marazzi became a favourite visitor at Queen Mary over the duration of the project, as well as a strong influence and good friend to the project.

In April, 'A New International Division of Labour' brought social theorist Sandro Mezzadra from the University of Bologna; Jane Wills, a geographer and community organiser from Queen Mary; and Xiang Biao, a young anthropologist from Oxford University.

Finally, 'Governance, Conflict, and the Production of the Common' (Harvey, 2002) saw talks and a conversation among Stefano Harney; Judith Revel of the University of Paris; Raul Sanchez, a community organiser from Madrid; and Alberto de Nicola, an organiser and education activist from Rome.

It is safe to say that no similar event had taken place in the United Kingdom at that time, bringing together Europe's autonomist thinkers from different fields. The semester marked out Queen Mary in these circles. This was not just a first in business schools but in British academia.

But most important for our purposes, the hosting of this programme was conceived and organised entirely as a result of the energies and commitments of the two doctoral students, Do and Pasquinelli.

Paolo Do would go on to produce critical work on the future of the university in Asia and Europe and to hold key curatorial positions in Italy and Switzerland, where he continues to produce original collaborations and writings.

Matteo Pasquinelli wrote a key text while at Queen Mary, *Animal Spirits* (Pasquinelli, 2008), and continues to be a scholar at the cutting edge, currently appointed at an art academy in Germany.[1]

They are examples not only of the leading role played by PhD students in the Queen Mary project but also of the success that doctoral students enjoyed after the school's project and despite its short life.

Two new research platforms produced by PhD students also warrant mention: a community geography project of visiting PhD students from the University of North Carolina, hosted jointly with the Geography

---

[1] University of Arts and Design Karlsruhe; see http://matteopasquinelli.com/teaching/.

Department at Queen Mary, and the collective that put together *The Paper*, a free newspaper on and for the student fees debate at the time and the mobilisations around them.

'Counter/Mapping QMary: The University and Border Technologies' (*Counter/mapping QMary*, n.d.; *Lateral*, n.d.; Queen Mary Counter-mapping Collective and the Counter-Cartographies Collective, 2012) featured a residency and three public workshops, all hosted by the Counter-Cartography Collective from North Carolina (Dalton & Mason-Deese, 2012). Funded jointly by the school and Geography Department, the collective engaged the Queen Mary doctoral students in a joint investigation of the university using the technique developed by the collective and bringing aspects of the discipline of geography to the heart of the school's PhD training.

The Paper, produced by PhD students, including Camille Barbagallo and Bue Hansen, was designed to provide real-time information to students caught in the grip of major changes through the introduction of market-level fees into the UK system. It provided everything from fiscal analysis to DIY advice (*We Are the Paper*, n.d.). Both projects contributed immensely to the feeling that to be at the school was to live the consequences of the curriculum, not just study them. Other doctoral students who influenced the project were Marina Vishmidt, Valeria Graziano and Manuela Zechner, all of whom would go on to make their marks in organising, theory and education, both inside and outside academe.

A significant publication project also had its origins in the doctoral programme at Queen Mary. Stevphen Shukaitis, now in a position in business ethics at Essex University in the United Kingdom, launched his imprint, Autonomedia, there (Minor Compositions, n.d.). Many of the imprint's noted publications originated in and around the Queen Mary project, including the *Nanopolitics Handbook* (2014); *Contract & Contagion: From Biopolitics to Oikonomia* by Angela Mitropoulos (2012), another highly original and talented doctoral student at Queen Mary; and *The Undercommons: Fugitive Planning & Black Study* by Stefano Harney and Fred Moten (2013). Shukaitis's (2015) own two monographs – *The Composition of Movements to Come: Aesthetics* and *Cultural Labor after the Avant-Garde* and *Imaginal Machines* – also show the influence of the period and his own influence on the project.

Adding to the milieu were visiting fellows such as Anna Curcio, a political theorist of feminism and social emancipation; David Graeber, the well-known anthropologist who was always a friend to the programme; and the dedicated postcolonial theorist Miguel Mellino, whose frequent visits inspired a rethinking of global business and its relationship to Frantz Fanon, Stuart Hall and colonial/postcolonial thought.

Other friends of the programme are too numerous to mention, but Tiziana Terranova, the brilliant feminist sociologist of media and work; Massimo De Angelis, founder of *The Commoner*, and feminist legal scholars Brenna Bhandar and Patricia Tuitt deserve special mention for the way they inspired the curriculum and its bold blend.

Public Programmes

The most remarkable aspect of the Queen Mary case was the holistic integration of a liberal management education curriculum and pedagogy with public programmes of research and with postgraduate research education. These elements combined not only to reinforce and nurture each other but also to provide a confidence, sense of collective endeavour and pervasive excitement that 'something was going on at Queen Mary'.

Like-minded interdisciplinary programmes such as Queen Mary's highly ranked Drama and Geography Departments collaborated with the school, attended events and shared PhD recruitment and supervision.

Discussions began on extending the reforms to postgraduate education, something that would be realised within several years, though unfortunately after the core of the experiment had been discouraged by a new senior leadership in the College, who focussed instead on metrics identical to the universities ranked directly above them. It may also have been that the sheer energy and activity emanating from the school during those three years from conferences to media appearances to alternative research platforms produced some jealousy among certain other departments, excluding the ones mentioned, and this may be one of the many lessons to draw from the case.

Among the positive lessons are the record of integrating public research events and platforms with the new liberal management education, mixing scholars, doctoral students and the public in a thrilling atmosphere of being on the cutting edge of interdisciplinarity. A brief review is therefore worth undertaking, beginning with the first major event, a conference investigating the rise of metrics, 'Measure for Measure' (2007). The two-day conference featured international speakers, including Patricia Clough, the head of Women's Studies and an important social theorist at the City University of New York. Its ambitious interdisciplinarity featured no less than nine disciplines, from art history to physics. It would set the tone for later events and especially for using the public programmes to think about curriculum reform. It took place just as the movement for curriculum reform gathered pace and became an inspiration and impulse to continue.

The mix of high-profile academics from across the liberal arts and management that characterised the 'Measure for Measure' gathering would become a regular feature of the public research profile of the school. People like Luce Irigaray, the eminent French feminist scholar; Michael Hardt, the social philosopher from America's Duke University; Maurizio Lazzarato, a theorist of 'immaterial labour'; Silvia Federici (2004), the influential author of *Caliban and the Witch*; and American sociologist Stanley Aronowitz all began to visit, give seminars and spend time in conversation with faculty members and students in the school between 2009 and 2012. Indeed, the school had programmed an all-day conference celebrating the work of Aronowitz, 'Future Promises' (Composition & Commons Co-research Project, 2008), the first of its kind in Britain for the sociologist, who most inherited the mantle of C. Wright Mills.

Other significant public research events included the 'Labour of Translation' organised by Dr Arianna Bove (2010) and featuring talks by translators of books such as a collection of interviews with the great African film-maker Ousmane Sembene, translated by Dr Bove (Busch & Annas, 2008), and works by the political theorist Antonio Negri (2003), by Dr Matteo Mandarini, also at the school.

A year later the school was still at the cutting edge of new scholarly conversation when in a new partnership with the Law School at Queen Mary, the school co-sponsored a conference around the work of philosopher Catherine Malabou on 'Sovereignty and Plasticity' in 2011.

One of the most influential visits was a weeklong shared residency with Cultural Studies at Goldsmiths of Cedric Robinson, the eminent political scientist from the University of California, Santa Barbara. His visit was sponsored by Professor da Silva and the Centre for Ethics and Politics and emerged out of the energies of the annual Postcolonial Capitalism symposium, discussed later. His work would exert a major influence over a number of scholars at Queen Mary and shape their writing and teaching.

All these extraordinary thinkers came to the school because of an interest in what it was trying to achieve, and they contributed significantly to that project in the process.

This list does not end there. The iconoclastic development economist Professor John Sender from SOAS, London, came to break down the truths of the fair trade movement, a visit facilitated by another doctoral student, Scott Cheshier, who was writing a dissertation on state firms in Vietnam that countered the orthodox literature.

Dr Marc Driscoll from UNC came to explain the nuances of Chinese political economy. Dr Campbell Jones, at the time the bad-boy of CMS, brought his knife-like analysis to the campus for a business ethics conference. But most important, all came into an atmosphere where the school's reputation preceded it. Most of our friends in other departments welcomed this. Perhaps a few other departments felt sidelined.

Postcolonial Capitalism

The first year (2009) of the liberal management education project also saw the first instance of what would become the school's flagship public research event and which would deeply influence its curriculum and teaching. In the first year it was called, simply, 'Postcolonial Capitalism: A Symposium' and was organised by Mellino, who had come on the first of several visiting scholar terms from Naples.

Together with Mellino, Ishani Chandrasekara, the postcolonial accounting scholar at Queen Mary; Yasmin Ibrahim, a postcolonial media theorist also at the school; and Stefano Harney helped organise this two-day event held, like 'Measure for Measure', at Goodenough College at the University of London.

The conference line-up was a who's who of postcolonial autonomists and black studies scholars, including Denise Ferreira da Silva, Nahum Chandler, Fred Moten and Sandro Mezzadra. It also featured an important contingent of scholars from Goldsmiths, initiating a relationship between it and the school that would grow as scholars and teachers from the two institutions recognised common causes.

The crucial intervention of the postcolonial capitalism symposium was to address the real lives of the Queen Mary students and the immediate histories of their families through attention to the role of colonialism and race in the making of capitalism and of postcolonialism and race in the practices to undo this past. Ideas and concepts from the symposium made their way directly into numerous course modules from strategy to academic skills.

But something else decisive to the completion of this experiment also resulted. Professor Denise Ferreira da Silva became founding director of a new Centre for Ethics and Politics at the school, in which she also taught the required ethics and politics modules on the undergraduate programme. The centre would become the fulcrum of new public programming and the research profile of the school, out of which many events grew, including the annual postcolonial capitalism symposia over the subsequent three years, organised by Professor da Silva and her doctoral student, Rashne Lemke. Particularly memorable was the 2011 iteration, 'Histories and Cartographies of Global Capitalism' (Queen Mary School of Business and Management Events, 2011), which took place several months after the 'London riots' of August 2011. The riots took place in Queen Mary's 'backyard'. The symposium had the chance to reflect on whether capitalism was delivering and for whom and where race and class and gender made the difference.

Several modules were adapted to reflect the crises outside the door of the school, just as earlier some lecturers had chosen to feature the imposition of fees as a lesson. But the most important revelation emerging from the intellectual foment of the annual postcolonial capitalism conferences might well have been the affinity between management studies and other fields, thematic rather than disciplinary in nature.

In other words, liberal management education, as it manifested itself in the public research profile, came to advance the potential of management studies as a thematic of modern life, not merely a discipline. Like women's studies, cultural studies or black studies, might it be the case that management studies necessarily range across disciplines in order to account for all the places we find the phenomenon of management in our daily life? After all, management is not at home only in the world of business.

The ideas and practice of management play a key role in the art world, in the history of the welfare state, in the household and the family, in popular culture, and in health and environmental sciences, to name a few areas of life almost at random. Just as women's studies acknowledge the role of gender in every walk and facet of life so too might management studies come to see itself as a thematic, or a structuring, of modern life, requiring all the liberal arts and social sciences to house it and given the precedent of feminist work in the sciences there too perhaps.

Of course, the presence of women's studies, gender and sexuality studies or black studies in the university is linked to social movements and demands for change in the hierarchy of knowledge taught in the university. Their examples raise the question of where pressure might come for a truly liberal management studies, not just a liberal management curriculum. But there is a provisional answer to this question too.

Business leaders are almost notoriously anti-business studies in their curricular tastes and opinions. This badly kept secret usually gets treated selectively or rhetorically by university leaders. But much more might be made of this support and potential co-operation. Queen Mary was on the verge of just such co-operation when more typical university leaders replaced the vice provost who had allowed the project to flourish.

But even more important, and certainly more probable, than a movement of business leaders for liberal management education would be one led by students – especially business students not at elite institutions, where any deficiencies in curriculum are compensated for by class privileges and high-level connections but by those who discover that they might have had so much more.

After all, the wealth of liberal management education lies in its value added. It teaches the business curriculum and the humanities and the social science curriculum. Students left Queen Mary and SMU for positions in banks and ministries just like most business students at good schools, but they left with other educational values too. Their curriculum had been enriched, showing the quotidian management education given to so many to be impoverished. That may well be reason for raising voices together.

Of course everything in this experimental project did not go to plan. Though we had the inspiration of older interdisciplinary models as outlined in the previous chapters, no contemporary business school had undertaken anything like this alchemy. Admirable programmes that integrated ethics and social responsibility, such as Thunderbird in Arizona, existed but none that so completely attempted a new blended curriculum across business, the social sciences and the humanities.

Mistakes were made. We often underestimated the insecurity and disorientation some faculty members and graduate students felt in encountering work from so many new disciplines and the intimidatory classics that underpinned many of these disciplines. This shifting ground caused some faculty to question whether their own work remained relevant, critical and cutting edge in the face of these radical shifts in pedagogy. Moreover, as much as we tried, we could not always reassure senior management in the university that being different could still mean excellence and rankings on which they depended.

The financial crisis, ironically, helped. The media was looking for something different in the face of the unprecedented fear that accompanied the crisis, especially in London. Our school was different, and we appeared on the BBC, commercial channels and in the major daily newspapers during this period (Harney, 2011; Harney & Dowling, 2012).

But this high-profile commentary on the financial crisis was not enough to convince some of our senior leadership, and sceptical colleagues, that we were a 'real' business school. Some of these problems are structural to the professional system of rewards and the competitive and marketised system of rankings. But certainly there were instances where more communication and sensitivity would have benefitted all sides. And as the leadership of this experiment, we often felt pressure to make quick decisions and sometimes could not consult in the collective spirit that otherwise animated the project. This was also a mistake, even if one we readily admitted at the time.

But there is also another, last issue that must be touched upon given the Queen Mary case study in particular, and it is a delicate one. What we discovered was the possibility, not proven, but suggested by the enthusiasm, broad reach and lasting impact of the public research profile: perhaps not only does liberal management education add value to management education but to management scholarship too.

Put inversely, perhaps management scholarship would benefit from an encounter with other disciplines. One must be delicate in raising this issue. It could be said that sociology would benefit from more of an encounter with literature too, or politics with drama. And we must be careful too because in some instances these encounters do happen. But nonetheless let us take one example.

In management studies the study of culture is associated with Geert Hofstede (Hofstede, 2001 [1980]; Hofstede & Hofstede, 2005); indeed, he helped to spawn a sub-discipline of cross-cultural management. And yet, what might be different in this work if he or his disciplines had been involved in a liberal management education project? What if they had not just encountered but engaged fifty years of scholarship in cultural studies, black and postcolonial studies, critical anthropology, ethnic studies and subaltern studies?

Instead, Hofstede and his disciples appear to have developed their work in isolation. And along the way they committed themselves to many positions and ideas that had long ago been called into question in these other fields, as was often discussed on the edges of the 'postcolonial capitalism' gatherings.

When introduced to Hofstede's work, many at the conference expressed surprise at the isolation of these views and what some characterised as their archaic qualities. But who knows how these other disciplines might have engaged Hofstede if they had been aware of his centrality, of the importance of the study of culture in management and of the general field of cross-cultural management? Seen from both directions, what could be a clearer call for liberal management scholarship?

The Queen Mary case study demonstrated the importance of support from senior management in the university for such a project to succeed. When new leadership failed to continue that support and sought a wholly new direction for the school, the project of a liberal management education could not survive. This withdrawal of support and insistence on mirroring the character and approach of other 'competitor' business schools was fatal in a way that none of the mistakes made in the experiment itself were. Trying to compete successfully with a product derivative of another product has of course proved illusory. But it is easy to understand how university leadership was convinced the 'metrics' were necessary, especially in the UK academic climate of the time.

Yet it must be said that senior leadership put careers in jeopardy as these metrics shifted suddenly. Students too were denied the breadth of learning and engagement with social, political and environmental issues that cut so close to them in the urban East End neighbourhoods of London from which they came. Soon the university would 'raise standards' and exclude most of these local students in favour of wealthier, whiter, more suburban students. Nonetheless, testimonies suggest that there were few faculty members or students who went through this curricular experiment who were not changed by it, often in profound ways.

Many came to see the society, the university and their relationships with each other against the grain of common sense. Certainly this molecular change in experience is reason enough to attempt such a liberal management education elsewhere and again.

Part II

The Liberal Heritage of Management Education

5   Forgotten Kinships

Today in many universities the social and institutional distance between business schools and schools of the humanities appears great. On many university campuses this distance seems to be reflected even in the architecture and landscape of those campuses themselves. The most famous example may be the Said Business School at Oxford University, located nearer the train station than other colleges and facing London rather than looking inward.

Of course, one could note that this physical and symbolic separation is only the latest example in a long history of estrangement. Harvard's business school was said to have been placed quite emphatically on the other side of the river from the rest of the Harvard campus. And most recently Oxford was in the news again as Peking University bought a nineteenth century manor to house a branch of its HSBC Business School.

Universities may be hard to separate from their real estate these days, but business schools appear particularly emblematic of this new manorial spread. Any visit to a first-tier research university in the United States will turn up very contemporary, very consciously designed business school classroom buildings and even on-campus business school hotels and conference centres, such as the business school hotel at the Fuqua School at Duke University in the United States – this in addition to Duke's already quite posh campus hotel for other disciplines and schools. However, on the campus tour one would quickly get the feeling that, *contra* the case of Oxford and Harvard, many business schools appear, with help from university administrations, to have instigated their own separate and sometimes unequal status. This topographical distance only reinforces the perception of a gap at many other levels.

The fortunes of business schools, reflected in their new buildings, have diverged sharply from the fortunes of the humanities, including the traditional social sciences such as anthropology, sociology and politics. Those fortunes in turn have led to very material differences – faculty pay scales and students who expect and receive well-paid offers on graduation, for example. The evidence that scholars like Christopher Newfield (2015) have turned up – that humanities teaching is among the most profitable business for most universities, far more so than the STEM (Science, Technology, Economics and Mathematics) subjects – is sadly not reflected in the facilities of most English Departments, at least at public universities.

These differences have also aggravated the differences in curriculum and pedagogy. At both the undergraduate and postgraduate levels, universities struggle to offer any kind of mutually satisfactory core curriculum across this gap. Business students are often impatient with having to take humanities courses, and business schools are often reluctant to share faculty and curriculum with other schools in the university for which those business schools can charge a premium, and for which they paid a premium on the market.

Humanities professors and students often perceive business courses to be insufficiently reflective in style for inclusion in a liberal arts education, and business school students grow impatient with what they regard as the political content of some humanities courses. The list goes on.

But beyond these questions of resources, content and style there is also the gap in teaching methods. Many business school courses rely on textbooks and case studies and teaching methods to fit these sources. Many humanities courses assign full primary texts and focus on close readings of these texts for interpretive challenges, the very opposite of a case study designed to deliver clear information for deliberation and decision.

Against the divisions only cursorily outlined here, the recent calls for a business education more fully infused with the humanities must seem noble but naïve.

At a time when many universities feel the strain of maintaining even the semblance of a cross-school foundation or core course, the ambition to integrate the humanities more fully into the business school curriculum at both the undergraduate and postgraduate levels appears fanciful. Yet that is the ambition of the present book, beginning in this chapter on teaching the foundation of an integrated intellectual history. As we mentioned in the introduction, we are emboldened to offer such a curricular and pedagogical recipe because of the evolution of the university in society.

For Kant, religion was a higher faculty for the university at the outset of the enlightenment; and so were the nation-building humanities for Humboldt and Newman a century later; so the sciences, agriculture and engineering in the last century; and so business studies is the higher faculty of this century.

We have tried to stress that this is not a value judgement but a historical observation about the place of certain forms of knowledge in capitalist
society today. It is not that business is the new religion but rather that
business knowledge serves to orient us today to our world as religious
authority did in Kant's. It is an operational, not a theological, connection. And as in Kant's time, the question remains of the relationship
between the higher and lower faculties. In other words, the very prominence of these business school buildings on campus prompts the Kantian
question of the relationship of the faculties and hastens our work.

But we are also encouraged by a certain recounting of history that
reads against the grain of the current gaps in our discipline. Thus in
this chapter we want to outline the beginning of an intellectual history of the twentieth century that reminds us of the common problems,
biographical connections and related theories of what would become
contemporary business studies on the one hand and on the other the
humanities and (especially in this chapter) certain social sciences, many
of which, after all, are not much older than the discipline of business
studies itself.

We will show that there is a forgotten kinship in this history that can
be the basis not only for encouragement in our present task but indeed
also a source for the practical purposes of developing exactly such a
curriculum.

As we stressed in the introduction, this chapter will thus serve as
both a prospective syllabus and a pedagogical tool. We will write as if
we were teaching or, perhaps more exactly, we will write as if we are
speaking to teachers who might wish to travel with us on this improb-
able path to the integration of the humanities into business studies. We
will assume that, like us, our readers see the Kantian imperative in reconciling today's conflict of the faculties for the benefit of our students
and our society.

The Pareto Circle at Harvard

To reintroduce this neglected kinship we will take the case of the Pareto
Circle at Harvard University in the 1930s, pairing it with the contemporaneous movement of New Criticism at Cambridge University
in the United Kingdom. Joel Isaac's (2012) excellent book, *Working
Knowledge,* will be our guide. This is a text that would also serve well
as a foundation for a course on the intellectual history of business and
the social sciences.

Isaac's book concerns the larger question of what he calls 'the intersti-
tial' in twentieth-century American universities. He is concerned with

the way the modern university became populated with disciplines and yielded its exclusive endorsement of the classics to include the social sciences and (pre-)professional programmes on an equal intellectual footing. But for our purposes his pivotal chapter on the Pareto seminars will serve to demonstrate to contemporary students that scholars of business, of science, of social science and of philosophy regularly shared not just a room, a course and a set of theoretical passions. And behind this co-operation scholars also shared some common concerns about the society in which they found themselves.

Perhaps this is the first lesson of any such intellectual history. The current division, the gap and isolation, between business scholars and scholars in sociology, biology or philosophy is not natural. It is historical. There was a time when such faculty did not have to be summoned to serve on university-wide committees in order to come together. There are other examples of cross-discipline co-operation and research. In the 1950s the Tavistock group in London, and in the 1970s the Aston group in Birmingham – to give but two examples – would prove highly innovative and productive in working across the social sciences on business problems. However, although they included psychologists, they did not have the benefit of natural scientists nor philosophers nor the sheer range of talents found in the Pareto Circle.

Isaac's chapter focusses on the extraordinary career of the biochemist Lawrence Joseph Henderson. In 1932 Henderson initiated a weekly seminar at Harvard on the work of Vilfredo Pareto. In particular the seminar members came together to study Pareto's *Treatise on General Sociology*, a work that marked Pareto's dissatisfaction as an economist and his turn to sociology to try to understand why in his view economics was not successful at predicting and modelling actual human behaviour.

Pareto believed that what he called 'sentiments' were the missing key to understanding systems and the problems of equilibrium in these social systems. Pareto was a complicated and multifaceted thinker and not an attractive one to many. He put forth a theory of elites as necessarily manipulating 'the masses' for good or ill that seemed to support antidemocratic conclusions, and perhaps sympathies. He reinforced this interpretation not just because of his noble background in Italy but by agreeing to be a senator in Benito Mussolini's government.

From the perspective of teaching business students about the relationship between emerging business knowledge and the imperatives of society – the historical urgencies of the time – this aspect of Pareto is crucial, and we will come back to it. But as Isaac points out, for Henderson and his extraordinary circle of participants in the seminar and its related activities – such as a jointly taught course called Sociology 23 – it was not Pareto's elite theory but his theory of scientific knowledge that attracted them, and it was from this scientific philosophy that most of their own works, in myriad emergent fields, would take their inspiration.

Who were these figures, and what was the substance of this inspiration that made the Harvard Pareto Circle so influential, so historic? The participants were a who's who in the making of modern American academic life. We quote Isaac:

From the Harvard faculty came Joseph Schumpeter, Pitirim Sorokin, Thomas North Whitehead, Fritz Roethlisberger, Hans Zinsser, Clyde Kluckohn, W. Lloyd Warner, Henry Murray, Elton Mayo, Crane Brinton, Bernard DeVoto and Talcott Parsons. Student members included Robert K. Merton, William Foote Whyte, Kingsley Davis, George C. Homans and James Grier Miller. (Isaac, 2012, p. 63)

Isaac also notes 'the seminar produced five future presidents of the American Sociology Association, and one each of the American Historical Association, the American Anthropological Association, and the American Economic Association' (ibid., p. 63). But alert business students will already have noted the names of the leaders of the research at the Western Electric Company, better known as the Hawthorne experiments – Mayo, Roethlisberger and Whitehead.

Indeed, these experiments and the classic business text *Management and the Workers* were heavily influenced by the scientific philosophy derived from the Pareto seminar. As Isaac shows, this seminal work was also significantly influenced by Henderson *qua* biochemist. In bringing together these different faculties, Henderson worked from an office on the business school campus. He was enthusiastic about the data being gathered and lent much institutional support for what he saw as a key application of Pareto's theories to an American context. Indeed, Henderson believed Pareto held the key to establishing a science of human relations and hence firmly establishing business studies as a proper academic discipline.

What Henderson meant by a 'proper academic discipline' brings us to the scientific philosophy of Pareto and why it meant so much to business scholars, sociologists, anthropologists and economists of the circle. Henderson drew from Pareto and, long before him, Hippocrates, the idea that things tend to return to a state of equilibrium. But equilibrium could only be measured if things are in turn organised in a system that is either out of balance or returning to it. Discovering, interpreting and assessing such a system could not be done at full scale, especially where that system was society itself. The object was too big. Thus specific and exemplary cases had to be developed to measure this equilibrium and tell us something about the system as a whole.

For example, the purpose of a personnel department was to ensure that employee sentiments did not disrupt this equilibrium, or if they did, the task was the manipulation of these sentiments. The Bank Wiring Observation Room would become the case that told us about the health of the larger industrial system. But though Henderson paid special attention to applying this scientific philosophy with his colleagues in the School of Business Administration at Harvard, he and the seminar participants adapted this common philosophy across a range of disciplines.

Bringing students to this moment in intellectual history, while at first perhaps a difficult sell, should begin to pay dividends in illuminating the history of how they came to be taught as they are, through case studies.

Indeed, in teaching students about the Pareto Circle one is also teaching about the formation of fields.

Rather than taking for granted that fields such as business studies are natural divisions – whereby knowledge changes over time within them but they remain constant as frames of reference – students instead observe that disciplines themselves are historically constructed. Indeed, they see that many of the participants are in the room together in the act of constructing the contours of a number of disciplines. Equally, students can observe that significant works that come to define different disciplines emerge less out of those disciplines than out of the pre-disciplinary mix. Only later do these texts become canonical as if they were organic to the discipline they in fact helped to shape. Of course there is a larger point about the way research creates its object, a point that is entirely different from the one business students are often taught – that they must merely be careful in their research not to affect an object they intend to study.

In the case of business studies, one of the most significant texts to emerge from the Pareto Circle and in a sense to create its object was, as we have mentioned, *Management and the Worker*, published in 1939 by Fritz Roethlisberger and William J. Dickson on the Hawthorne Works. We will return to this work when we look at the rise of English studies at Cambridge University and particularly at its crystallisation in the 1930s around the work of F. R. and Q. D. Leavis, T. S. Eliot and Ivor Richards.

There are many other teaching opportunities presented by the Pareto Circle, including those concerned with the development of knowledge and those spotlighting the context of history and society. In the area of knowledge development, one of the truly significant influences of the Pareto Circle and its faculty seminar and course for students was its development and spread of the case method. Contemporary students introduced to this history have the opportunity to see that the case method unites business studies not only with legal studies and medical studies but also with important methodological movements in anthropology and sociology, where cases were introduced with a new and more scientific application as a result of the Pareto Circle.

As Isaac rightly notes, Harvard Law School began developing the case method in the nineteenth century in response to the problem of systematising teaching and research in the school. Common law began not like continental law from principles that could be applied with scientific and logical rigor but with precedent and constant interpretation of opinions. Thus early law schools appeared as a collection of views and counterviews with no way to systematise either the knowledge or the teaching. The strategy of adopting a case method in law schools thus anticipated much of what Henderson would synthesise under the influence of Pareto.

That is, it took specific opinions and made them into exemplary cases that in a sense stood in for the principles of Napoleonic law. Those cases in turn gave focus and consistency to teaching. Students would now learn through studying these exemplary cases, the opinions of which could be more generally applied. The cases came to stand for the system. Get the cases right, and the system would stay in equilibrium. Henderson grasped the usefulness of the case method for bringing together his interest in systems equilibrium with a specific method of study in the case, with teaching based on rigour of analysis.

Teaching the case study method created a virtuous circle in which the case stood for a specific position in scientific philosophy; equilibrium implied systems that could be known through their cases, with a specific object of study for each discipline, whether a town for sociology or a factory for business studies. As Isaac also notes, it is little wonder that each week of Sociology 23, the course developed out of the faculty seminar for undergraduates, featured a case, whether taught by a sociologist or scientist.

It would also be useful at this point to raise in any such class on intellectual history the question of whether the case method was indeed as easily applied in other disciplines as it had been in legal studies. Or does the conversion of opinion into principle in legal studies exhibit something unique that needs to be approached with more caution than Henderson's enthusiasm allows?

Medical schools went through a transition towards cases based not on patients but on their test results, a necessary advance in the clinical efforts of the science of medicine. But they have subsequently spent many years trying to bring the patient back into focus, to say nothing of culture, society and even politics. It could be useful to read some of the narratives of this return to the patient, or her voice and environment in the medical literature.

One obvious place to start would be with the pioneering work of Carol Gilligan (Gilligan, 1982, 1990; Gilligan et al., 1989). Her efforts at freeing women from the limits of case study led to new methodological exploration, as we will see in a subsequent chapter on the relationship between management studies, psychology and gender studies. Of course, students will be well prepared for these discussions because they are likely to have encountered the case method firsthand in their business education. Here, then, is an opportunity not only to explore its origins and its multidisciplinary career, but also to ask questions about how the business case differs from the legal case, how business cases have attempted to adjust for these differences and whether they have been successful.

While business studies has its own discourse on the method of the case, widening the view of the student to include this history adds a dimension they are not likely to encounter otherwise. This is especially true given that the discourse is often the preserve of business scholars and not shared with students for fear of undermining confidence in the method itself. Few business lecturers begin with a preface on problems in scientific method when they introduce their first case study.

However, an intellectual history of business studies can come at the question another way. Joel Isaac's work is not the only one, obviously, in a group as important as the Pareto Circle. Other works place much less emphasis on scientific philosophy and the emergence of the case study method and much more on the historical context in which this group of Harvard professors found itself working.

Annie L. Cot (2011) of the Sorbonne in Paris, in her groundbreaking article on the Pareto Circle, notes many of the protagonists, including the famous sociologist George Homans, admitted the study group was set up very much in opposition to other schools of thought, in both economics and philosophy, at Harvard. In particular, the Pareto Circle, led by Henderson's own political sensibility, saw themselves in direct opposition if not confrontation with both the institutionalist and Marxist groups in these disciplines at Harvard and elsewhere.

Here is a chance, then, to talk with students about two levels of context or what we might call disciplinary politics and societal politics. To what extent was this knowledge forged within an antagonism to other approaches to knowledge? In other words, it is an opportunity to introduce students to the idea of partisan knowledge; not to discredit such knowledge but to deepen our understanding of its production and deployment.

As Cot points out, Henderson believed the systems approach, with numerous sentiments and variables affecting the equilibrium of that system, blunted what he and others called the cause-and-effect approach. This terminology was his way of characterising historical materialism, though no doubt the historical materialists, who in turn called Pareto the Marx of the bourgeoisie, would not agree with this characterisation of their own method. For our classroom such antagonisms are more than historical trivia. They are warnings to look for the antagonisms today that lie beneath knowledge formation.

Beyond the antagonism of university politics, however, stood another larger set of forces seemingly arrayed against each other in the era of the Pareto Circle. Interestingly, Cot tells us, Wallace B. Dunham, the dean of the Harvard Business School during this period, gave a lecture in Sociology 23 on the unionisation of streetcar workers, and Chester I. Barnard, the famous business historian and later author of *My Years at General Motors*, gave a lecture in the class on a riot by the unemployed in New Jersey. Needless to say, these are not topics commonly covered in today's business school seminars. In other words, we have the opportunity to teach about the way theory responds to the pressing challenges of politics in the society in which it is developed.

Dunham and Barnard chose to focus on what they would have understood as disequilibrium in part to present an alternative to a theory of class struggle, coded as Henderson's belittling of the cause-and-effect theory. This too is the context for the development of business knowledge studied in business schools today. (Think, for example, of the free-market, anti-regulatory sentiment in business scholarship that has only recently ebbed with the recognition of how much wealth disparity inhibits growth.) It is a context that requires an awareness and familiarity not just with other disciplines but also other ideologies and societal antagonisms outside the business school.

But there is also a way to lead the students in this intellectual journey across disciplines and ideologies into an unusual alliance between the Pareto Circle and their small but threatening Marxist opposition. There is another way to interpret the urgency of the Pareto Circle aside from acknowledging its trepidation that stepping off the green peacefulness of Harvard Yard might be to step out into a strike or riot.

Both groups shared another, related, concern. This was the industrialisation of science, or what might be called its secularisation. The rise of industry had for a century drawn more and more on science for its advances, but the full power of industrial capitalism by the 1930s was such that questions about the heady combination of commerce and science began to be asked.

How was it possible for science to remain independent of these commercial forces? The automobile was reshaping the landscapes of the United States and Europe. Fantasies of speed and travel made possible by advances in science and technology were reflected in everything from Art Deco architecture to art movements such as Futurism. Both the Pareto Circle and its rival Marxist colleagues sought assurance that science could remain neutral in the face of this onslaught of worldly temptations. Of course, their analysis was different, but they both needed, for their own authority and for the society they wanted to see, a form of science that could stand above and apart from this profane world. The Marxists thought they found this in the science of history. Henderson's group sought it in Pareto.

Although cases might involve one in the day-to-day life of society, the method of abstracting from cases aimed to return to a systems analysis. Students can be asked to consider whether, for all their differences, these scholars did not seek a common form of authority in this objective concept of science, a form of authority that points uncomfortably to their status as what Pareto would have called 'circulating elites'.

Cambridge English

If business students are unlikely to know the history of the Pareto Circle at Harvard, they are even more unlikely to have heard of Cambridge English, New Criticism or the protagonists we now wish to introduce. Perhaps more dauntingly, they may struggle to see the relevance of such a focus. The previous discussion at least makes explicit the relationship between disciplines and makes the case for studying across them as a way to understand business studies better. But English at Cambridge?

However, if it is clear that business studies emerges in a moment where social sciences are struggling to define and consolidate their research and teaching within the university, where rival epistemologies such as Marxism have taken hold, and where the emerging objects of study are in societal and political turmoil, then these are also the conditions at Cambridge, albeit perhaps stereotypically, in a more restrained way. Moreover, as we shall try to show, some of the attempted solutions to this conjuncture of challenges have certain similarities with those proposed and worked through in the Pareto

Circle, while also offering students an expanded set of ideas and methods from the humanities.

The 1930s and 1940s at Cambridge University saw the emergence of a new, vigorous form of criticism. It was not modelled on the sciences, but it did attempt to systematise criticism and to take the individual work of literature, whether poetry or prose, as a unit that could be dated, ordered within a canon and read closely for what it might reveal about that system and about society. Literature and literary criticism in particular would respond to the problems of mass culture in the United Kingdom by providing a model of 'composure'. The very different figures of T. S. Eliot, F. R. and Q. D. Leavis, and I. A. Richards did not form a reading group, but they were said to have transformed their discipline in much the same way as the Pareto Circle transformed business studies and sociology and had profound effects on economics and anthropology.

They responded like Henderson and his colleagues to what they perceived as a lack of rigour in their field, and they responded with urgency, conviction and great energy because, again like Henderson, they saw the stakes as going well beyond the university. Cambridge English was a national programme, whether the nation accepted it as such or not. There was something both radical and conservative about their approaches.

Ivor Richards (2004 [1929]), for instance, would insist on the possibility of different interpretations in the close reading even as he also insisted that every great work ultimately had a 'composure' or, we might say, an equilibrium. Like his colleagues at Harvard, where he would also lecture, Richards offered the radical freedom of the individual sentiment with the security of the system returning to equilibrium. On the way, students will have the opportunity to be introduced not only to brilliant literary theory but also the poetry of T. S. Eliot (1997 [1920]), for reasons that go well beyond poetry's edification in its own right.

Richards's efforts in particular revolved around developing a theory of interpretation.

In his book *Practical Criticism,* he sought to put the interpretation of poetry and literature on a solid methodological footing. Interpretation, in Richards's view, had been neglected to that point in the history of the discipline in favour of biography, history and bibliographic details. The ability to interpret was thought, until that time, as something that one simply possessed if one were educated. But how then to teach it, especially beyond the circle of gentlemen who were comfortable with their circular argument?

Students should be able to see a parallel here to early business studies where the emphasis was on the practical skills, equivalent to the footnoting and textual annotation that Richards saw predominate in his day.

As has become widely accepted because of disciplinary histories such as Rajesh Khurana's (2007) *From Higher Aims to Hired Hands*, early business scholarship struggled for the equivalent of a theory of interpretation, that is, a theory of the enterprise: not just know-how about it. Richards's (2004) strategy of reading for interpretation was akin to the search for generalisable, theoretically sound business knowledge then occurring. But Richards also once said that it was not only poetry and fiction that could benefit from a theory of interpretation but also that 'direct training in reading' would also be beneficial to 'economics, psychology, political theory or law, and philosophy' (p. 337).

Richards, then, believed he could produce a science of interpretive reading, a science of the meaning of words on the page. And he believed this science could be generalised and, indeed, that it must be. Richards, like Arnold before him and like his contemporaries, F. R. and Q. D. Leavis, saw criticism as the foundation for the modern claim to expertise. Though like the others he believed in the spread of education, he was no democrat about this education. He worried instead that those who had true ability, expertise and professional knowledge needed a persuasive way to assert their views with the masses, one that was not based on privilege but on superior intellect.

For Richards, critics would be the managers of the population's opinions and tastes – of their inner lives – only if such management was put on a scientific footing, only if experts could argue that their superior interpretations were based on something rigorous and systematic.

We will close this chapter with a look at how similar this view could be to contemporaneous management theorists by suggesting that students could be introduced to a comparative reading of selections of *Practical Criticism* on the one hand and Roethlisberger and Dickson's *Management and the Worker* on the other.

Matthew Arnold and Raymond Williams

The great Welsh critic Raymond Williams, a Don at Cambridge towards the end of this period, would famously say that there was no Cambridge English before himself going on to identify three characteristics of that movement. He very much valued the advent of close reading as a method made famous by Richards, and he could not deny the advances in historical evaluation of literature associated with F. R. Leavis, though he added that it often became overshadowed by attempts to reach universal truths at every stage. But he could not abide the third aspect of Cambridge English, the discourse on reading initiated by Q. D. Leavis.

Williams wanted to know about the non-reading public, the public he came from, the majority public. He believed in their literacy, another kind of literacy, and he is justly famous for his exploration and elaboration of the culture of ordinary people. But what he saw in Cambridge English was not the agency *of* those people but a programme designed to work *upon* those people. In this sense we could say that Cambridge English – whether it was truly a coherent programme or not – had much in common with the Pareto Circle.

We are talking also, and primarily (as for a while Cambridge English did), about an intense crisis of culture and society: a crisis diversely defined and diversely met, but in any case, much more than an academic problem. The 1930s in Britain witnessed labour unrest, the rise of fascist sympathies in some quarters (including royal quarters), economic depression and the new ubiquity of mass popular culture such as movies and music. In a sense, with all this urgency and noise outside the windows, it is remarkable that the Pareto Circle or Cambridge English found time to think – a point that may be made to impatient students today.

But if religious authority was no longer at the centre of the university, many universities remained removed from the secular world. Williams (1983), of course, was never comfortable with that remove. He wrote of his senior colleagues in the department:

> Yet in its own ways Cambridge English, especially through Richards and Leavis, recognised the central practicality which is so often now forgotten: that the object of the course is not to reproduce its instructors, by imparting the habits that made them instructors. Most of those who take it go on to very different work, in which new and much more severe tests of perception and value are the real practicalities. They should never have to contrast the soundest academic instruction with a world of more pressing real choices. In English studies, and in its convergences with other humanities and human sciences, there is so much active knowledge, so many active skills, which are both valuable in themselves and which really can connect with a world of practice and choice and struggle. (p. 8)

However, we could also say that Williams is in conversation not with what the literary historian Chris Baldick called the social mission of English at Cambridge in the 1930s but rather, as Baldick and other scholars like Pamela McCallum also point out, with Matthew Arnold. And it is perhaps with the great Victorian critic that one would want to start with students.

It was Arnold who first attempted to lift literary criticism and what would become the discipline of English or English Literature from a gentleman's set of ineffable and personal, yet cultural, sensibilities to an objective and communicable – that is teachable – set of procedures. Arnold was especially interested in the social mission of such a criticism but also worried about the obstacles to that mission.

His book *Culture and Anarchy* (2009 [1869]) argued that it was the mission of civilised men to determine and disseminate 'the best that has been thought and known' (p. xxii). He saw culture as the study of perfection but also as a check against our received wisdom, lesser habits and accepted routine knowledge. He spent much of the book criticising 'philistines', and students can reflect here on the vexed relationship between phrases like 'the best and the brightest' and a forthright elitism but one that seeks not to draw away but to spread its universal values. How different indeed is this combination from the mission statements of the contemporary elite universities in which many of them study? How much does the university remain, for all the talk about profanation, 'Arnoldian'?

But how could culture – which in his view had become increasingly separate from society – provide a moral compass for that society? Williams, of course, would quarrel with the premise. Not only did culture exist among ordinary people, but it was a moral economy of its own.

Students might be directed here to think of the similarities between some of Arnold's statements and positions and those of the earliest management theorists who sought also to place management on a more procedural footing, less reliant on common sense, trial and error, and personal methods.

Taylor's phrase 'the one best way' epitomises this shift, as does Henri Fayol's (1930) position that 'administrative doctrine is universal' (p. 6). Reading excerpts of Arnold alongside Frederick Taylor and Henri Fayol shows students how two very different systems of knowledge were consolidating themselves in very similar ways. Both Arnold and the earliest management theorists did not see themselves as copying the hard sciences but rather as creating equivalent sciences, filled with their own standards, proofs and universal claims and applicability. And they saw themselves as producing a way of thinking in which numerous causes and effects jostled each other, none dominating for very long.

Critics would call it the scholarly equivalent of liberal democracy, a pluralism of positions but all within an unexamined system.

Indeed, Arnold appeared to anticipate Henderson's disparaging phrase about cause and effect in heterodox scholarship when he said, 'I hate all over-preponderance of single elements' (Lang, 1998, p. 370). Arnold did not have the benefit of the case and systems model that both Cambridge English and the Pareto Circle would attempt to introduce, and he is sometimes accused of haphazard positions. But he was consistent in his belief that the new middle classes needed to be drawn into debates that considered what today would be called multiple variables and interpretations and not hold on to singular prejudices by which they made their judgements.

Indeed a very productive seminar might include reading and contrasting Arnold's *Culture of Anarchy* with Raymond Williams's later, and not accidentally titled, *Culture and Society*. Students could be directed to the Preface in particular in which Arnold (2009) writes:

Great changes there must be, for a revolution cannot accomplish itself without great changes; yet order there must be, for without order a revolution cannot accomplish itself by due course of law. So whatever brings risk of tumult and disorder, multitudinous processions in the streets of our crowded towns, multitudinous meetings in their public places and parks – demonstrations perfectly unnecessary in the present course of our affairs – our best self, or right reason, plainly enjoins us to set our faces against. It enjoins us to encourage and uphold the occupants of the executive power, whoever they may be, in firmly prohibiting them. (p. 72)

This preface can be productively placed beside Williams's essay, 'One Hundred Years of Culture and Anarchy' in *Culture and Society*, written in the 1960s and beginning with a play on whether he is discussing the 1860s or the 1960s. Williams not only reads the 1860s to speak of the 1960s but allows us to speak with the students about 2010s. He notes that many of the same issues of 'the franchise' that sparked debate in Arnold's time could be grasped in the tumult of the 1960s. Arnold, like the management theorists and English professors of the 1930s – another period with many similarities concerning the franchise – proposed his criticism as a response to this tumult.

In the mid-Victorian time of Arnold, only one-third of British males could vote. This number would rise to two-thirds towards the end of Arnold's life, meaning that well less than half of the total British adult population could vote. In contrast, the 1960s saw the attempted expansion of democracy into other spheres, including universities, workplaces, and among migrant and marginalised communities. Yet Williams notes that something can be learned from Arnold's shortcomings. In response to Arnold's appeal to executive prohibition in the face of what he calls 'tumult and disorder', Williams (2005) writes that we have to prevent this 'short-circuit' in Arnold's thought:

> The attachments to reason, to informed argument, to considered public decisions, and indeed, in Arnold's terms, to learning from all that has been thought and said in the world, requires something more than an easy rhetorical contrast with the practices of demonstrations and of direct action. (p. 8)

Here is an opportunity to engage students on this question of the openness to new knowledge in business and in society in their contemporary world. For all the emphasis on disruption and innovation, large sectors of the economy, from oil and gas to banking, would better fit Williams's description of the short circuit in Arnold's thinking. Indeed, our students live in a time, and increasingly in a place, whether the United States, Turkey, India or Russia, where Arnold's executive can be said to make precisely this easy contrast between the public interest and 'practices of demonstrations and direct action'.

From learning about the attacks on university professors in Turkey to feminist activists in Russia to university students in India and to immigrants and just about anybody else in the United States, students should be able to make the connections between this debate across a century between Arnold and Williams.

But just as important, they should come to situate the production of knowledge, of disciplines and of systems of thought, including business studies, squarely within this dialectic.

Concluding his case, Williams (2005) writes: 'Arnold is different, and so are our own little Arnolds. Excellence and humane values on the one hand. Discipline and where necessary repression on the other' (p. 8).

Instead, what was required, according to Williams (2005), was that 'those who believe in reason and in informed argument are able, within the noise of confrontation, to go on making necessary distinctions. It matters also whether, in the inevitable tensions of new kinds of argument and new kinds of claims, the defenders of reason and education become open to new and unfamiliar relationships, or instead relapse to their existing habits and privileges and then – as is now happening, but as significantly didn't happen to Arnold – manoeuvre and combine to restrict, to purge, to impoverish education itself' (p. 8).

Though no fan of John Stuart Mill's liberalism, Williams credits him and those who took his position for avoiding the impoverishment of education Arnold seemed ready to countenance in the name of order. Students can begin to reflect on the relationship between change and order and the relationship between order and what Michel Foucault would call the order of things, the disciplining of knowledge, whether knowledge of literature, or business. Such a line of inquiry might return to the twentieth century properly as a next pedagogical step.

The Dark Side of Management

One might then pair those readings with excerpts from Frederick Taylor's (1967 [1911]) less well-known text, *Shop Management*, together with Peter Kropotkin's (2014 [1901]) essay, 'Brain Work and Manual Work'. Or one could even ask students to read *We* by Yevgeny Zamyatin (1972), a dystopian vision of what would happen according to the novelist if Taylor's ideas, much favoured in the Soviet Union in the author's day, were ever fully implemented.

The introduction of an anarchist text might be thought to be mischievous, but on the contrary it gives us the opportunity yet again to remind students that the production of disciplinary knowledge does not take place in a vacuum. As Gerard Hanlon (2015) points out in *The Dark Side of Management*, Taylor was very explicitly anti-democratic and moreover proposed his system as a new system of equilibrium that would not only create a balance between human and machine on the shop floor but also a new psychological equilibrium in the worker, anticipating what Antonio Gramsci would call 'Fordism and Americanism'.

Taylor had the influence of anarchist thought among immigrant American workers very much in mind, to say nothing of the industrial relations of the moment. It should be pointed out to students that Taylor was working and developing his methods at the Midvale Steel Works during the famous Homestead Steel Works strike at the Carnegie and Frick steel operations in Pennsylvania, the defining industrial event of his era and certainly his time in the state. It involved gun battles between thousands of steel workers from numerous factories and Pinkerton private guards and later state militia for the company. It included an anarchist-inspired assassination attempt on Frick. Taylor was not just founding a science in those years but a science to restore equilibrium to a system in the middle of a civil war between labour and capital in his time and at his address.

In this he was a precursor to Elton Mayo, who some decades later, amid other influences on the workers, would say explicitly that the control of what he called 'reveries' was the best defence against worker unrest. Mayo already believed in the need to restore equilibrium in these writings from the 1920s, influenced indirectly as many social scientists were by Ricardo himself. He believed these worker reveries had to be kept in balance.

His exposure to the Pareto Circle would help him systematise his intuition about how to deal with symptoms of class struggle in his workplace. Both Taylor and Mayo were addressing the rise of mass society in much the same way Arnold anticipated with the rise of the middle classes, while Leavis and Richards responded with a social mission for English criticism in British society.

Yet for all his efforts Taylor never achieved a science of the internal equilibrium of the worker. Nor did he found an academic discipline. Nor did Arnold found English as a field of study. That would be left to Mayo and other social scientists influenced by the Pareto Circle.

It is interesting to note in passing that the field of business studies' own most competent disciplinary history, Rakesh Khurana's aforementioned *From Higher Aims to Hired Hands,* makes no mention of the Pareto Circle – though obviously some of the characters from the Harvard Business School make an appearance in his narrative. It is perhaps for this reason that for all its merits, Khurana's book cannot give students the sense of the commonality of the social sciences in their drive for disciplinary status and respect through theory and methods. We are left with an almost anachronistic singularity. But this singularity echoes a contemporary solitude that is hard to dispute and to which we will return in a later chapter.

It is to Hanlon's work rather than Khurana's that we must also refer if we are to have some proper historical sense of the antagonisms producing the discipline. What Hanlon's work documents in particular is that the drive to theorise management, to give it, in Richards's phrase, a theory of interpretation, was always very much bound up with a pitch to corporate leaders, congresspeople, investors and America's circulating elite.

The solution to conflict in society could be found not in new arrangements of that society, whether the Progressive Era reform, or New Deal intervention, never mind social revolution, but inside the factory, the office and the workplace. Discontent needed to be addressed from whence it emanated. Students who learn this lesson learn something of the high stakes behind the sometimes-mundane operations of human resources management.

Franchises

But before we leave these pre-disciplinary discussions, there is one more direction in which we are obliged to take our students, not only for the sake of some kind of context in the current discussion but also as a foundation to lessons we will want to teach subsequently, especially in our chapter on the humanities beyond business ethics teaching.

Although we said earlier that during the time of Matthew Arnold only one-third of the British population could vote, we neglected to say that for the millions of people living under British rule in colonies at that time, from Ireland to India to Barbados, any kind of meaningful franchise was beyond the imagination of the colonial masters, while being less imaginative than what was in the minds of increasing numbers of the colonial subjects as the Victorian era wore on.

It is in this expanded context that we might say that the first business school at Oxford was not the Said School but the Indian Institute, which opened its doors in 1883 in a new building constructed especially for it by Oxford University. The Institute was conceived and built to train young men for duties in the Indian civil service. It was intended as a place of learning for both British and Indian students, though funding and sometimes the will for Indian students proved unsteady.

As Richard Symonds (1993) tells us in his *Oxford and Empire: The Last Lost Cause?*, the Institute started with a strong emphasis on the classical subjects such as Sanskrit, but soon the demands for a more rigorous and systematic training of colonial lawyers, scientists and administrators came to dominate the school. The business of running the empire was after all not purely, or even chiefly, a political one, much less a scholarly one. It was an administrative one.

This is especially the case when we remember that Indian colonialism began as a business enterprise and was run that way throughout the nineteenth century, even after the 1857 Mutiny when the business was turned over to the British state.

Colonial civil servants were in every case trained in administrative techniques for overseeing legal codifications, physical infrastructure works and education. As Gyan Prakash (1999) notes in *Another Reason* the administration of public works under Lord Dalhousie from 1848 to 1856 produced what Michel Foucault called a governmentalisation of the state. That is, the state became an administrator of daily life, shaping daily existence through the ways it managed the population using these public works. In other words, the state became managerial and civil servants needed management training, something some of them now began at the Indian Institute, rather than haphazardly in the field as in the earlier days of colonial rule.

Bernard S. Cohn (1997) in fact links the more scholarly efforts to categorise and separate various Indian cultures, languages and arts with the creation of a system of administrative law that used this local knowledge to build its system of colonial management. Indeed, we might say that the Indian Institute's curriculum, spanning subjects such as Sanskrit and Indian fine arts to the management of engineering

works and the harmonisation of legal procedures, was a far more uni-
tary curriculum linking business studies holistically to the humanities
than the Said School would be able to manage 120 years later.

We must also teach the other side of this argument, however, especially to prepare students for contemporary debates on globalisation.
Although colonial administration was replete with business administration, scholars such as Elizabeth Kolsky (2010), in *Colonial Justice in
British India*, remind us that despite the claims for the imposition of
British law as an essentially civil and administrative act, a matter of
good public management, legal violence was necessarily present precisely because this was an imposition.

Moreover the 'Subaltern Studies' school of Indian historians (see for
e.g. Chakrabarty et al., 2015; Ludden, 2001) will also not let us forget
the connection between colonial law and colonial forms of economic
production and accumulation. Here law did not so much administer
business as frame the very terms of the market under which actors were
forced to act in unequal conditions.

Our own students might also be directed to the current debates
in India about the Uniform Civil Code, a legacy of this systematising administrative effort that nonetheless used cultural and traditional
variations to build its system. As the feminist scholar Nivedita Menon
(2016) has pointed out, the current call for more uniformity might well
be a cover for an attack on differences still encoded in that law, especially differences protecting Muslim minorities in India.

But we could also say to students that something like Fayol's philosophy of universality of administration lay behind this systemisation
and that so much of early supply chain management – which begins in
earnest as commercial logistics with colonialism and the slave trade – is
learned in the colonies.

It is not uncommon in today's business schools to remind students
at the outset of a course of International Business or Global Business
Environments that the East India Company could be considered among
the world's first corporations. It differed, of course, from the twentieth-
century corporation but it was already a global concern, dealing in
foreign markets not only in India but also in the Malacca Straits and
Chinese ports. Less commonly have we taken the opportunity to look at
colonial India as an important precursor in general to the systematisation of business knowledge, though work on the legal origins of British
law in the colonies, and the work of Anjali Arondekar (2009), ought to
be noted. But the Indian Institute, the efforts at public works, creating
legal frameworks and setting up and running of schools were all a piece.

Perhaps the founding document of this ambitious administration of India was Thomas Babbington MacCaulay's (1835) 'Minute of 2 February 1835 on Indian Education', written a full fifty years before the founding of the Indian Institute. This infamous letter proposed to use a system of teaching English literature, history and culture to create 'a class of persons Indian in blood and colour, but English in tastes, in opinions, in morals and in intellect' (p. 724). In short: a colonial management class. It also disparaged Indian and Arabic literatures in a way that would have dismayed and angered scholars of these traditions, as opposed to the Orientalists on which he built his opinion.

Not surprisingly, postcolonial theorists have focussed on the imposition of an education from the imperial centre onto its periphery. But given our discussion of the importance of administrative science in Indian colonial history we might also focus on something else. Indians who came to occupy this class of persons, including those attending the Indian Institute, and who become known as 'MacCaulay's children', were intended to be 'a professional' management class, in much the same way scholars of management would call for the same a few years later in the United States.

MacCaulay was clear that such a class had to be produced because the British could not administer the Indian population of such a size directly. Such management would have to be sub-contracted. Business schools, an (ex)patriate management class, public and private partnerships, and market making in colonial India – about which we have only skimmed the surface – need to be required curriculum for any business student seeking a sense of historical context for her or his own critical thinking.

Comparative Methods

Equilibrium systems thinking was widespread at the end of the nineteenth century and beginning of the twentieth century, influenced not only by Ricardo but by Darwin too. To give just two prominent examples that might be shared with students: Freud's theories relied on the idea of the release of psychic energy to restore equilibrium between the conscious and unconscious mind, to release enough energy from the unconscious to keep it from overwhelming our conscious life. Indeed this was precisely his interpretation of the role of dreams – they allowed for a release of psychic energy while we slept, without overwhelming us as they might if we were awake. And with dreams our waking served as a safety mechanism if this release threatened our equilibrium too much. Emile Durkheim, too, defined his famous search for solidarity in society, a founding approach to sociology, by means of balance.

Students could at this point also be introduced to the postwar work of the French theorist Georges Bataille. His theory of a general economy, as opposed to a restricted economy, was a more or less explicit reaction against equilibrium thinking. Bataille suggested that there is always the need to expend excess energy in a system and that the way a society 'wastes' this energy tells us much about the society. It might be through pleasure or it might be through war.

Rather than beginning from scarcity, then, Bataille (1988) suggests 'the accursed share' – his name for this excess – should motivate us to live in exuberance and not as rational actors. It is an opportunity for students to reflect on just how much of our thinking revolves around scarcity and how scarcity structures what is valuable. Bataille does not escape the systems thinking on energy and waste Freud also promulgated, but he wanted to.

Still, teaching students about systems thinking without emphasising the unique contribution of the case study method would be teaching them only part of their own intellectual heritage. The case method, in all its diversity and whatever its faults, introduced a controlled way to talk about divergent influences and causes and as such more or less explicitly excluded a dominant cause – characteristic of what Henderson called the cause-and-effect school. In part this is why we could suggest to students that while Freud wrote case histories, he did not really embrace the case method.

Let us then finish this chapter with a close reading. Ivor Richards (2004) once advised the American poet and critic Cleanth Brooks to ignore Freud's theories and instead to concentrate on Freud's cases and on the way Freud interpreted the words in his sessions. Brooks (1981) notes that for Richards this method of reading, this science of interpretation, was not designed to replace science itself but to accompany it. He writes that 'it could keep us in mental health so that we could function as sensitive, flexible, resourceful human beings' (p. 594).

But this separation from science did not mean Richards did not employ science, starting with psychology in his early works, and even including later in life Claude Shannon's communication theory and the physics of Niels Bohr.

Let us conclude this chapter with a discussion of two texts, written in the same year, one by an English critic and another by a sociologist and working manager. At first look, students will find no obvious similarities, despite our discussions. Richards's text is over 300 pages and covers a multitude of terms, choosing and discarding them according to the internal logic of his argument. Roethlisberger and Dickson's text is a slim volume, seemingly just reporting the results of interviews and observations with workers at a plant in Illinois. But students might be invited to recall our premises. Each text represents a discipline searching for its rigour in both theory and method. Each text finds that method in the case and that theory in a science of equilibrium. And each text is responding to the changes in the world around it, changes that are tumultuous at the end of the 1920s and beginning of the 1930s.

In Richards's case, each poem he offers becomes a case study in the proper close reading for meaning in the words of that poem. In the case of Roethlisberger and Dickson, it is the observation room and each unit of workers who are studied inside it and outside in the larger plant. Moreover we could say that for Richards what the latter call the technical organisation of work is what he means by practical criticism – that is, the rules and procedures by which one ought to read a poem, just as the technical organisation in the plant are the formal structures through which work ought to flow.

Yet a close reading of the final sections of each book unveils an important difference, and perhaps to the approval of our students we might show something more perspicacious in our management thinkers. After dismissing problems with productivity in the plant as merely a matter of mismanagement, Roethlisberger and Dickson (1939) turn to the tension between the technical organisation and the human organisation of the plant. They note that the workers are often the victims of changes in the technical organisation. These changes have intentional or often unintentional negative consequences for their working conditions. To protect themselves from these forces workers develop solidarities. The authors write that 'it is a mistake to neglect the social factors involved. The real question is what gives rise to these informal organisations' (p. 394).

They note that even if some of these changes might be beneficial to the worker, the workers band together to resist them. The reason, they conclude, is that the worker's 'established routines, his cultural traditions of craftsmanship, his interrelations – all these are at the mercy of the technical specialists' (Roethlisberger & Dickson, 1939, p. 16). What they call his social codes and customs are 'not the product of logic but are based on deeply rooted sentiments' (Roethlisberger & Dickson, 1939, p. 407). They conclude therefore that:

Any plan to promote collaboration among the workers, therefore, has to be thought in relation to its effect on the actual social organisation of the workers and not merely from a logical viewpoint alone. Successful management of any human enterprise depends largely on the ability to introduce more efficient methods without disrupting in the process the social foundations on which collaboration is based. (Roethlisberger & Dickson, 1939, p. 000)

Or as they put it in the negative:

In so far as industrial disputes are often attributed either to the perversities of human nature or to the logical defects in the technical organisation alone, the result in terms of diagnosis or remedy is bound to be inadequate. (Roethlisberger & Dickson, 1939, p. 407)

Meanwhile, here is Richards:

It was interesting to observe the wide range of quality that many individual readers varied through. They would pass, with contiguous poems, from a very high level of discernment to a relatively startling obtuseness, and often force one to consider very closely whether what appeared to be so stupid did not mask unexpected profundity. (Richards, 2004 [1929], p. 316)

In fairness to Richards, he then goes on to make a number of qualifications for why this might be and how in fact it may not be stupidity. But finally, despite this generosity, he does seem to conclude,

On the whole evidence, I do not see how we can avoid the conclusion that a general insensitivity to poetry does not witness a low level of general imaginative life. (Richards, 2004 [1929], p. 320)

Without the benefit of Mayo's warning, Richards then suggests,

When nature and tradition, or rather our contemporary social and economic conditions, betray us, it is reasonable to reflect whether we cannot deliberately contrive artificial means of correction. (Richards, 2004 [1929], p. 320)

Then finally we must quote this passage at some length to suggest our point and how this point might intrigue students. Richards speculates as follows:

It is arguable that mechanical inventions, with their social effects, and too sudden diffusion of indigestible ideas, are disturbing throughout the world the whole order of human mentality, that our minds are, as it were, becoming of an inferior shape – thin, brittle and patchy rather than controllable and coherent. It is possible that the burden of information and consciousness that a growing mind has now to carry may be too much for its natural strength ... Therefore, if there be any means by which we may artistically strengthen our minds' capacity to order themselves, we must avail ourselves of them. And of all possible means, Poetry, the unique, linguistic instrument by which our minds have ordered their thoughts, emotions, desires ... in the past, seems to be the most serviceable. (Richards, 2004 [1929], p. 320)

We might now note with students that poetry for Richards could be understood now in light of management theorists' distinction between technical organisation and social organisation. Is not poetry here precisely his blueprint for a technical organisation of the mind?...

And if so what takes the position of the informal social organisation of the workers? Is it not all of the kinds of reading that Richards considers bad reading?

Next, students might notice a contrast – a kind of respect management theorists show for this informal social world, versus a kind of disrespect or at least disappointment in Richards.

The purpose of this chapter has been twofold: first, to use the common origins of several disciplines to offer teachers of business studies a convincing historical argument to make to students. That argument is that business studies should not be studied in isolation because it was not born and did not develop in isolation.

The second purpose was, of course, to offer students exposure to lessons in history and literature that present different ways of thinking of societal problems and new methods of confronting them – in particular in this instance the close reading of texts. Our task will grow more complicated in the next chapter as the kinship of these fields grows more estranged in the 1950s and 1960s. But as we will argue it is well worth keeping up with the relatives who, it turns out, continue to share many concerns and to feel the pressures of these two formative decades in the humanities and the social sciences and indeed in our contemporary world.

The first book business students ought to read in a course that brings the humanities, the social sciences and business studies (back) together in the 1950s is Arthur Miller's (1952) *The Crucible*. The last book students should read in a course looking at these disciplines in the 1950s is *I, Tituba: The Black Witch of Salem* by Maryse Conde (1994). Or perhaps we should reverse that order.

In other words, to bring alive the scholarship and the important intellectual ideas of the 1950s, it is vital for students to have some idea of the overwhelming sense of menace that the Cold War came to spread in Europe as well as in the Soviet Union and its allies. At the same time as the decade progressed, civil rights and decolonisation provided powerful winds of change amid this paranoid standoff. It is for this reason that not just Miller's work but also Conde's re-imagination of the witch hunt stand as part of what Silvia Federici (2004) understands as the very modern purposes of the witch hunt: to order and drive primitive accumulation for emerging capitalism in the towns of Europe and the slave labour plantations of the New World.

Business studies arise to a great extent in the Atlantic world, one where the continuities from its origins to the Cold War and onward to the civil rights movement are the context for the development of the modern university and in the twentieth century the maturation of many disciplines.

Business studies was far from immune to these larger forces and indeed can be read largely through them. But even if it were isolated from these structuring social and political conditions in its concerns, its intertwined institutional relationships and cross-fertilising growth with other disciplines directly concerned with the tenor of the times would have shaped it nonetheless. The 1950s, and, for that matter, the 1960s, as we will see later, continue to provide us with examples such as the Pareto Circle of the folly of trying to study the development of business knowledge or business schools without thorough attention to the other disciplines of the university. And put more positively, these decades continued to provide us with instances of both real and fictive kinship with these other disciplines in order that students might gain not just a more accurate understanding of where academic business knowledge comes from but a fuller education in preparation for producing future business knowledge and practices more rounded and adequate to our equally challenging times.

In his book *The Cruel Peace: Living Through the Cold War*, Fred Englis (1992) takes us back and forth across the Atlantic to examine key episodes – what we would more likely call cases – that exemplify the dangerous equilibrium of the long 1950s. These cases include focusses on specific historical events, specific indicative biographies and specific novels, films or plays of the time. One such case is that of Arthur Miller's play. Today in the United States this play is still taught in high schools across the country. As Englis points out, but as any American kid knows, the play is used to teach students about the threats to American individualism and the dangers if we do not stand up for that individualism as an ideal. We could say that the play, an extended metaphor of all that went wrong in the Cold War, is still taught, ironically (or more accurately without any irony) in a Cold War fashion, what the American political scientist Seymour Martin Lipset called the 'paranoid style'.

In fact, Miller's play is not a defence of individualism (as even most American students came to discern) but an attack on the fear, superstition and ignorance that the Cold War bred in all its protagonists and antagonists. Few escaped this paranoia, and there is little surprise in saying academia must be included here. Indeed, we could say that academia was one of the more visible victims of this paranoia, especially in the United States.

The 1950s could be said to open in the late 1940s with the purges at the City University of New York, in which without evidence and against any claims to a community of free thinkers, the university purged hundreds of professors and students it deemed to be 'communists'. As Ellen Shrecker (1986) shows in her important study, *No Ivory Tower*, CUNY was but the start.

What is most telling in Shrecker's account, however, is what cannot be told. She notes that we can go through the records to see the number of professors dismissed across the country, but we can never know the chilling effect these events had on scholarship. Students ought to be asked to consider this problem of the counter-factual. What might academic knowledge have been like without this fear, a fear Shrecker and others demonstrate without a doubt coloured every aspect of the Cold War university from the late 1940s to the early 1960s where it would take on new tones in opposition to new 'enemies within'?

Indeed, in the important collection *The Cold War and the University* (Chomsky et al., 1997), we also see that fear was not unfounded or unfunded. As students become more familiar with this history of the Cold War, it will also be possible to discuss with them what survives, lingers and takes on new life from the Cold War and how history is never really past. Such a point will be made even more forcefully when we come to consider the subsequent civil rights and anti-colonial movements and their influence on academic thought.

Reading Arthur Miller's classic play can also give students a feeling for how personal history can be and how great social forces can also be intimate. Miller wrote his play in response to the testimony of his friend, the director Elia Kazan, in front of the notorious House Un-American Activities Committee.

Kazan 'named names', including some in Miller's theatre troupe. The friendship ended, and research for the play began. Kazan would respond, defending himself through the plot of his most famous film, *On the Waterfront*, starring Marlon Brando, finally giving us the individual character with a conscience that Miller refused to write so simply. The ubiquity of paranoia during 'the McCarthy era' combined with the personal nature of its wrenching loyalties and disloyalties is the right frame of mind for students with which to approach a case study from business studies on scholarship and the Cold War – that of Abraham Maslow.

To guide us through this case we will turn to the scholarship of an underrated management historian, Bill Cooke (2002), whose seminal work on slavery and management we will also have occasion to utilise when we come to the 1960s and the relationship of management studies to race and social justice. Cooke and his colleagues examined Maslow's work in its historical context. Their argument is that the history of the Cold War is important to understanding that work and is too often omitted in management theory. We are less interested in entering the debate about whether the Cold War or any historical context gets its due in management scholarship (though clearly we want to give history its place in our teaching) than in the results Cooke and his colleagues produced.

Maslow's diaries show a scholar with a lively awareness of social and political situations in his formative period in the 1950s and his coming to fame in the 1960s. They also show constant interplay with theorists living and dead, from Herbert Marcuse and Kate Horney to Sigmund Freud and Karl Marx, which belies any simple relationship between psychology and management alone.

There was tension between these disciplines despite friendship with Warren Bennis and others and Maslow's own sense that management studies was a fruitful place for his research, as his diaries also make clear. We can use this research by Cooke and his colleagues and by such scholars in psychology as Ellen Herman, who is indeed cited by them, to teach students about the way all the social sciences were drawn into the Cold War and later social movements formed in the 1960s in part against this war, which was in fact both cold and hot, especially for emerging postcolonial states. Moreover, these social sciences existed not just in the Cold War political climate but also in its cultural climate, as Fred Englis teaches us.

Thus this narrative is also an opportunity to extend students' vision to the humanities during the Cold War as they reflect, challenge, divert and re-imagine that Cold War political climate. As the historian of science Audra Wolfe (2013) argues, the use of the term *Cold War* to describe a scholar's work is often heard by others – those who may have been influenced or even mentored by these senior scholars as well as those who rely on that work as foundational to their own theory-building – who have a tendency to hear an accusation. The accusation is that somehow a scholar's work was in the service of the military-industrial complex and discredited American foreign policies, or even domestic examples of repression.

Wolfe rejects this objection precisely in the name of history and social science – if we observe the influence of the Cold War on the work of scholars we cannot refrain from an honest account simply because it may cause embarrassment or hurt and in any case the term is used as a descriptor of a period not of an individual.

In our case, the debates are an opportunity for students to learn something about the politics of scholarship as well as the politics under which scholarship often occurs, and therefore the need to have an understanding, from disciplinary sources that can provide it, of history, sociology and politics.

Cooke and his colleagues did not have the benefit of a superb collection brought out eleven years after their research was published. *How Reason Almost Lost Its Mind: The Strange Career of Cold War Rationality* (Erickson et al., 2013) allows us to extend our discussion from Maslow to Herbert Simon and any number of other management theorists and social scientists and hopefully to generalise the conclusions of Cooke et al.

But first, let us look a bit closer at Abraham Maslow through this research and think about the way students can come to contextualise and examine their own attraction to Maslow. Every business school teacher has had the experience that when students forget everything else in their business school education, they remember Maslow. Or worse, one is in a bar and someone finds out one is a business professor and without fail one has to hear about how someone still remembers Maslow's Hierarchy of Needs (unless it is Douglas McGregor's X and Y!).

Why is this? That is one of the questions Cooke and his colleagues have. They note that Maslow's appeal comes from the way he seems to confound questions of being on the Left or the Right, liberal or conservative or in the language of the 1960s, establishment or counterculture. Famously, the Yippie leader Abbie Hoffman saw Maslow's concept of self-actualisation as compatible with the social revolution in the United States that he and others were advocating in the late 1960s, and indeed Hoffman said he spent many evenings as a student talking to Maslow and eating dinner at his house.

On the other hand, Maslow is known to have dismissed the student movement in both public and private comments and to have been a supporter of the American war in Vietnam. Cooke and his colleagues consider those who have written before them trying to understand Maslow in historical context and conclude that he was a Cold War liberal: that is, he held ideas that could be said to be contradictory.

Cold War liberals expressed a commitment to the individual but saw a strong state as necessary to enforcing that freedom. Maslow embodied this spirit in his theories. He thought everyone had the right to self-actualise, but he also thought, based on his primate research, that some led and some followed, some dominated and some were dominated.

For Maslow, his diaries show this applied not just to people but also to nations. In other words, Cooke and colleagues' argument implies that to teach Maslow to students, and for them to make sense of contradictions in his theories as well as in how those theories were and continue to be received, we should teach students some history of the Cold War as part of their training in management studies.

We would go further to say we need to teach some history of what Raymond Williams called the 'structure of feeling' in this period, and for that we will need also the humanities, starting with Arthur Miller.

The scholars brought together by the Max Planck Institute who wrote *How Reason Almost Lost Its Mind* start their collectively written book with a quote from the 1958 novel *Red Alert* by Peter George and a reference to Stanley Kubrick's *Dr. Strangelove, or How I Learned to Stop Worrying and Love the Bomb.*

This is a marvellous moment in a discussion of curriculum where we imagine our colleagues will be full of ideas for novels, plays and movies that convey the structure of feeling of the Cold War to students. We might suggest our own materials.

The Book of Daniel by E. L. Doctorow (1991) introduces students to a modern master of American prose while at the same time placing them in a deeply affecting story of the execution of the Rosenbergs, accused of being Soviet spies. In contrast, another master of modern English prose, Graham Greene (1981 [1958]), produced one of the funniest books on the absurdity of the Cold War in *Our Man in Havana*. Greene's book was also made into a near perfect movie by Carol Reed (1959), starring Alec Guinness.

Other emblematic films we would want to show are Alfred Hitchcock's (1959) *North by Northwest* and John Frankenheimer's (1962) *The Manchurian Candidate*. Both raise questions of identity, the fear that anyone could turn out to be communist, anyone a spy and give us the sense of the paranoia of the time. The documentary *The Fog of War* (2003), about Robert MacNamara, one of those figures who links business, think tanks such as Rand, and government during the Cold War would also provide more historical context than there would likely be time to discuss, and the documentary could also act as a bridge to the discussion of management in the 1960s and its encounter with the American war in Vietnam.

But, of course, beyond assigning and discussing such material in an integrated business curriculum, there are the pedagogical questions of what one might want to imagine would be, in that unlovely phrase, the 'learning outcomes' of including such material.

All these course materials carry the same contradictions and ambiguities we find in Maslow's theories. Students cannot only be attuned to great prose and to the visual composition of shots but to the themes of loss of identity, the absurdity of life and death, the way power operates in society and how gender performs under the duress of such power – to name but a few teaching moments.

Yet what of the question we raised of the seemingly unique popularity of Maslow and his odd memorability? One of the more interesting ways to try to understand Maslow's ideas on self-actualisation as the basis for a theory of motivation is through the comparison that has sometimes been made, and is taken up again here, between his hierarchy of needs and the major economic development theory in the United States during this period – modernisation theory, where each stage builds on the last.

Modernisation theory, students should be taught, stood in contrast and in conflict with other theories of development at the time, including most of the actual histories of revolution on the other side of the Cold War.

Some postdevelopment theorists, eager to make the point that both sides of the Cold War had theories of modernisation, faith in progress and a teleological approach to history, miss the facts of what was once called 'Actually Existing Socialism'. Russia, China and Cuba did not go through these stages and then take a wrong turn towards socialism. The Soviet Union caught, in some cases surpassed, American science and technology without following any of Walt Rostow's stages or creating any of the institutions and conditions he advocated for postcolonial states.

Indeed, in order to help students understand the Cold War – and through it much of the scholarship, literature and history we are discussing – it is important to stress just the opposite. These places had revolutions that 'skipped steps' and 'jumped paths'.

Cuba went from a corrupt plantation economy to a socialist country almost overnight. This is what postdevelopment theorists who want to paint both sides with the same brush miss. And more important for our discussions with students, this is what fear looked like for American theorists of modernisation such as Rostow. He was not afraid that countries in South East Asia would take the wrong path. He was afraid there would be no path – that there would be revolution because of the legacies of colonialism – and he had every right to be afraid.

When we encounter social scientists such as Rostow or Maslow claiming, as Cooke et al. quote the latter, 'enlightened management as a form of patriotism' (Cooke, 2002, p. 14), the stakes of patriotism and the fears of the Cold War must be accounted for to give his work and the management studies of the 1950s context.

As the authors point out, Maslow was very 'pro-American' and 'anti-European', but he was not particularly what one would call a 'Cold Warrior'. Yet his thinking did parallel Rostow's in interesting ways.

His hierarchy of needs was staged, just like Rostow's take-off theory, and Maslow's utopian finish to this hierarchy was like Rostow's contented consumer society, the end of history. Maslow himself saw a parallel with the promise of Marxism here, but both Rostow and Maslow – dedicated as they were to all the pieces of culture or society being in place and being built and developed – were haunted by the idea that a society might instead leap, rather than take off, into another system altogether.

But understanding Maslow in the context of the Cold War and modernisation theory also allows us to discuss him with students in the context of other disciplines and key scholarship that could also be best understood in this historical and political context. Perhaps the two most famous anthropologists of the postwar period emerged in the 1950s, Clifford Geertz and Claude Lévi-Strauss.

Geertz's first work is a conscious application of modernisation theory to the field of anthropology. Lévi-Strauss's masterpiece of the same period, *Tristes Tropiques*, is a work of what came to be known as 'structural anthropology'. The prominence of these two anthropologists, which would grow through the 1960s and into the early 1970s, is a good opportunity to introduce business students to anthropological thought and method as it was clearly conditioned by the Cold War and by the changes wrought by decolonisation. By looking at them we can give business students a sense of their affinity with Maslow and others working in the same period such as Herbert Simon and James March, whom we will come to shortly.

But we can also broaden our discussion of methods as we did with Richards's close reading in the last chapter. Geertz is most famous for his introduction of what he called 'thick description', a term he borrowed from the Cambridge philosopher Gilbert Ryle. Thick description was proposed by Geertz more or less directly in opposition to the methods he saw in Lévi-Strauss's American early counterparts, the componential school of anthropologists, and he later deployed his method directly against Lévi-Strauss in his critique *The Cerebral Savage*.

For the purposes of working with our students, just as with the rise of Cambridge English, we have to be somewhat schematic and say that while Geertz valued the interpretation of culture and the search for its social meaning above all else, Lévi-Strauss insisted there was something beyond or below meaning, a structure to culture that gave rise to meaning among other things.

Parallels with emerging thinking in business studies should be obvious but are worth restating. While the Tavistock Institute of Human Relations in Britain could be said to adhere to the Geertzian search for meaning, the opening of the Sloan Management School at MIT – and with it in the emergence of operations research and management science – channelled the obsessions of Taylor's project and the systematic analysis of data we will also find in Lévi-Strauss's *Laboratory of Social Anthropology*. Along the way we will have cause to teach students about the way management theory, as a social science, came to be nurtured by a series of Cold War US administrations keen on using those social sciences as a weapon. In the process the entanglement of management studies, the other social sciences and public policy would come fully into view, providing ample opportunity to demonstrate the relevance of these other disciplines to the study and teaching of management.

We will begin with Clifford Geertz. Geertz started his famous studies of Indonesia while at MIT's Center for International Studies, where Walt Rostow was developing his influential modernisation theory. He would continue his work at the University of Chicago.

Clifford Geertz was a part of the Committee on the Comparative Studies of New Nations, a kind of interdisciplinary think tank on modernisation theory that also included Edward Shils and David Apter. Both centres received significant funds from foundations to pursue knowledge about how newly independent nations might be encouraged and helped to move through stages of economic development towards a Western-style market economy. It was not at all clear Indonesia would move this way.

Under President Sukarno there was a tolerance for a large Indonesia Communist Party until 1965, when it was the subject of a horrible systematic massacre following a military coup (Melvin, 2018; Robinson, 2018). But in the 1950s the direction of Indonesia, like many newly independent nations at that time, was unclear. Geertz (1963, 1971) wrote two books based on research in the mid-1950s, considered companion pieces. The first was *Peddlers and Princes* and the second *Agricultural Involution*. Both were explicitly written using the modernisation framework – that is, both asked why development had not 'taken off' in Indonesia and why 'leadership' had not emerged in the economy through an economic elite, two key assumptions of 'take-off' theory. Both books sought to find the answer in the conditions and culture among the peasants and small traders.

Agricultural Involution made use of the notion of shared poverty, (akin to anthropologist Oscar Lewis's subculture of poverty in his study of Mexican peasants. Lewis's study, which would have strong ramifications in American social policy, was taken up infamously by Daniel Moynihan and his colleagues to blame black American culture for its socioeconomic predicament, enraging civil rights activists and intellectuals.

Geertz, however, was not the polemicist or politician of this later moment. He maintained that it was for historical reasons that peasants tended to share risk rather than take individual risk and to share poverty by intensifying their methods in the fields rather than breaking out into some new economic forms.

In *Peddlers and Princes*, students should note that Geertz suggests his two case studies help bolster and explain his general conclusions in *Agricultural Involution*. These two studies are of towns in Bali and Java. The contemporary economists Daron Acemoglu and James Robinson – authors of the influential text *Why Nations Fail* – note that what Geertz was really doing was a study of firms and why they succeed or fail in different business environments.

Significantly, Geertz discovered cultural failings in both environments. In Bali, the cultural traditions were too strong for new forms such as the independent business firm. In Java, the firm could emerge but the lack of a culture of trust and the proper background to create a business environment for a firm led to its failure. Students should be able to recognise, even without the prodding of Acemoglu and Robinson, that this anthropologist has transferred some very modern thinking about economies and firms to what were then called traditional societies.

Students could read passages from his work for a sense of anthropology in that moment and how it looked at the firm in particular. At the heart of Geertz's work as a modernisation theorist are two ideas to explore with students.

First, one needs a cultural change to have modern economics.

Second, cultural change has to be based on sufficient 'substitute' solidarity, common purpose and shared understanding to replace the culture it is supplanting.

In other words, Geertz, like the sociologists he was trained by and among Harvard and MIT, relied on Max Weber's idea of a work ethic and Emile Durkheim's idea of a solidaristic society, a *gemeinschaft* as Ferdinand Tonnies called it. Key passages from these giants of social theory could here be introduced. But can either such change or such solidarity be consciously fostered using the research knowledge of social scientists?

The answer then, as now, seems to be a combination of private doubt and public confidence, of academic caution and political bravado. Though Geertz himself always defended his work and his independence, history was not to be kind to him, and students might want to reflect on that lesson.

As Nils Gilman (2002) points out, Geertz's work would be taken up in the political context of modernisation theory versus communist development in the 1960s in two ways.

First, his implication that peasants in South East Asia were generally passive and risk-averse in their economic strategies reinforced the US government's position in southern Vietnam that if peasants in the south were rebelling, it was because of outside agitators from northern Vietnam.

Second, Geertz's suggestion that colonialism had produced a single peasant culture in Indonesia (and perhaps elsewhere) that valued stability over change led to the conclusion by some policy specialists that development was going to require a technological intervention. The Green Revolution of the 1960s was precisely this kind of outside stimulus, according to its backers in the modernisation camp.

Geertz lived long enough to see his reputation called into question, including his work at the Centre for International Studies (CENIS) and in Chicago, both of which were institutions that took CIA money at a time in the United States when many were beginning to question its role in the world. But anthropology in general, students should be advised, would also change radically in the next decade.

On the one hand, 'peasant studies' would change, and peasants would be shown to be active, rebellious and open to opportunity for change in their own right. The work of Eric Wolf and James Scott could be used to contrast with Geertz. Wolf's work in particular could easily be excerpted to present another argument.

On the other hand, the work of Talal Asad and others asked American anthropologists in particular whether modernisation theory was not in fact a kind of neo-colonial, paternal approach – an American version of the colonial enterprise, even as Americans allied themselves with a history of being colonised rather than holding empires.

Asad and then later James Clifford raised the question most directly of the relationship between anthropology's objective search for knowledge about these societies and the very interested position of the foundations, government agencies and political masters who often made this research possible in the 1950s and 1960s.

Had the story ended there we might have another important synergy to teach students around the common pursuit of knowledge across disciplines in the 1950s and early 1960s but nothing more. However, as with Cambridge English, we also have an opportunity to talk about method. Because although Geertz refers to his study of the two towns in Java and Bali as cases, his idea of what a case entailed was to evolve in a way that has brought him a lasting reputation far more positive than the infamy these early works have endured.

In the late 1960s and early 1970s Geertz (1973) would begin to elaborate his idea of 'thick description'. Students might be given his introductory chapter in *The Interpretation of Cultures*. The first half of that chapter may contain philosophies of knowledge that evade students, but the second half lays out his method beautifully. As Richards's close reading sought meaning in the text, Geertz's interpretation sought meaning in the social situation of the 'text', most famously a Balinese cock-fighting contest.

Geertz's *Agricultural Involution* was published in 1963, and as we have said and Gilman rightly noted, whether this is Geertz's fault or not, it was largely received within a new phase of the Cold War in the United States – the American war in Vietnam.

In retrospect the scale of the changes that were coming could never have been anticipated by Geertz or other social scientists, working as they did with models of implied consensus and equilibrium as norm. This transition in the way scholarship was received might be characterised for students as 'bringing the war home'.

Now scholarship found itself not just in a structural antagonism with an imagined enemy abroad, but 'politicised' by the conflict of analysis and values domestically. Two years later, for example, Abraham Maslow would watch his colleague, the Marxist sociologist Herbert Marcuse, be 'let go' by Brandeis University.

Some of Maslow's colleagues resigned in protest. Maslow did not. The US academic world was becoming as polarised as the political world outside its door. In the same year as Geertz's book appeared, James Baldwin (1995) published *The Fire Next Time*. It is to this work that students might next be directed. The reading of the book might be accompanied by Raoul Peck's (2016) recent film, *I Am Not Your Negro*.

One might turn to Richard Wright or W. E. B. Dubois before Baldwin for an explicit connection between the Cold War abroad and the increasingly domestic civil war that would culminate in 1968, a year of revolt and repression not just in the United States but also in Mexico, France, Czechoslovakia and Brazil. We will return to this year as one to teach students when we move on to the later 1960s in our management studies curriculum.

Wright and Dubois had been making the connection between instability caused by continued colonisation and instability caused by the suppression of civil rights since the war and much before in Dubois's case. But for students the elegance of Baldwin's text and the way it announces that the world cannot continue as it had been is perhaps the pedagogical object we would want here.

Before we leave Clifford Geertz and anthropology, however, we can also offer students the chance to think about organisational culture through his insights. Geertz criticised Lévi-Strauss, as we have said, for suggesting that we could find the answers to how culture worked in the deep structures of the human mind. Lévi-Strauss was trying to develop a new humanism where primitive and industrialised minds all shared these deeper human structures of meaning-making. But Geertz (1973) objected. He wrote in his elegant prose, and we quote at length to emphasise to students the value of such prose in itself:

After a century-and-a-half of investigations into the depths of human consciousness which have uncovered vested interests, infantile emotions, or a chaos of animal appetites, we now have one which finds there the pure light of natural wisdom that shines in all alike. It will doubtless be greeted, in some quarters, with a degree of welcome, not to say relief. Yet that such an investigation should have been launched from an anthropological base seems distinctly surprising. For anthropologists are forever being tempted – as Lévi-Strauss himself once was – out of libraries and lecture halls, where it is hard to remember that the mind of man is no dry light, into 'the field', where it is impossible to forget it. Even if there are not many 'true savages' out there any more, there are enough vividly peculiar human individuals around to make any doctrine of man which sees him as the bearer of changeless truths of reason – an 'original logic' proceeding from 'the structure of the mind' – seem merely quaint, an academic curiosity. (p. 353)

By contrast, Geertz insisted culture is public because meaning is public. There is no private or psychological culture. Culture is enacted by individuals, but it was the product of joint activity. And this meant culture is messy and always in formation. These are lessons that the best of the organisational change and development literature also contain, and these might be fruitfully compared.

Later feminist anthropologists such as Joan Vincent (2002) and Laura Nader questioned whether the public was as 'whole' or visible as Geertz and others presumed or whether the culture that anthropologists sought to make public was not a much more contested and conflicted site.

It is worth noting that Nader's (1972) work on 'studying up' was highly influential in changing what kinds of cultures and what kinds of cultural conflicts would be studied. She advocated ethnography in the industrial organisation, the laboratory, office, bank. Her work in the 1970s anticipated the work on organisational culture in management studies in the 1980s and 1990s and could well form another interanimated lesson beyond the scope of our discussion here. In other words, the rich vein of thinking about culture, and the field of anthropology in general, allows us to talk about the twists and turns of thinking about organisational culture over the past century in management studies too.

From the GSIA to the University of California, Irvine School of Social Sciences

The intellectual biographies of Abraham Maslow and Clifford Geertz show us a way to teach students about the postwar decades of the 1950s and 1960s while at the same time establishing key methodological and theoretical foundation stones for contemporary management studies.

These biographical itineraries are especially useful for teasing out the Cold War context of these key theories. They help us stress the importance of context in the production of theory and reveal the way theorists work within specific historical problematics. Conversely, we can add that to be unaware of this historical context and uninformed about the interdisciplinary influences and confluences of management theory is to be not fully educated in management studies. Indeed, in the figure to which we now turn, we see a culmination of this very awareness.

No one was more alert to the importance of historical necessity and intellectual cross-fertilisation than one of the pre-eminent management theorists to emerge in the 1960s, James March.

A theorist as contemporary as he is historical, his work on leadership, decision making and organisational design remains widely cited and widely influential. But he is also an important actor in the shaping and development of business knowledge institutionally, socially and politically, not only reacting to his times but also sculpting them. His intellectual and institutional journey thus marks another salient opportunity to teach students two of the central lessons of this chapter: social and political context as crucial to understanding the emergence of the problems management theorists set out to solve and the intellectual and interdisciplinary influences with which they undertake these urgent tasks.

In what follows, we will use the original and important research of Donncha Kavanagh (2013), an Irish management scholar who has done primary research on a unique, but not isolated, institutional experiment that helps set the direction of today's management scholarship and moreover offers some reminders of the importance of questioning institutional structures of knowledge production in an era when business schools have become increasingly homogenised by rankings and competition for students, faculty and corporate attention.

James March (1972) may already be known to students, but tellingly, he will likely be known for his research independent of its institutional origins and influences. His 'garbage-can' article and his distinction between exploration and exploitation are probably as close to canonical as anything in contemporary management studies, much like Maslow's hierarchy of needs.

But his institutional work and the social and political context of the development of his ideas are often severed from this popular knowledge. Yet we can use his travels in academia to extend our lessons on the 1960s beyond the Cold War and into issues with which March was grappling throughout the 1960s, including the American War in Vietnam, the civil rights movement and the restructuring of the US economy amid labour unrest and shifting global geopolitical realities.

Between 1964 and 1969, five of the most tumultuous years in modern American history, and five years that included what is sometimes called 'the global year of 1968', March was the inaugural dean of the School of Social Sciences at the University of California, Irvine (UCI). In this capacity, he carried out a bold and revealing experiment in institution building and in the production of academic knowledge, prominently in management studies.

By the time he took up this position, March had already been an integral member of two other seminal institutional arrangements, both highly interdisciplinary and both seemingly beyond the imagination of most universities today.

March received his PhD from Yale University, which, Kavanagh points out, had housed the Institute of Human Relations, an interdisciplinary programme that encouraged co-operation between the hard sciences and the social sciences. March's own institutional experiment would be characterised by an insistence on mathematics, modelling and computing at the heart of social science research. The Yale unit was perhaps at the time the second-most-famous social science conglomeration in the United States, behind only the equally interdisciplinary but less scientifically focussed Department of Social Relations at Harvard University. Harvard's programme was run by Talcott Parsons and was influenced by the Pareto Circle's intellectual agenda.

Under Parsons it maintained a focus on the interpretive, in partial contrast to the more quantitative approach at Yale. Students could be directed to see this split as one March pursued in allying his Irvine project with mathematics and often criticising qualitative theory, especially ethnomethodology as it was emerging in California at the time in Harold Garfinkel's and Harvey Sacks's work, building on Erving Goffman.

Students might also be led to ponder the contradiction here. The author of the garbage-can model might be thought to be more sympathetic to the interpretive school of sociology represented here. But perhaps this contradiction is less thorny than it at first appears. For as we shall see in the construction of the interdisciplinary curriculum, March was keen that social observations be 'empirical'. The ethnomethodologists might quarrel with the definition of empirical, but for March it clearly meant observations that could be converted into data.

While this idea of the empirical might seem common sense to most business students, and indeed business faculty, today, the victory of this definition of the empirical as quantifiable was hardly a foregone conclusion. Theory building in much of the social sciences to this point was much more heterodox and would remain so through the 1970s, as we will see. Large areas of anthropology – as we have already seen – will reject this idea of the empirical, despite Geertz's own early flirtations, focussing instead on the 'interested' qualities of knowledge creation.

Sociology, influenced by a combination of the structural functionalism of Talcott Parsons, the radical sociology of C. Wright Mills, and the ethnomethodologists would continue to resist the idea that social observation could be converted to mathematics. Even psychology, which clearly had an affinity for such data-driven approaches by the 1960s, continued to be divided by psychoanalytic approaches, especially through the influence from Europe of Jacques Lacan and his disciples.

Students might be directed to research current debates in psychology that have seen precisely this resurgence in the psychoanalytical clinical approaches resistant to data deductions. We will cover this movement in the allied disciplines of psychology and psychoanalysis in a subsequent chapter. But for now, it is worth noting with students that March's bold insistence on mathematics as an integral part of social science observation and its application in the world was far more innovative then than it might seem now that it is so hegemonic in management studies.

The Graduate School of Industrial Administration (GSIA) at Carnegie Mellon University in the United States is perhaps more familiar to business students because it was the home for so long of one of management studies' other founding figures, Herbert Simon. Simon himself, of course, cannot be claimed solely by the field of management studies and is widely recognised as pioneering a number of disciplines and sub-disciplines. GSIA was itself both interdisciplinary and multidisciplinary, and symbiotically, Simon was both enabled and enabler in this polymorphous structure of knowledge production.

Simon and the GSIA would make another worthy case study of the vital pedagogical importance of teaching interdisciplinary, historically informed management studies. Like March, Simon was not only a product of such a milieu but also a major protagonist in the creation of these forms of learning and teaching. Today we largely take their work out of context, if not in our scholarship then structurally in the way we teach them within a canon that seems to have no time for the conditions of its own making or the many hands that assembled it.

Like Simon, March was not guilty of this neglect. Just the opposite.

When James March was appointed to launch the School of Social Sciences at the University of California, Irvine, it had yet to enrol its first student. As Kavanagh explains, it was a *tabula rasa* for March's experiment. He set out to create a school with no disciplinary borders and indeed no disciplines. Instead, he set the school up around common problems, emerging paradigms and co-operative projects.

March hired mostly young faculty who, while bearing traditional titles, were to contribute an openness and a lack of rigidity befitting his projects.

These hirings included appointments of political scientists, psychologists, anthropologists, specialists in industrial relations and economists.

The curriculum they created together bore the mark of the urgency of the day. Their first catalogue stated:

Important new problems confront society; and social scientists have a responsibility to assist in the development of solutions to these problems'. (UC Irvine, 1966, p. 79)

What were these problems?

Kavanagh writes: 'the instability within the University of California system was symptomatic of wider sociopolitical upheavals of the time, which centred around United States foreign policy, especially United States involvement in the Vietnam war, which was escalating in the early 1960s, the Civil Rights Movement (the Civil Rights Act was passed in 1964), and a turn to alternative understandings of the human condition (the Esalen Institute opened in California in 1962), and a popularisation of radical (often Marxist) critiques of society and social science' (Kavanagh, 2010, p. 5).

March was also a pioneer in a way that today seems less remarkable – he was a leader of an organisation that studied organisations, and this was rare at the time, in the days before strategy scholars became deans. Kavanagh goes on to list another level, an epistemological/political level, at which March felt the challenge of his times.

Kavanagh (2010) continues: 'There was also an emerging hostility towards organisation. For instance, the Free Speech Movement in the 1960s often cited Paul Goodman, who attacked the "organised system" proffering a utopian anarchist alternative (Goodman, 1960), while C. Wright Mills's *The Power Elite* was also hugely influential (Mills, 1957). And while March was in Irvine new movements emerged such as the poststructuralist, postmodern worldview and the romantic enthusiasm for "flower power" and other countercultures' (p. 5).

Kavanagh's contextualisation is exactly what we are driving at. Still, it is unlikely that the reception of poststructuralism or postmodernism would have reached US academia in March's time, especially the social sciences. Little had been translated, and much was still being written during this time.

But Kavanagh might have mentioned other figures and movements. The feminist movement, the presence of Herbert Marcuse only just south of March at the University of California, San Diego (having found a new home after being fired at Maslow's Brandeis) and Ivan Illich's deschooling of society all cast their shadows and influential critiques over the value of 'traditional' social science.

March is a fascinating figure to study in this context because of how he incorporated much of this foment while remaining faithful to the idea that the social sciences could indeed deliver solutions to these emerging problems cited in his first course catalogue at Irvine. In this sense, students can learn something about the resilience of the social scientific model, particularly the quantitative model.

Students should be reminded that the wind was at March's back when he arrived at Irvine. As many intellectual histories of the modern social sciences attest, the postwar period in the United States (but also in the Soviet Union) saw a great deal of faith being placed in the social sciences by the federal and state governments. The social sciences were understood to have helped greatly with the victory of the Second World War in tandem with the sciences and industries. Scholars such as Simon and March were thus ideally placed to receive support. They were social scientists, advocating more use of the sciences, and aimed much of their work towards industry. But students should understand that had changed by the time March left Irvine in 1969. Not only was industry, and capital accumulation more generally, in crisis by that point, but also the social sciences had suffered, along with the government that promoted them, the ignominy and shame of the war in Vietnam. Their proximity to power, once regarded as a well-deserved position, now looked to be a vulnerability. That March persisted in the face of these changes says a great deal.

The 1967/1968 catalogue seemed to be in spirit with the rebellious times when it stated:

The Division of Social Sciences has no great confidence in a college education that consists solely in regular attendance and grades in a specified list of courses … enrolment in a course is simply a commitment on the part of the student that he will educate himself (with such faculty assistance as is required.) When the education is complete, the course is complete. (Kavanagh, 2010, p. 10)

Indeed, the only 'normal' course was Social Science 1, invented and largely taught by March to all undergraduates and ranging across disciplines to address problems in society.

These problems were to be solved 'with models, some equations, some graphs, maybe a computer programme' as Kavanagh (2010, p. 10) reports one informant saying.

Significantly, because of the presence of linguistics, anthropologists, and sociologists among the young academic staff, several global field sites were engaged too, including Samoa, Mexico, Liberia and Brazil. That a management scholar of March's stature should be engaged in overseeing these international interdisciplinary economic and social development projects presages some of the current recognition that management knowledge or business-led solutions are not enough when addressing international development issues.

Students might be directed to compare current interdisciplinary efforts re-emerging in business schools in areas such as financial inclusion.

At Irvine March also oversaw the development of an experimental farm on campus, which was to provide further opportunity for social observation that could be empirical but soon took on a life of its own more concerned with precisely the kinds of approaches, alternative forms of knowledge and spirituality that March battled in his own experimental organisation.

March is, however, dismissive of the farm in a retrospective interview with Kavanagh. But this is perhaps also symptomatic of some of the paradoxes of the School of Social Sciences and also perhaps one reason the memory of the school is the source of conflicting interpretations, with the next well-known figure to serve at length as dean, William Schonfeld, less than flattering about the experiment, considering it manipulative of younger faculty and students.

March's dismissal of the farm and its inhabitants – he calls them damaged people who endlessly debated questions of leadership and organisation on the farm – reflects some of the ideological divide into which his particular experiment was thrust.

Whether or not Schonfeld and others are right to say that it was too much directed and controlled by March, the form of his leadership was no accident. March was asserting an idea of leadership that was much in contention in his time, and he was asserting a commitment to the social sciences under this leadership model that was equally under attack. What was so noteworthy was that he did not do this in a conservative or reactionary way, as did many professors who found themselves on the wrong side of student movements – like recalcitrant faculty, for instance, at more establishment institutions like Columbia, where Hannah Arendt voiced her notorious opinions of the black liberation movement, and Chicago, whose economic and politics disciplines would forever be attached to the 'Chicago Boys', who carried forth the true religion. Rather, March saw this combination of strong leadership, mathematics, interdisciplinary research and curricular experiment as a form of radical innovation worthy of the changing times.

Perhaps the final lesson students can learn from March and his experiment is something that presages the rise of management studies to its current prominence and may even help explain this rise. Though it might horrify other social science disciplines that fancy themselves as more 'progressive' than management studies, we might suggest no discipline of the time, exemplified by figures like Maslow,

Simon and March, was more committed to interdisciplinary work, experiments in the production of academic knowledge or adapting to the times than management studies. Its subsequent rise, today overshadowing other social sciences, might be, if we follow this curriculum carefully, about much more than the influence of money and corporate resources.

Perhaps no one exemplifies this flexibility and attunement to the times more than the figure we will discuss in the next chapter on the 1970s and management studies, Peter Drucker.

Teaching Peter Drucker in his time and in his milieu will once again provide students with a curriculum that does not stop at the walls erected on the border of today's business schools. But before we leave March, and before March leaves for Stanford and a more conventional career as a management guru, we have the opportunity to give students a sense of the very high stakes involved in what March and Simon before him were trying to do. Because just down the coast in California in March's final year at Irvine, the US national media, and much of the international press, declared another University of California social science professor 'the most famous intellectual in the world'.

Marcuse and March

That man was Herbert Marcuse, and the global year of 1968 turned him from a philosopher with a small but dedicated student following to a global celebrity. His name was evoked by protesting students from Paris and Berlin to Berkeley and Mexico City. Slogans from his books were painted on the walls and left as graffiti. His most famous student, Angela Davis, would herself shortly become a world icon.

But this is not a story of fifteen minutes of fame. From 1968 until his death in 1977, Marcuse sparked a remarkable return of a school of thought, and a project in academic knowledge production, begun in the 1920s in Frankfurt, Germany. Named after the city, the Frankfurt School in fact worked only briefly there before its members began fleeing the rise of the Nazis. They ended up as refugees in the United States and after a spell at Brandeis University, Marcuse found himself at the University of California's San Diego campus, ninety miles south of March and his School of Social Sciences.

In contrast to the support and resources March enjoyed, Marcuse was always on the outs with US universities. As we mentioned, a number of his colleagues quit Brandeis in protest when his contract was not renewed at that university. And the renewal of his contract in

San Diego became a national news story, with then-Governor Ronald Reagan weighing in against the reappointment, joined by the very powerful American Legion, the veteran's organisation, and a local newspaper company.

But it is not for his fame or notoriety that business students would do well to study Marcuse, especially as a rival to figures such as March and Simon, but because of what he had to say and the way his message resonated with so many students in the 1960s and early 1970s.

Marcuse's message was this: why, as society becomes more affluent, do our lives appear to become more impoverished? His was perhaps the first and most direct message aimed not at the working class, the poor or the colonised, but at those who were supposed to have benefitted from the rise of wealth in many countries. Students at American universities counted themselves among his audience, therefore, as did many privileged to go to universities around the world in the 1960s.

Marcuse provided not only the question, but also an answer. Societies were producing a 'one-dimensional man'. We were developing only one side of our personalities while the other side – enjoyment, fellow-feeling, aesthetics and an appreciation for the natural world of which we are a part – was neglected or degraded in importance. Marcuse put the emphasis on the individual and his alienation, and he combined both Sigmund Freud and Karl Marx to make his analysis.

It was, of course, for the latter that he was so broadly condemned in some quarters for influencing students around the world. Yet, for our own students in business school today, Marcuse can feel a very contemporary figure in at least three important ways.

First, the fear that our personalities were being shaped by the drive for material success to the exclusion of other values remains with many business students today. Marcuse's premonition that consumerism would come to dominate and control us through our own desires for more, that all art would be put to use by business and that technology would develop a rationality that we could only follow in its internal logic are so prescient that they appear almost common-sense concerns to the average business student today. But that does not mean they are any less intransigent or vexing.

Second, his work and the work of his colleagues in the Frankfurt School are largely responsible for the circulation of the term *critical* in critical thinking through their espousal of 'critical theory'. Again, the term *critical* is commonly espoused in business schools today as a key component of any student's skill set, and questions of the meaning of the term continue to be influenced by its original proponents.

Third, Marcuse's interdisciplinary social science research group was the original one: before the Pareto Circle, before Carnegie, Tavistock or of course Irvine, there was the Frankfurt School. Moreover, that research group developed the seminal idea of the authoritarian personality (Adorno, 1950) through broad survey research and predicted the rise of fascism, an issue they would link to the other problems they identified in affluent societies and one that our students should not be tempted to ignore in our world today.

Given the unnerving rise of neo-fascist sentiments and organisations around the world today, Marcuse now as then seems, fairly or unfairly, to be addressing more urgent issues than the mathematical modelling of the social problems approach championed by James March or indeed most business scholars today.

With the United States, India, Turkey, and much of Central and South East Asia all seeing a marked upturn in neo-fascist activity and governance models, today's business students have the misfortune of understanding some of the divisions in 1960s knowledge production. Questions of political urgency were not easily put aside, and March's work is much better appreciated in this atmosphere. Marcuse's emergence from the Frankfurt School gives us the opportunity to teach students about the very first and perhaps most well-known interdisciplinary social science programme of research, an urgent one.

Among his colleagues were experts in law, sociology, philosophy and economics, all working together on common problems such as the question of what came to be known as the authoritarian personality, the culture industry and the fate of what they would have called working-class politics. All of this research was collective, interdisciplinary and, in the case of the famous authoritarian personality study, both qualitative and quantitative.

This last area is worth spending some time on with students as a way to link the contexts of management studies across this century and the last. Theodor Adorno, a prominent sociologist in the Frankfurt School, began his research into the authoritarian personality in Germany, stimulated by the clashes between Left and Right forces in that country at the time.

He wanted to understand what led one person to identify with a revolutionary position and another with a fascist position. By the time Adorno continued this work and developed the full study in the 1950s at the University of California, Berkeley, he had taken to calling the revolutionary position the democratic position. The study also become more psychological in its approach.

Initially Adorno and his colleagues sought to understand these personalities in terms of both psychology and class or economic condition.

But perhaps as the world became increasingly irrational, culminating in the Holocaust, Adorno and his new American students felt that only a psychological explanation of such evil personalities could obtain an explanation. Clearly, whether phrased in terms of rational acting and self-interest or class for itself and class in itself, economic explanations seemed inadequate to explain the madness.

The study was published in *The Authoritarian Personality* in 1950 and has been widely debated since. Prominent American political scientists such as Daniel Bell and Seymour Martin Lipset used the term to describe the followers of Republican presidential candidate Barry Goldwater in the 1960s. Though flaws were found in the methodology, recent political events in the United States have led to renewed interest in the psychological composition of authoritarian and fascist personalities.

There is an instructive contrast to be taught around the question of institutional and societal stability here. Herbert Marcuse and James March obviously shared something with all such scholars of the 1960s who did not put their heads in the sand. They saw the interplay of stability and instability in the institutions around them and in society at large. But they read the two conditions differently.

For March some recognition of instability was necessary to stability. For Marcuse some recognition of stability was necessary for instability. For March, as for Simon, Maslow, Douglas McGregor, Elton Mayo, and any number of management scholars who might loosely be classed under the behaviourist category, organisations – and private firms especially – were already subject to a great deal of external instability.

A theory of the firm that expected the organisation to represent stability, clarity, even singularity of purpose and a unified sense of itself, risked adding to the actual instability faced by a firm by placing unrealistic burdens on it and on its leadership in particular. Much of their work as management theorists was to help managers recognise, accept and work with the inherent instability in organisations rather than imagining these organisations in contrast to the instability of markets or society at large.

Thus we could understand many of the concepts March invented or with which he was associated.

Bounded rationality, coined by Simon, became an important term for signalling the limit of information, or potential for stability, and the unknown beyond this available information or the potential for instability. 'Satisficing', invented by March and Cyert, acknowledged that there were always going to be potential conflicts of interest within firms just as there were outside in society.

The garbage-can model went further, suggesting that firms themselves were essentially unstable, and management's job was to try to stabilise enough of the firm to keep it working. These were seminal contributions to management's theory of the firm. But they were also a recognition that even affluent societies would continue to be plagued by conflict and instability. These management theorists saw it as their task to stabilise the firm through advice to leadership that would allow those firms to be sources of stability in a conflictual world. Of course, not least among those attributes of stability was the capacity to sustain production and generate wealth, jobs and shareholder value. But firms were also to be symbols of the way instability could be managed.

Herbert Marcuse took these theorists seriously. But he was concerned with how successful they were and the unintentional consequences of their success. In his analysis, society's problem was that it had been stabilised. He shared with many of his contemporaries a view that a society that was set up around a price-making market (including the pricing of labour) was inherently unstable and so too were its institutions.

In this assumption they differed from those theorists of the 'classical era' who believed in equilibrium, even if they too confronted instability. Equilibrium, with its balance, full information and symmetry, was a possibility for classical thinkers in a way that postwar thinkers could no longer believe. There might be structure, role and function, and even systems, but equilibrium existed only in models. However, Marcuse saw systemic instability as symptomatic. Manifestations of instability were just visible signs of something wrong in the way society was set up, socially and psychologically.

Marcuse believed that work was structured in a way that alienated people from themselves and that, increasingly, other aspects of life, especially consumption, leisure and culture, were also developing in an alienating way for the human psyche.

Consequently, Marcuse did not want to see what he regarded as symptoms suppressed. We could say that each successful management or leadership advance was for Marcuse dangerous in that it misled us into thinking our work and our lives did not require serious healing. Management innovations were for Marcuse a form of repression of the symptoms, a coping mechanism for an inherently unbalanced world. In this he bore the influence of Freud.

It might be easy for students to assume this conflict was one between the practical approaches of the management theorists and the idealistic hopes of Marcuse. But it is important for eliciting a strong pedagogical debate to ask students to consider that his widespread fame and influence at the time suggested that many people, including many students at many world-class universities, considered trying to satisfice the current system to be the truly unrealistic position.

Such a contrast also allows us to discuss with our students the final contribution of Herbert Marcuse and his colleagues in the Frankfurt School – critical theory and the injunction to critical thought that derives from them. And vital to understanding critical thinking as it emerged in the Frankfurt School is that it was a methodological position. Just as we have suggested to students that understanding methods from English and anthropology – close readings of texts and thick description – can help us to historicise, contextualise and 'defamiliarise' our own methods, especially the case studies, so too we can do this with critical thinking as it emerged here.

Critical theorists saw their method as emerging through a distinction in how knowledge is acquired and what status it has in the world. (This distinction might be opposed to one based on *which kinds* of knowledge are best – such as the quantitative/qualitative distinction or historical/comparative, etc.).

One view, the dominant one today and certainly the dominant one in business schools, holds that it is possible to create social scientific knowledge about people and society and to test and falsify that knowledge, again whether through quantification, qualitative observation, theory-building and logic, or historical or comparative and ethnographic means. James March and Herbert Simon were among those scholars to give this position an even more scientific basis with their integration of mathematics.

But as we will see, even with a more anecdotal management theorist like Peter Drucker, the underlying idea of objective knowledge about society, and about management in particular, remains fundamental. The Frankfurt School, students will probably be surprised to be taught, did not believe in the idea of objective knowledge.

Marcuse and the Frankfurt School saw knowledge production the same way they saw all production in and of society. The standpoint from which you viewed knowledge and judged it to be true depended on one's place in the world of work.

Bosses had one standpoint, workers another and consumers a third. The unemployed, small farmers and large landowners all had different standpoints. The same knowledge claim might be adjudicated very differently according to experience, and what was judged true for one class or group might not be judged valid by another. Such 'situated knowledge' would later be developed and refined by feminist thinkers, including most importantly black feminist thinkers such as the Combahee Collective.

But in the 1960s, Marcuse's challenge to social science was this: it is not that truth is relative, nor that it depends on your perspective. Truth is real for one group and false for another. In other words, knowledge is not only in conflict, it *is* conflict. One might even say knowledge production creates instability. March and Simon, and almost unanimously all business scholars today, do not agree with this philosophy. Few business students are likely to do so either.

But it is equally true that few humanities students would disagree with it today. The reason to teach this view, however, is – as we have said – its implications for critical thinking. For the Frankfurt School, critical thinking was a negative enterprise with none of the policy implications of Clifford Geertz, for example.

In particular, critical thinking exposed 'interests' in what was said to be the truth, the interests behind the claim to be objective. Critical thinking did not simply propose new thinking where old thinking no longer worked. Such a knowledge production process goes under the anodyne name of 'design thinking' in business schools today, where the classroom copies not so much Silicon Valley as a Silicon Valley advertisement.

On the contrary, students will be made uncomfortable about the original intentions of critical thinking because they do raise questions about power, authority and leadership, suggesting these are much more partisan endeavours than students will be used to thinking through. But given the failure of business ethics in business schools, a subject to which we will return in a later chapter, a genealogy of critical thinking might be worth teaching as a method of approaching knowledge.

Asking who benefits from the judgements of truth, objectivity, proof of validity or professional consensus is an uncomfortable business but perhaps one that for that very reason can save business ethics from itself.

Certainly we will propose such a critical genealogy as part of a more general rescue of business ethics by the humanities subsequently. But for now we turn to a figure where truth and objectivity are not foregrounded, though they do anchor his epistemology. Instead, management studies in the 1970s and 1980s is inaugurated by the re-emergence not of science but politics, not Marcuse's but one nonetheless with a demotic flair. A good teaching tool for this transition might be the screening of *Herbert's Hippopotamus*, a film ostensibly about a hippo that Marcuse used to like to visit in the San Diego zoo. It is not, of course, that alone but a life of this sociologist of all that management studies would claim for its own.

7   The Demotics of Management

As we argued in the introduction, the business school today is at the heart of the university because business is at the heart of society. We stressed that this was not a political stance on our part, any more than when Kant named religion as the higher faculty or what Cardinal Neumann identified as national culture.

Business knowledge, business discourse and thus management theory occupy such a central role in the contemporary university because students have always gone to university under conditions wherein enlightenment and career were entwined. This was true of a religious education several centuries ago and also of a scientific education 100 years ago (and still today). Such a scientific education came with the promise of more than just a position as an agronomist or engineer but also as an enlightened citizen of a new world of progress, empiricism and rationality.

Even the classical Oxbridge education combined the education of gentlemen with preparation for the mission to use their cultural superfluity to rule at home and abroad, and as we know, many a colonial official was fond of quoting Wordsworth or Coleridge. Boris Johnson, a degraded product of that tradition, parodied this education by quoting Kipling in a Burmese temple recently, but in its original form it was taken as both erudition and qualification in one. Later, in the United States, the liberal arts came to serve as preparation for the emerging 'professional managerial' class after the Second World War.

But soon the difficulties of managing large organisations armed only with Melville and Hawthorne came to the fore for the professional managerial class (PMC), and that of course is where our story began.

The rise of business education, and the at least partial eclipse of the liberal arts, seemed a necessity of history. And yet it bears repeating that this book is written out of the belief that new and (abiding) necessities dictate that this specialised education in running organisations – and latterly in understanding finance and marketing – is itself no longer fit for the purpose. Business is still at the heart of society, and history

128

tells us management studies will therefore remain at the heart of the university. But the question today is, to borrow from C. L. R. James on cricket, what do those know of business who only business know?

Like religious education, where the church grew distant from the parishioners, or scientific education, where the laboratory drifted away from nature, business education separated itself artificially from society sometime in the 1980s or 1990s. How did this happen? And how can we enact an education of and for both business and society? How can we invent a faculty appropriate to our day at the foundation of our universities?

In this chapter we attempt a first effort at this ambitious goal by trying to investigate with students how we got to the point where much of university education became reduced to what Peter Drucker called 'economic performance' by placing this change in a broader context.

With the publication of his classic *Managing for Results* in 1964, Drucker is largely thought to have invented the field of business strategy, a claim he also makes himself. Eventually we developed a term for this kind of writer – the management guru, of which Drucker was the first example and perhaps still the most famous.

Drucker is an interesting figure with which to begin this chapter, helping students to chart the rise of management education to such a hegemonic position within the university today. Studying his work and career can help us introduce to students something of the split between business and society that currently afflicts the university and its curriculum, despite many efforts to overcome the division. The rise of management gurus, culminating in the rise of Michael Porter in the last decade (and the fall of his consultancy firm), can be contextualised in at least two ways valuable to practising the kind of pedagogy of business and society that we seek in this book.

First, management gurus are the most prominent examples, and exponents, of what we might call the demotics of management. It is not just that management became popular in the 1980s and 1990s, and with it business school education, but that management became both popular and democratic – hence the term demotic, denoting both popularity and availability. It became common sense, as we suggested in the conclusion of the last chapter.

Indeed, it is not too much of a stretch to suggest to students that something of the struggles we discussed in the chapter on the 1960s unleashed demotic forces in subsequent decades. They showed themselves, in perhaps an unlikely way, through the rise of demotic management discourses and practices.

Second, another result of the struggles we referenced to contextualise James March, Abraham Maslow and Herbert Simon in those decades was the emergence of challenges to academic discourse, its specialism, its objectivity and its privileges. Management gurus are one result of that challenge. They defy discipline, style and protocol in much of their writings and references. Again Drucker is exemplary here, and exceptional.

Drucker is exemplary in his insistence on the range of influences he brings to his writing, regardless of disciplinary borders or sometimes even disciplinary context. But at the same time, he is one of a kind in that he had an education precisely in the areas of history, sociology, law and literature that have become marginalised in the business schools that embrace him. (To be sure, some of this embrace is precisely based on his appearance as a polymath, an appearance exaggerated by the very narrowness of today's business school discourse.)

Drucker and the management gurus who followed him also represent in their promiscuity the contemporaneous spread of management theory and practice throughout society, now as much at home in public sector and civil society organisations as in the private sector.

Drucker is again especially prominent – beginning in 1969 with his prescient call for 'deprivatisation' (what we came to call privatisation) – in the promotion of such management thinking across sectors.

We can show students that the demotics of management is but one form of change in the 1970s that will come to define the end of the century and the first decades of the twenty-first century.

Drucker comes to devote more and more space in his writing from the end of the 1960s into the early 1990s to the rise of civil society, or what he terms in a more limited way the nonprofit sector. Drucker's point is that civil society organisations must be well run; and being well run means sticking to the objects of such organisations. We will return to his position; the key point for students is that Drucker's attention is drawn in this direction by the growth of the state, especially in the United States through the War on Poverty and the explosion of organisations coming out of other demotics in the 1960s.

Though the growth of the state in Europe and the United Kingdom takes a similar trajectory, there are important differences that eventually manifested in the way in which the United States and United Kingdom 'broke away' towards neoliberalism in the 1980s. But for our purposes we will stay in this section with Drucker and his American context.

With students we can address three new ways society became organised here: through gender, the environment, and the common sense of management practices themselves, personified by Drucker.

The rise of women's organisations, accompanied by the emergence of new forms of feminist scholarship, should be the first introduction students receive to the transition from the 1960s, when second-wave feminism forms, to the 1970s and 1980s when it reorganises much of our thinking and again our common sense. We will use the example of the pioneering feminist Carol Gilligan to illustrate this challenge to method and privilege in society and in academia and the new forms of knowledge her methods introduced and how her work influenced these new organisations of civil society.

As Gilligan was doing her important research, historians in the United Kingdom such as Hilary Wainwright and Sheila Rowbotham were asking questions about the voices and appearances or disappearances of women in history. Meanwhile collectives such as the Combahee River Collective were exploring the contributions and experiments of Black feminists in the United States and trying to link to global feminisms. By the end of the 1970s the United Kingdom's most famous feminist organisation of women of colour, Southall Sisters, had been founded.

Students might be encouraged to see their own inclusion in rapidly expanding business schools in the subsequent decades as part of this general demotics, this democratic expansion of rights and possibilities.

Nor was it only people whose rights became more demotic. The earth itself came to be understood as having rights. The environmental movement cannot, in fact, be separated from the rights being won by people because it has been and remains so connected to indigenous rights. But nonetheless, the 1970s are also marked by the rise of environmental organisations in and of society and their rapid expansion as common sense.

Greenpeace, the Sierra Club and World Wildlife Fund were started or vastly expanded in this decade, as were Woodland Trust and Friends of the Earth in the United Kingdom. The civil society landscape has been utterly changed by the rise of women's and environmental organisations. Add to this after the Stonewall Riots the emergence of what would come to be called LBGT+ organisations, the re-emergence through AIM of indigenous organisations, to say nothing of civil rights, human rights, and consumer rights organisations, and our students may begin to see a picture of society very much transformed. The crystallisation of so many movements into formal organisations gave the issues and concerns of these movements a permanent presence on the landscape, and increasingly in universities too, where programmes in gender studies, black studies and environmental studies became mainstream.

Peter Drucker

Drucker's career spans six decades. But as those who praised him argued when he won the Presidential Medal of Freedom in 2002 and those who mourned him when he died three years later at 95 confirmed, his career can be seen as a complex whole with much continuity and consistency.

For our purposes we want to put Drucker in context for our students the way he himself was often praised for putting management in context. Drucker is remembered for his efforts to read the wider conditions of society and economy in order to recommend the most appropriate forms of managerial and leadership action. It has been said by his biographers and followers that his central problematic was found in his origins, in the Austro-Hungarian Empire where he was born into a family of intellectuals and professionals, and in his youth, where he encountered the scourge of National Socialism and the spread of Nazi evil.

Henceforth, Drucker would be dedicated to the preservation of the dignity of the individual in the face of the organisation. He would try to find a balance between institutional imperatives and individual freedom. Unlike many others of his generation, including the Frankfurt School, who came out of the same situation a few years later, Drucker sought this balance in modern management techniques. His concerns were always by definition about more than management, more even than business enterprise or the market.

Students might be directed to the parallels with other scholars who lived through fascism and fought it from near or far.

Drucker sought his solution in management, particularly what he called management by objectives and self-control (the latter what today we might call self-management or even entrepreneurship). By contrast, other prominent intellectuals confronting this problem sought other solutions.

We have spoken already of the dominant sociologist of the postwar period, Talcott Parsons, who was studying at Heidelberg University in the late 1920s. Parsons believed social scientists must pay attention to the way individuals achieve meaningful roles in society and that it was the task of social scientists to ensure that the institutions of society – schools, families, religious houses, clubs – continued to integrate individuals into meaning in society. Other public intellectuals in the American context who might be compared to give students a sense of the uniqueness of Drucker's approach would be James Baldwin (1998), who as we have seen, already saw citizenship and human and civil rights as the key to fighting fascism, including the homegrown kind. H. L. Mencken and Walter Lippman (2007) pointed to a free press and free speech; John Dewey (1977) to reform in education.

While Drucker would quarrel with few, if any, of these approaches in any alliance for the individual and against fascism, students might be reminded that most of these others we mention, though many were also anti-Communist, would not see management as the key to such a struggle.

Yet it was not just management but a certain open, democratic, popular crusade about organisations being well run that really describes Drucker's lifelong passion for balancing individual freedom with institutional power. And it is for this reason of demotics that we can draw an unlikely line between Drucker and the movements of the 1960s and the organisations of civil society in the 1970s.

Drucker was far from attuned to them in many cases at the level of content. He has very little to say about race, though his most famous practical book on how to manage came out in the year of the Civil Rights Act (also the year James March began his institutional experiment at Irvine). He was equally quiet about feminism throughout his career. And for all his reputation as a prophet, he is not very enlightening on the environment. Nor do areas like consumer rights, freedom of information or business and international human rights figure in his otherwise cosmopolitan thoughts. He tended to prefer to talk about uncontroversial organisations such as the Girl Scouts and the Christian church. But at a deeper level, he shares an affinity with all of these movements for change.

One useful exercise with students would be to go through some of the criticisms made of Drucker's work and help students identify the way these criticisms, whatever their merit, misread Drucker's intent. If Drucker does indeed share a common sensibility with all these movements for change, inclusion and fairness, as his commitment to the nonprofit world would suggest, then maybe what are seen as weaknesses or problems in his work could also be viewed with the students as attempts to realise a demotics of management.

If we take seriously Drucker's belief that well-managed, well-led organisations were the key to striking a balance between individual freedom and institutional prerogative, and a society of such organisations the key to preventing any emergence of fascism, then Drucker can perhaps be seen as dedicated above all else to the spread of good management practice beyond the cadre of private-sector managers he first addresses – in other words, in a movement towards a demotics of management.

Drucker is sometimes accused of being too general in his advice, too anecdotal in his examples and too casual in his arguments. But seen from the perspective of someone who is promoting a society of managers, not just an elite class, his approach makes sense. It is a popular approach in the best sense of seeking to reach those outside the top echelons of private firms.

Certainly he speaks to such established leaders and uses them as examples (as he later does managers of nonprofits) for a wider set of lessons that can be learned by this society of managers and self-managers. *Managing for Results* (1964) emerged from engagement with established managers going all the way back to his time at General Motors.

Students could productively compare his General Motors book to *My Years with General Motors* by Alfred P. Sloan (1972). Drucker claimed the book was a response to his, though no mention of his book is made by Sloan. Such a joint reading would be an opportunity for students to apply some historical and contextual analysis to a management debate in the age of what President Dwight D. Eisenhower would call the 'military-industrial complex'.

Drucker's book concerns itself with the legitimacy of emerging corporate managers, as opposed to owners, and he seeks this legitimacy as part of his desire to find a stable balance in society through good management practices. Sloan's book was published twenty years later.

Two theories of the firm are competing: one that sees the firm as a substantial entity with responsibilities, and Drucker at first appears to side with this idea.

But gradually the other theory, the contractual theory of the firm, where the firm is just a legal structure to deal with transactional costs, an empty firm as it has been called, becomes dominant, and Drucker later seems to side with Ronald Coase et al. In fact, again we could see Drucker's fluid position as trying to stay with the managers as they redefined themselves while promoting good management as the key to harmony, individuality and societal stability.

Drucker also wrote books that concerned themselves with the context of management in history, technological change, culture and politics. Two famous examples are *The Age of Discontinuity* in 1969 and *Post-Capitalist Society* in 1993.

Students might be encouraged to see these books as another part of the strategy of spreading good management practices through society. It was not just that Drucker believed in context as a precondition for good management, although he certainly did so. If we take seriously his own ambitions for management – that it should be a leading practice in stabilising our society and smoothing the transitions into any new society – then we might say to students that he meant these books as the necessary accompaniments of knowledge managers needed to fulfil their roles as societal leaders. Today it is commonplace to see business school mission statements that suggest students should become leaders not just in their fields of business but also in society. It is worth noting how relatively new this sentiment is.

As we have suggested, students might be reminded that in decades past societal leadership was more likely attributed to politicians, journalists, educators and military figures than to business leaders. Drucker was among those who influenced this change, one he believed in deeply because business leaders would bring the key management practices that he thought would keep a society of organisations healthy.

Again his books on politics, technology, culture and history have not been without their critics. For instance, Drucker's well-known criticisms of both John Maynard Keynes and Karl Marx do not stand up very well as scholarly critiques. He himself admitted he did not like the mathematics at a seminar by Keynes that he attended, and there is little attempt to engage either figure through an in-depth reading of their prose or their models.

Many of Drucker's statements about Keynes and Marx are contradictory. Drucker noted that Keynes was interested in commodities while he was interested in people. To say the least, this is an odd statement to make about someone whose work was so dedicated to employment. He claimed Marx's model was applicable only to nineteenth-century industrial capitalism. Aside from the fact that Marx said much the same himself, this easy dismissal of Marx's concerns perhaps did little service to the managers whose ears he had in the 1970s, 1980s and 1990s, who were outsourcing such industrial capitalism globally. Many of the issues Marx identified have come back to haunt such managers, from sweatshops to environmental degradation. A more nuanced approach to Marx might have served Drucker's clients better.

But his dismissal of Keynes and Marx could again be attributed to a certain enthusiasm rather than ill will for either state bureaucrats or labour unions. Drucker believed managers need to be free to manage and that they could develop ways to do so responsibly in a knowledge economy.

It may be true that the knowledge economy has not swept all before it. (The largest job category in the United States today is truck driver.) It may equally be true that knowledge did prove itself, *contra* Drucker, to be vulnerable to monopoly as we see with Alphabet, Amazon, Facebook and other virtual information monopolies. Drucker's praise of Japan now looks misplaced, and his call for privatising services naïve, as funding failed to follow in so many polities.

It may even be true that the defence of the firm as being primarily about wealth making has suffered under a history of public bail-outs and tax evasion cases. But at the time of putting forward each of these positions, Drucker was addressing managers and trying to get this expanding population to think beyond 'management by objectives' and think about economy, society and politics. He was preaching to the choir, but a growing choir, and one that he felt needed to hear an expanded version of events.

No one who seriously studied Keynes or Marx would be discouraged by Drucker's critique, but his critique was not directed at them. No one who understood the intricacies of social policy around poverty, race or crime would be convinced by his remedy of contracting out. But he was not writing to such people. He was writing to create an enlightened manager, a population of knowledge managers in 'employee capitalism' that would be responsible because they would see themselves as the stabilising force providing leadership in society.

Students might thus be encouraged to see the utopian side of Drucker's project, not least in themselves. In other words, students might be reminded how much the world of a television imaginary such as *Mad Men* has gone.

The professional managerial class has been dispersed from a class to a much more general condition. The rise of management gurus, popular management texts and business schools are products of this dispersion.

Today millions of students study SWOT, PESTLE and Five Forces – not just in the United States and Europe but in China, Peru and Zambia. There still exists a core of students in business schools who follow March and Simon into a more scientific and mathematical world of strategy and finance; certainly the majority of business schol-ars prefer this approach, even in fields such as organisational behaviour and human resources (OBHR). But Drucker's project was not this. He wanted all to have access. He saw good management as a social mission.

And access meant not just more but different too. The white male middle- and upper-middle-class managers of *Mad Men* look unlike any business school today, anywhere – not least because they are men. The emergence of the women's movement, of what is termed second-wave feminism, out of the 1960s was a global phenomenon, uneven but global, reflected, for example, in the international institutions that arose subse-quently to tackle gender inequality. The accompanying rise of feminist scholarship provides us with another opportunity to place management studies in context and to look comparatively at methods across disciplines.

In particular, we can return with the students to several of the cri-tiques of Drucker we just mentioned – not this time to reflect on the demotic impulse behind Drucker's strategy but to introduce some methodological questions and with them some new methods for stu-dents to consider.

We have mentioned that Drucker's work was sometimes considered anecdotal, too full of stories and too subjective. It obviously lacked the objectivity sought by James March or Herbert Simon, who themselves were admirably careful about the difference between objectivity and rationality. His work could be said to draw too much on personal experience.

But we have already introduced the students, through the work of Herbert Marcuse, to a certain scepticism towards objectivity; and with feminist scholarship we have another chance to question assumptions of achieving objectivity and connect it to other forms of writing and thinking, not entirely unlike Drucker's style.

Feminist Standpoint Theory and Carol Gilligan

What by the 1980s would be called feminist epistemology or feminist standpoint theory was already being explored in the 1970s by figures such as Cherrie Moraga and Carol Gilligan. Feminists began to raise the question of what kind of unrecognised values go into 'objective' research questions, 'objective' scholarly debates and 'objective' curricula.

As more and more of the assumptions in more and more walks of life came to be questioned by feminists, who suggested these assumptions held unspoken gender bias, it was inevitable that academic scholarship would also come under scrutiny.

What was more fascinating was that it entailed not a mere critique of male blindness to privilege or prejudice about how society should be structured but also the emergence of other techniques, forms of knowledge and experiments in methods.

To illustrate this we look at the work of the psychologist Carol Gilligan, who not only questioned the objectivity of psychology and raised issues of its unseen male bias but also pioneered new methods, in part by including styles of speech and argument that would be familiar to Drucker.

We might suggest to students that, unlikely as it might seem, this similarity has its origins in a common project to expand access, knowledge and power in society. Gilligan's work revolutionised the field of psychology along the way – and for this reason alone is worth teaching to students in our effort to expand the curriculum and promote interdisciplinary knowledge. Gilligan (1982) was a promising student in the world-famous psychology department at Harvard University, studying and conducting research under a number of prominent names in the field such as Lawrence Kohlberg. She soon came to notice, however, that the classic studies upon which the field was largely based routinely excluded women from the studied populations. She noted in her own classic work, *In a Different Voice*, the culmination of her work in the 1970s and published in 1982, that 'the disparity between women's experience and the representation of human development, noted throughout the psychological literature, has generally been seen to signify a problem in women's development' (pp. 1–2). Thus women were often left out of studies on moral development because they did not fit the model or had failed to develop sufficiently in the eyes of the researchers making the initial assessment of data. Gilligan noted this failure of women to 'meet the theories' that male psychologists had developed goes all the way back to Sigmund Freud and Jean Piaget. But she suggests that instead we should see that 'the failure of women to fit the existing models of human growth may point to a problem in the representation, a limitation in the conception of human condition, an omission of certain truths about life' (Gilligan, 1982, p. 2).

Thus her challenge throughout the 1970s was to account for this limitation, and to try to overcome it, in order to present other ways of understanding morality, ways that women for reasons of history and culture had kept alive and cultivated. These human qualities tended by women needed not only to be acknowledged and respected but also made available to men, for the sake of the species. Gilligan summarises her project this way:

At a time when efforts are being made to eradicate discrimination between the sexes in the search for social equality and justice, the differences between the sexes are being rediscovered in the social sciences. This discovery occurs when theories formerly considered to be sexually neutral in their scientific objectivity are found instead to reflect a consistent observational and evaluative bias. Then the presumed neutrality of science, like that of language itself, gives way to recognition that the categories of knowledge are human constructions. The fascination with point of view that has informed fiction in the 20th century and the corresponding recognition of the relativity of judgment infuse our scientific understanding as well when we begin to notice how accustomed we have become to seeing through men's eyes. (Gilligan, 1982, p. 6)

Gilligan will also make very good use of literature, together with her clinical studies, to make this case. Students might be directed to this technique within her method. Literature and film from Virginia Woolf, to Henrik Ibsen and Ingmar Bergman are not so much made to serve social scientific investigation as they are to interrogate the social scientific.

In other words, literature is regarded as a source for trying to overcome limits in the social sciences. It is not merely an adjunct to a scientific education, some exercise in thinking more flexibly or more ethically. Rather, students could come to understand literature as another way to investigate the world, giving it a status alongside science.

This lesson would be a valuable one in business schools, where the humanities are often relegated to being useful only in support. But this lesson is not the central lesson of Gilligan's methods. She notes something about her clinical studies too:

> Both these studies expanded the usual design of research on moral judgment by asking how people defined moral problems and what experiences they construed as moral conflicts in their lives, rather than focusing on their thinking about problems presented to them for resolution. (Gilligan, 1982, p. 3)

One of Gilligan's studies focussed around an abortion clinic in Boston in the 1970s. She interviewed women before they made the final decision to have an abortion and also a year after. The other study focussed on university students and asked them to comment on a moral dilemma: A man must obtain a drug from a pharmacist to save the life of his wife. But he cannot afford the drug. Students are asked if he should steal the drug.

What Gilligan did in both cases is allow those asked to begin to construct their own moral problems around their real situation, in the first instance, and the perceived problem in the second. The second study involved both male and female students.

What Gilligan discovered is that when psychologists begin to listen to women and allow them to construct the problem, rather than imposing problems and logics developed among men, something very interesting is observed:

> Women's moral weakness, manifest in apparent diffusion and confusion of judgment, is thus inseparable from women's moral strength, an overriding concern with relationships and responsibilities. The reluctance to judge may itself be indicative of the care and concern for others that infuse the psychology of women's development and are responsible for what is generally seen as problematic in its nature. (Gilligan, 1982, p. 16)

In the study with students, Gilligan noted that when women were allowed to construct the problem, they consistently prioritise not the rules nor the rationality of the question but the relationships in the story. These results in turn led her to ask whether a moral vocabulary could be discovered that was based on the construction of human relationships, rather than principles or procedures, as the basis for moral development:

> But to derive developmental criteria from the language of women's moral discourse, it is necessary first to see whether women's construction of the moral domain relies on a language different from that of men and one that deserves

equal credence in the definition of development. This in turn requires finding places where women have the power to choose and thus are willing to speak in their voice. (Gilligan, 1982, p. 70)

The abortion clinic became such a site. Women had the power to choose but with moral dilemmas that had to be voiced in their own vocabulary. Again Gilligan found that rather than focussing on religious or legal conceptions of morality, women tended to voice the issues in terms of responsibility. She noted that growth and development could here be understood as the movement towards a strong enough sense of self to insist on the mutuality of this responsibility in relationships. Often women began by voicing their responsibility to others, but only after some time, including in some instances after the event, did they begin to construct a moral universe in which responsibility flowed in many directions. As Gilligan put it, 'care becomes the self-chosen principle in judgment that remains psychological in its concern with relationships and response but becomes universal in its condemnation of exploitation and hurt' (Gilligan, 1982, p. 74). Thus care requires no scaling to become universal.

We have spent time with Carol Gilligan's work as part of an effort to show students that this expansion of the definition of moral development, resulting from the energies and insights of the second-wave feminist movement in the 1960s and 1970s, gives us a new context for understanding the concomitant rise of popular management discourse, the demotics of management signalled by Peter Drucker.

But we can also go deeper here. We can recall for the students that the specific form of management Drucker advocated from at least the mid-1960s and into the 1990s was Management by Objectives (MBO). It is very clear that this technique was a form of listening to employees, constructing objectives together and giving employees the right to define how they understood these objectives. As much as his management books seem focussed only on the world of managers in firms or later government and nonprofits, Drucker was clearly and crucially influenced by his times and the history making going on around him in the form of these movements. All of these movements at the most general level emphasised opening up the way situations were defined, the participation in those situations and the judgements in those situations.

One could say this also separated Drucker's MBO from its predecessors. In fact, focussing on the part of MBO that frustrated Drucker himself by being the least taken up by practising managers – self-control – makes these connections and contexts even clearer.

We can recall for students that self-control meant that all managers became responsible for the results that they themselves helped to generate with their own managers. Moreover, we can note that since first identifying knowledge workers as a class of worker in the late 1950s, Drucker moved increasingly towards an inclusive workplace where more and more employees could be understood as managers and included in this system of MBO.

Self-control meant being able to act on certain agreed principles, but those principles were agreed through relationships and involved the growth of a network of responsibility in which senior management was responsible to those below in the organisation and those below to senior management. This relational form of management was key to how Drucker understood the role of management in ensuring that fascism would not re-emerge through organisations in society or because people were alienated from those organisations.

Drucker would eventually move away from the workplace as the glue of society. But in the 1960s and the 1970s and up to the 1990s, he sought forms of moral responsibility in those workplaces, through MBO and its self-control mechanism, that mirrored the larger forces in his society seeking to expand a sense of people's responsibility to each other and to escape the technological rationality against which Herbert Marcuse warned.

Carol Gilligan refers to her findings as the emergence of 'an ethics of care in responsibility'. She anticipated the re-emergence of an ethics of care in philosophy and other academic fields twenty years later, but she also read the times in which she lived. Those times saw movements that students now take for granted, but they changed the way we think about organisations.

Participation, trust, inclusion, diversity and constructive criticism are all now accepted parts of corporate organisational culture. But the very idea of corporations having a moral development that could be nurtured was not even accepted by Drucker himself originally. That he became, indirectly at least, a proponent of such organisational moral development through MBOs may be viewed by students with some irony, and justifiably, but it might also be interpreted as evidence that scholars work within an intellectual ferment that is heavy with the concerns of the day.

Even if Drucker and Gilligan would never find themselves in a common research project in the mode of those who worked at Irvine or Carnegie-Mellon, they nonetheless found themselves reacting to the same intellectual weather.

But it was not just the moral development of the person or the corporation that was at play in this weather. It was also the relationship between the two. The rise of logistics in the 1970s and 1980s and its incorporation into operations management as a field can, and should, be taught to students as an example of this coming together of the moral development of individuals, of citizens and of the corporation. Tracking the rise of the environmental movement, of indigenous movements and the rise of logistics – and of what would come to be called in the 1980s supply chain management – provides us with another way to emphasise to students how vital it is to understand something of politics, culture and society if they are to understand the origins of fields of management.

Operations management may seem at first to be an unlikely candidate for such an expansive view, though today it is quite common to think in terms of green logistics and ethical sourcing and supply chains. The origins of this happy development in operations management lie squarely in the context of its development in the 1970s amid the burgeoning global environmental movement. It does not end there, of course, and today we continue to see the need to teach logistics in the context of global issues in labour, environment and consumption. But there it begins.

The Environmental Movement

As with the relationship between the feminist movement and the work of Peter Drucker and the management gurus, we ask students to look below the surface of the discourse to its deeper structure when considering the environmental movement and its relationship to logistics, operations management and supply chain management.

Environmental thinking is perhaps the most popular contemporary form of systems thinking. But with Drucker, as with film and media and feminist theory, we do not assume with the students an original equilibrium but an intervention in disequilibrium. Drucker was certainly no feminist in method or theory, yet at another level the demotics of management he promoted ran parallel and in the same spirit as the democratic demands of women for lives that allowed for the full development of every individual against the plaintive objections of patriarchal myths of the past. Moreover, that full development was grasped by Drucker in his MBO schema and by the feminists in the development of a feminist ethics of care in which men and women were to be bound to each other by mutually agreed responsibilities – not the same as but not structurally unlike managers and employees.

Students could be encouraged to look for the same deep structures of homology in the rise of supply chain management (incorporating logistics and integrated with operations management) and the environmental movement. We have already addressed equilibrium systems with students when discussing the origins of management thinking in the Pareto Circle. Such equilibrium systems, even when acknowledged to be disturbed or incomplete, as in the seminal work of both James March and Herbert Simon, were nonetheless understood, like all equilibrium models, to be closed systems. The environmental movement made more popularly available another kind of systems thinking, open systems thinking.

In open systems thinking equilibrium and integrity are not assumed. An open systems way of thinking is more than acknowledging external shocks to a system; it is breaking down the very idea of a discrete system separate from its environment. The rise of the environmental movement does not mark the first time open systems had been introduced to management theory, but the ubiquity of the environment movement in the 1970s and 1980s must be conveyed to students to give a proper appreciation of its influence on common sense and the way it began to persuade management theorists that neither economies nor firms could be taken as self-contained entities.

It is important to note at the outset of our discussion of open systems that this way of thinking should not be confused with mere open and closed supply chains, a business strategy that simply involves trying to monopolise some technology or industrial technique. We are speaking instead of a different world view, where firms are no longer seen as separate boats in a sea of equilibrium. It was this world view that led management theorists to deal with what Drucker himself called in 1962 the 'distribution problem', not as a problem of the firm but one of relationships of knowledge and action.

The connection of logistics to operations management and operations management to supply chains was a result of this change in world view and went well beyond a strategy or even a solution to the distribution problem.

Of course, today with disruptive thinking and chaos theory and any number of theorists who have made their way into management thinking – Nikolas Luhmann, Humberto Maturana and Francis Varela, for instance – we are required to remind students that open systems thinking was jarring to management thought in its day. The environmental movement may be studied as the context for this abrupt message of changed thinking. Coming to define organisations by what Gregory Bateson would call their family of relationships departed from the century or more of interest in establishing equilibrium. Supply chain management – if not in the exact language – was the first discipline in business to suggest that perhaps a firm is nothing more than its relationship not with itself (as the theories of the firm suggested) but with its environment. And the use of the term *environment* is not accidental. There are at least two ways to give students the sense of the social environment created by the environmental movement in the 1970s and 1980s. One way is to take students through some of the land-mark environmental crises of these decades. Sometimes the urgencies of climate change suggest wrongly that environmental crisis is new. A lot of these decades dispel that 'presentism'. Climate change may be the worst crisis humankind has faced, but it has had competition.

The second way lists and describes the incredible amount of environmental activism, heroism and tragedy of these same two decades. Regardless of which approach is chosen, environmental issues were a matter of nightly news and daily headlines in those decades and came to influence our cultures of thought and our structures of feeling. This social environment was reinforced by a steady flow of films, television and novels on the subject – as well as the retrieval of classics like Henry David Thoreau's *Walden* – that now become resources in the classroom. One thinks of the excellent film made of the life of activist Karen Silkwood – *Silkwood* (1983) directed by Mike Nichols with Meryl Streep or the environmental dystopian film Soylent Green (1973) with Charlton Heston and Janet Leigh, for example, both of which convey the mood of their times for students. But let us begin with an events-based summary of environmental history in these decades.

The first Earth Day was celebrated in 1970 with millions calling for attention to the environment and for cleaning the air, water and soil. But it was to be also a decade of environmental disaster. In 1972, we had the first examples of widely read environmental journalism, W. Eugene Smith's photographic essay of mercury pollution in a Japanese town, Minamata, after which Minamata disease took its name. In West Virginia the first of a series of dam disasters, killing 125 people and displacing 4,000, took place the same year. This was followed by the Canyon Lake Dam failure, killing dozens more and destroying 1,335 homes in June of that year.

The next year environmental issues mixed with health and safety issues as a liquefied natural gas plant exploded, killing forty workers on Staten Island, New York. In 1976 the Grand Teton Dam would fail, killing fourteen and shaking people's faith in these mega-projects to control the environment. The Liberian-registered tanker *Argo Merchant* crashed off Nantucket, releasing nine million gallons of oil. The next year the Ecofisk oil well blew out in the North Sea, and the Laurel Run Dam gave way, killing forty people in Pennsylvania. Then in November of that year, the Kelly Barnes Dam collapsed, killing thirty-nine college students and staff.

In 1978, the Love Canal story broke, highlighting how many people around the world lived atop contaminated water and soil. The founder of the environmental justice movement, Robert Bullard, also wrote his ground-breaking reports that year, called *Cancer Alley*. Bullard drew attention to the way African-American communities, lacking representation and conventional political power, were targeted for dumping of DDT and PCB-laden soil.

The next year, the Three Mile Island nuclear plant melted down.

These were only the headline environmental disaster events of the 1970s. Many, many other smaller events contributed to the change in how people understood their relationship to the earth and systems that were not in equilibrium.

The Love Canal scandal continued into the 1980s, when residents were finally relocated. Internationally, the plight of the Amazon forest and its inhabitants entered public consciousness. Unfortunately, this awareness emerged as news of rubber tappers trying to defend the forest being murdered by ranchers became public.

Then in 1984, the global impact of unsafe environmental practices reached a tragic peak with the Bhopal disaster. Over 10,000 people died from leaked chemicals, and 50,000 required long-term care. The site remains toxic. Union Carbide (later bought by Dow Chemical) was found criminally negligent by the Indian government, but no serious compensation or clean-up was ever committed.

The next year, 1985, the *Rainbow Warrior* bombing was revealed to have been the responsibility of the French government. The destruction of the Greenpeace ship killed a photographer on board and made international news for weeks.

Then in 1986, there was Chernobyl. Anyone who had been sleeping through the past decades of environmental consciousness was unlikely to remain so.

To top off the two decades, the Exxon Valdez oil tanker ran aground in Alaska, dumping eleven million gallons of crude oil.

There are, however, many ways to teach this history other than as a litany of disasters, as much as that litany does make clear that no one writing any scholarship in any field would have been immune to the changes in thinking about the earth and its relations. There is also a history of progress that, students might be led to understand, first informs the open systems thinking of supply chain management and later more intentional developments such as green logistics and sustainable supply chains.

The 1970s and 1980s also saw a series of victories for the environmental movement and environmental thinking of open systems. The United States, one can now say nostalgically, led the world in these victories during this period; 1970 saw the creation in the US, for example, of the Environment Protection Agency. And the same year saw the creation of both the National Oceanic and Atmospheric Administration and the Occupational Health and Safety Administration.

The civil societies of both the United Kingdom and the United States were also places of great organisational innovation in these decades. The Natural Resources Defence Council was created in 1970. The next year Greenpeace was founded in Canada. In 1972 the United States passed laws protecting water quality, coastal areas, marine mammals and people (against insecticides, fungicide and rodenticides, though most of the reviews of dangers posed by these agents never happened). DDT was also banned in the United States, although American companies continued to export it.

The global community was also active in these years, creating the United Nations Environmental Programme in 1972, a year after a landmark treaty brokered by the UN on wetlands, the Ramsar Convention. In 1973, eighty countries signed an agreement on endangered species, and the United States passed its own Endangered Species Act. Numerous indigenous movements to protect forests and waterways emerged into the consciousness of the media and public in these decades as well, though many had been working for decades, even centuries, and served as inspirations for many Western and Northern efforts.

Influential environmentalist books were also published in this decade, including *Small Is Beautiful* by E. F. Schumacher and *Gaia* by James Lovelock.

In the 1980s the United States implemented its Superfund to clean up toxic waste sites. More militant environment groups also emerged, such as Earth First and People for the Ethical Treatment of Animals. Diane Fossey published *Gorillas in the Mist*, on which a Hollywood movie would also be based, providing a resource for students who can track the growing consciousness of issues through such hit films.

The 1980s also marked the end of US leadership on environmental issues, symbolised by a vote in the UN against a World Charter for Nature (the vote was 111 to 1). However, civil society continued to be entrepreneurial on the environment with the founding of Earth Island Institute, the International Rivers Network and the World Resources Institute in the early 1980s. The decade ended on a hopeful note, despite Chernobyl, with ratification of the Basel Convention against the international shipping of toxic waste and the Amazon Declaration.

And in a symbol of the global strength of environmentalism, already vibrant in India, Brazil and elsewhere, an important book by Chinese journalists on dams on the Yangtze River was published.

Just as the feminist movement had caused a new valuation of relationships as a way to understand moral development, the environmental movement emerged out of the unavoidable.

These decades of environment crises created a sense of humankind as based on a set of mutually dependent relationships rather than as an individual as a fully self-regulating system. This change in thinking had an undoubted impact on management theory's view of the firm, the leader, the employee, the economy and most visibly on the understanding of logistics, the distribution problem and supply chain management.

We have an opportunity to teach students about the environment, therefore, not as a matter of stewardship or corporate citizenship or the triple bottom line, but as an epistemological turn, a way of seeing systems and the systematisation of knowledge that is a discipline differently.

As we have suggested, to reach this level of understanding, where our way of thinking begins to change, students might be challenged to look at the environmental movement through film. This would also be an opportunity to introduce one of the newest branches of the humanities: film and media studies, not as it has influenced marketing and communications in management theory but in its own right as a way of understanding a changing world.

And no times were more full of change than the 1970s and 1980s when it came to environmental, open systems thinking. Our guide for this pedagogical journey will be the leading media theorist Toby Miller, who is an especially suitable guide because he not only is a recognised expert in film, television and media theory but is also a thought leader in considering the relationship between the growth of electronic media and its impact on the environment.

Film studies, media studies and new media studies enjoyed some notoriety at the turn of the twenty-first century in the United Kingdom. As the idea of the university shifted from a public to a private good, we began to see attempts to apply a more instrumental cost-benefit analysis to the higher education of students. As a public good, the university resisted this kind of calculation. How could one measure readying students for citizenship or preserving and extending national culture? More important, such benefits would not accrue in any case to the individual but to the collective.

However, with the introduction of more and more fees and the increased measurement of academic staff productivity, gradually the notion of the university as a private good came to take hold. Students should pay for education, the argument went, because each student is the beneficiary of this institution. The question of how much a degree was worth led to measures of employability and in turn to the idea that some degrees might not lead with any certainty to employment. Media studies, already known for its recalcitrance to the assent of such privatising logic, quickly became a shorthand for politicians and policymakers eager to make the point that universities need to be re-aligned with the new individualised cost-benefit thinking.

At the same time, it would be a shame if one of the most important technological and social forces of our time, the rise of multichannel media and especially of social media, should be clouded by this particular ideological debate.

Of course, business schools should be praised for the speed with which they have picked up the importance of social media, as well as the importance of media infrastructure to economies. However, the very urgency with which business schools have engaged social media and the massive global 'mediascape' more generally has often meant that more considered questioning of the role of social media and critical examination of big media has not received the attention it deserves.

For this very reason, we turn to media studies, including film and television and social media studies, to give students a perspective from the humanities that they can integrate with the operationalised learning they gain in business schools on the topic. We will also have occasion to introduce students to new methods as a result of this foray into media studies. The case study of Queen Mary shows how marketing and media studies could be blended as part of a larger curriculum experiment.

Miller (2009) is widely recognised as a definitive expert on the development of media studies and its allied disciplines. He also writes about environmental issues as they affect and are affected by the media. He has written numerous 'state of the field' articles. As we saw in his intervention in the debate on humanities teaching, his work is highly accessible in style and available through his website for curriculum use. We will attend to just one, entitled 'A Future for Media Studies'.

In this article Miller traces the history of media studies *avant la lettre* by distinguishing what he calls Media Studies 1.0 from Media Studies 2.0. The rise of popular media dates back several centuries, of course, to the pamphlets and broadsides of the Reformation and the French Revolution and so too, Miller points out, does concern among intellectuals and academics with the possible negative or uncontrollable effects of this popularly available media on the population.

Later these concerns would be known in media studies as effect studies, and today they continue to ask questions such as whether violent video games produce violent children – a question that was being asked about 'penny dreadfuls' in London nearly two centuries ago. But media effects thinking also has a history of positive correlation, particularly in the attempts to create citizens through a national media, such as the BBC and PBS.

The recent 'Oscars So White' protest in the United States represents the persistence of this kind of effects thinking. Representation, it is both hoped and supposed, will correlate with positive change in society. Miller notes that much sociology and social psychology, concerned with issues such as the rise of urban crowds in the nineteenth century, could not help but turn their attention to the effects of media, whether newspapers in that century or the emergence of film (and popular music) in the twentieth century.

We would recommend viewing Adam Curtis's (2002) film *The Century of the Self* as part of this introduction to media studies. It provides a parallel track of the rise of marketing, seemingly intent on maximising the effects of media even as social scientists worried about the damaging constructs produced by marketing and media. But not all media studies would question the embrace of media effects one sees in the marketing field, including in e-marketing.

Miller notes that Media Studies 2.0, influenced by cultural studies, celebrated the rise of popular media and saw those who consumed it not as victims of its effects but what today we would call 'prosumers'. For Media Studies 2.0, consumers of media and participants in social media code and recode what they consume, giving what they see and hear new meaning, making their own communities and developing their own novel forms of communication and expanded outlooks on a global world.

Miller notes that for these media theorists, new media, including new participatory coding platforms and social media, represent the best chance to build a new global citizenry. Rather than pointing to the protest over the Oscars, these theorists might point to the organising abilities of Black Lives Matter or recent protests in professional sports, made possible by social media.

Of course, there is much debate about the role of social media, in particular in global citizenship movements, whether the Arab Spring or the Umbrella Revolution. But what Miller wants to do is to show us that both versions of Media Studies have limits and need to be combined to produce what he calls Media 3.0. We can situate our lesson with students in this call by Miller. Because what Miller sees as the missing glue that might hold these together and build them into something durable is work. The very work that our students do and train to do.

What media studies can do – taught in the way Miller teaches it to us – is to illuminate the real lives of our students who can then be in a position to view films that they see as part of their education in a much more demystified way and one that allows them to connect to the importance of the environmental issues they seek to foreground. Miller argues that Media Studies 1.0 sees the media as too powerful, monolithic and agential. He says this view neglects the work of interpretation people do when they encounter media, but he does not therefore side with Media Studies 2.0. That is because 2.0 sees this interpretation but not as work. Or as Miller puts it, not as an activity that might contain conflict, differences and issues to be worked out in society. For Miller, 2.0 is naïve about people just as 1.0 was, only in opposite ways: one school thinks too little of people and the other perhaps too much.

Miller's remedy is to introduce the real case of people working at Electronic Arts (EA), the game industry giant behind the FIFA video games, among others. EA was exposed for overworking precisely the kind of creative employees we hope to produce in business schools. The point was not to condemn EA but to give us the perspective we need to educate our students in preparation for the media sector.

Media is neither a great force manipulating us nor a playground of the future. It is a workplace from the perspective of our students, and as a workplace it must be studied with the seriousness with which management studies has undertaken to study other workplaces. Students working in areas such as e-marketing are producing a product powerful in itself (and not just a tool for other products), and they can benefit from understanding the world of media as a workplace, even if that workplace does not stop at the traditional door of the office or factory.

But that is not all. We can take what Miller calls Media 3.0 into our discussion of the environment and especially into our viewing of films on the environment to help us teach students about film theory and about environmental issues at the same time. While film theory and environmental issues may seem quite distinct, in fact Media 3.0 can help us to make the links and develop more connections between disciplines and more holistic thinking among our students in the process. Such holism will still be interpretive – especially by introducing the idea of the documentary witness, where seeing is believing but also, as film, the suspension of disbelief.

But first a word about teaching environmental studies to students of any kind, including business students, who often possess a strong disposition towards problem solving and practical, immediate solutions. We could say that the demotics of management continues to spread, especially now, into other parts of the world that had previously been outside the orbit of contemporary business scholarship and business schools. We will discuss some of the challenges of spreading this knowledge in our chapter on an African integrated curriculum. But the story is one of progress in management's reach.

However, the history of the environmental movement recounted here in summary from the 1970s and 1980s has not enjoyed the same fate. Many reversals, including recent high-profile examples such as the United States withdrawing from the Paris accords, characterise the lifetimes of most of our students. Some positive developments are available, like the rise of indigenous movements' visibility. But students can come away with the idea that environmental issues are intractable and getting worse, even if all they do is follow the news on climate change or perhaps especially so.

We often say to our students that we have to keep changing films on climate change each year because each film becomes quickly out of date for not being pessimistic enough!

Media Studies 3.0 can help us here. As it allows us to talk about a workplace with different and sometimes opposing interests and a topic that should neither be seen as overwhelming in its force or entirely benign in its malleability, we have the basis for approaching the environment, and the films about it, differently. If one approaches the issue of environmental disintegration as Media Studies 1.0 does, then the films we see will overflow with doom and require on the other hand that everyone come to agree we should turn the ship around. Here the environment is a powerful and unified force, and we can only stand against it together (and of course students notice how little evidence there is that this is or will happen).

On the other hand, if we veer to the tradition of Media Studies 2.0, as outlined by Miller, we will then be susceptible to naïve case studies (some alas produced by business schools) and individual stories of heroism that will make students feel good. But those among them paying the closest attention may yet raise the question of whether such anecdotal inspiration is really the point. And this leads us to Media 3.0.

Conversely we may now also be at the point where we can rethink the relationship between the anecdotal and the scientific, between admissible and inadmissible evidence, between recognised and dishonoured forms of knowing. Such was the promise of certain autonomous moments like those that erupted in the 1970s and continue to erupt where they are least valued but most valuable.

Management theory of the 1970s shared a certain affinity with this autonomous movement, even if it could not bring itself to face some of the contradictions. It may be, as we shall see later in the chapter on Africa, that in the next decade it will find itself produced by a new generation of struggles, and it will again have the chance to explore its demotic, vernacular side.

Part III

The Future of Liberal
Management Education

8   From Ethics to Liberal Arts in Today's University

Speaking of a shift in the business curriculum is often misunderstood by many colleagues and university leaders as a brief for ethics. This misunderstanding may typically take two forms.

First, any discussion of the idea in the liberal arts sounds abstract to some business school ears and is automatically associated with the one area of business school curriculum allowed some licence to be abstract, ethics. This is the less distinguished position and speaks to the deficit of true conceptualisation in what Thomas Kuhn would call the normal science of business school thought and scholarship.

Second, a more engaging reason for associating liberal management curriculum reform with ethics takes the purpose of liberal arts education to be ethical. At least in this instance, one starts with a partial truth. Ethical reasoning runs deep in the liberal arts, but it could by no means be said to summarise them. However, it might be interesting to make the opposite point as well: ethics education in business schools can by no means summarise the need for liberal management education.

In what follows, we will point to one such insufficiency that reliance on business ethics is likely to encounter if not buttressed by a full and rigorous liberal management education capable of deploying a complete range of imaginative, creative, critical and dissenting thinking.

It may be observed without controversy that most leading business ethics journals focus more on research than pedagogy. In this, they follow journals devoted to other fields within the discipline of business and management, which also routinely give more space to research than teaching. Some would argue that those interested in pedagogy have other outlets or that ethics journals do occasionally feature special sections devoted to teaching and curriculum. However, in what follows we will make the case that in the field of business ethics in particular it is more important than ever to try to see business ethics 'whole' and to bring teaching and research together around this question: is it possible to teach business ethics effectively within what has been widely diagnosed as 'the corporatisation of the university'?[1]

Indeed, is it time to take the corporate university as a prime case study in the problems of ethical behaviour in organisations; even more controversially, our argument goes, is it possible to teach ethics in the university without being undermined by the very teaching environment today? We argue business ethics as a field has not come to grips with these questions, and we urge our colleagues to do so in what follows.

The Academy of Management Learning & Education (AMLE), for example, has periodically featured articles and special sections on teaching business ethics. Section editors have used the unique scope of the journal to include a range of meditations on the obstacles to teaching and learning ethics in the business school (Bell, 2009; Egri, 2013; Giacalone & Promislo, 2013; Kenworthy, 2013; Starik et al., 2010). The organisational context of the business school itself has featured centrally in many such articles, especially the way that another set of values, less conducive to ethical reflection, is expressed through the rest of the business curriculum (Giacalone & Thompson, 2006). Business ethics scholars have asked pointedly whether the business school is itself an ethical context for the teaching of business ethics, whether the ethos of most of its curriculum is compatible with, or even tolerant of, such business ethics teaching and learning, even after all the public and professional attention business schools have received on the matter. In returning to these vexed questions, authors and editors in AMLE are not unique.

In a recent review of twenty years of ethics scholarship in the *Business Ethics Quarterly*, written in the wake of the 2007 financial crisis, Edward M. Epstein (2010) reminds his readers with some resignation that 'calls to "retrain the business schools" to emphasise the ethical responsibility of business professionals are hardly new'. Nonetheless, after conducting a recent and comprehensive survey of the state of business ethics

---

[1] We will offer a range of citations on the corporatisation of the university – the now almost uncontroversial assumption that a traditional university can be managed, and indeed understood, in much same way as a private for-profit corporation. A short list of such citations would include the classic work of Sheila Slaughter and Gary Rhoades, *Academic Capitalism and the New Economy*. This follows the pioneering work of Stanley Aronowitz's *The Knowledge Factory*. Some other key citations would include former Harvard University President Derek Bok's *Universities in the Marketplace*; Frank Donoghue's *The Last Professors*; Marc Bousquet's *How the University Works*; Gaye Tuchman's *Wannabe U*; and Gary Rolfe's *The University in Dissent: Scholarship in the Corporate University*.

education within business schools, Larry Floyd and his colleagues (2013) again reissued a call in the *Journal of Business Ethics* 'for those who have the power to improve business ethics education (to) reflect on their obligations to business schools and society in using that power'. This reissued call has a slight feeling of despair about it, made all the more poignant by the many references by Floyd and his colleagues to the powerful business educators who have indeed called for reform of the business school to change the ethical context of business ethics teaching. If the business ethics journals have sometimes veered towards a dignified resignation on ethical reform of the business school, the media has been more impatient with its criticism of the ethical limits of business schools, their capacity to teach business ethics effectively and their ethical impact on the world of business.

The *Harvard Business Review Blog* (admittedly a hybrid animal of media, academia and social media) has been serially concerned for several years now with question of blame after the financial crisis, and business schools have figured prominently as the usual suspects. Meanwhile the financial press has in recent years sensed the opportunity for a little sensationalism with, for instance, *Bloomberg.com* featuring this not atypical salacious headline: 'Do Business Schools Incubate Criminals?' (Zingales, 2012). At the same time there has been increasing room given to more sober reflections on the *zeitgeist* enmeshing students and faculty in today's business schools (Harney, 2010, 2011a, 2011b).

This critique of the context of the business school tends to be tied to two related lines of inquiry. On the one hand, there is the extensive literature on organisational or workplace 'context' of ethical decision making in business ethics scholarship. A recent comprehensive review of this literature can be found in Valentine et al. (2013) in the *Journal of Business Ethics*. We will not rehash that literature here because we want only to mark its importance as a line of inquiry. But Birtch and Chiang (2013), writing in the same journal, have reconfirmed the specific importance of the business school context on business students' ethical decision making.

On the other hand, there is, as Epstein goes on to say, a forty-year tradition of criticism of management education in the context of ethics and its failures, including the persistence of corruption, exploitation, discrimination and environmental abuse in the world of business for which business students are being prepared.

Readers of this journal will be familiar with the most prominent of these arguments, extending from Jeffrey Pfeffer and Cristina Fong (2002) through Henry Mintzberg (2005) to Rakesh Khurana (2007).

Gabriel Abend (2013) reminds us that these critiques are as old as business ethics teaching and go back to the turn of the twentieth century, though this makes them no less urgent.

Contextual analysis of the business school has, to be fair, prompted some of the most interesting experiments in business ethics education. These experiments take holistic approaches to reforming the business school curriculum, as for instance, in the two programmes reviewed by Sandra Waddock and Josep Lozano (2013) at Boston College and ESADE in Spain recently in this journal.

In these exemplary programmes, the potentiality of ethics education was strategically bound to the educational environment of the organisation as a whole. These programmes were 'total' programmes in which all of the curriculum was integrated and aimed at 'a holistic perspective on the role of the individual leader or change agent in building a better world and asking them to find ways of working toward effecting what is meaningful' (2013, p. 227). For Waddock and Lozano, the general critiques of management education must be addressed to create the right environment for teaching ethical leadership aimed at 'building a better world' (p. 281).

Attention to the ethos of the business school as a context has also led to an expansion of what we might call the context of the context itself. Robert Giacalone and Mark Promislo (2013) in their article assert that students come to the business school from a context in which there is a predominance of what they call 'econophonic' language in which all societal values are phrased in terms of money.

Students also learn, long before they come to a business education, to despise those in need and to be suspicious of anyone placing moral values ahead of personal or organisational material gain. But like much of the best contextual analysis of business ethics education, there is a context that is left out, even in this most comprehensive indictment, and this context is the university.

Few have asked this obvious contextual question: is the university itself an ethical organisation conducive to the study of ethics in the classroom? More specifically, do students studying business ethics experience the university as an ethical organisation?

This contextual question has rarely if ever featured among the preoccupations of business ethics scholars. We might speculate initially that the reason for omitting this question is precisely because of all the public focus on the business school as the problematic ethical component within the university (something that our colleagues in other divisions of the university are not above rehearsing). Or perhaps because we accept too quickly the often-unstated premise that the university is founded as a space that is somehow in but not entirely of this world, that it retains some of its monkish roots and that what is left of this ethos is to be found not in the business school but in the liberal arts, the putative heart and soul of the university.

Indeed, the business school needs to deal not only with its self-critique but often with the accusation that its influence is undermining the rest of the university, either by bringing the university too close to the world of business or bringing business too close to the university through the influence of its management, leadership and accounting techniques and theories.

But the attention on the supposed sins of the business school or its influence on the rest of the university has perhaps detracted business ethics teachers from raising this larger question: do our students experience the university as a whole as an ethical organisation?

In some sense this question would have seemed an obvious one to ask, and the university has in fact rarely been free of robust confrontations over its ethical character. For example, when we were undergraduates at Harvard College and at Georgetown, the lawns in front of our dormitories were strewn with 'shanty towns' protesting these universities' investments in apartheid South Africa. Long before we arrived inside those ivy walls, our predecessors protested the presence of ROTC recruiting offices or defence contractors on campus during the Vietnam War. For our younger brothers and sisters, campus protests would burgeon around the use of 'sweatshops' to produce university caps and sweatshirts, or campus gentrification plans for urban neighbourhoods.

Student occupations and protests continue to today on campuses in the United States and globally around any number of issues. But we want to draw an important distinction here. Many of these campaigns took as their premise this assumption: that the university was a more ethical organisation than most and one that ought to be held to a higher standard, and that on the issue in contention the university was failing to live up to its true nature. In that sense, then, the question of the fundamental quality of the ethos of the university was not raised in those instances where the university was asked to live up to its presumed organisational values.

Many education scholars would say that something has fundamentally shifted in this premise in recent years, and this viewpoint is especially present in much of the scholarship of the last fifteen years, which has been highly critical of the university.

However, before turning to the rise of critical literature on the university, we should caution ourselves against imagining a nostalgic past, or indeed romanticising the history of the 'idea of the university', to borrow the title of Cardinal Newman's (1852) influential lectures. Despite the pejorative stereotype of the ivory tower, the university has rarely been conceived in the Western tradition as a world apart. From Kant to Cardinal Newman, to Charles Eliot and Clark Kerr (Kant, 1992; Kerr, 2001; Trumphour, 1989), the university has always been understood to exist in a kind of suspension between obligation and freedom, authority and independence (Thomas & Harney, 2013). It was never conceived as a pure ethical space and so by extension these are not the stakes of what critical education scholars see as the shift. It might better be understood not as a profanation or disenchantment but as a shift in the balance of power.

This balance of power has itself hardly been stable or reliable for those seeking to dwell in the limited freedoms it has historically allowed. We have only to remember the history of purges and restrictions on academic freedom documented in books such as Ellen Schrecker's (1998) *No Ivory Tower: McCarthyism and the Universities* or indeed Craig Steven Wilder's (2013) *Ebony and Ivy: Race, Slavery and the Troubled History of America's Universities*. Or in more recent history we might remember the analysis in the speeches of Mario Savio, leader of the Free Speech Movement at the University of California, Berkeley, when he accused Clark Kerr's 'multiversity' of being nothing more than a factory for producing employees. Or even more disturbingly, we might refer to struggles at San Francisco State University of California ten years later to implement a black studies curriculum, a suggestion that was met with billy clubs and expulsions.

If something has shifted, it has not been from a space of purity by any means but rather from a space where such expectations of ethical superiority were persistently raised even in the face of the university's own failure to exhibit these qualities.

So what, according to education scholars and commentators writing over the last 15 years, has shifted the balance of power in the university away from this expectation of ethical superiority, even in the breach? And how are students experiencing this ethical shift in the university?

For some of the most critical scholars of the contemporary university, the answer is that the importation of market behaviour, or more precisely more market-like behaviour, shifted the balance.

And for them the beginning of this shift is precise: 1980. This is the year the United States passed into law the Bayh-Dole Act. This act permitted universities to privatise publicly funded research results for commercial gain. Here lie the origins, according to some, of the drive to commercialisation in the university, what some of the fiercest critics have called 'academic capitalism'.

Sheila Slaughter and Gary Rhoades (1999) published their influential book, *Academic Capitalism: Politics, Policies, and the Entrepreneurial University*, in 1999, and the term quickly gained currency as a way to name what Slaughter and Rhoades called the 'involvement of colleges and faculty in market-like behaviour'. Both scholars have gone on to run high-profile centres on education research studying this market-like behaviour in the contemporary university at the University of Georgia and the University of Arizona, respectively.

This work followed two other books of notable impact by David Noble and Bill Readings, though they approached the subject with very different theoretical tools. Noble's (2002) *Digital Diploma Mills: The Automation of Higher Education* was an indictment of what he saw as the de-skilling of university teachers through digitalisation, modularisation and what today we would call blended learning. It was a book as shocking for the way that it talked about the university as a workplace like any other as it was for its condemnation of the technologies so many university administrators hoped would improve the efficiency and scope of their institutions.

Noble saw the university as merely aping the private sector and seeking efficiency and scale like any corporation in part through the reduction of labour costs rather than attending to its higher calling.

Equally important was the sophisticated and erudite work of Bill Readings, drawing on a knowledgeable reading of the history of the liberal arts and using post-structuralist thinking.

The University in Ruins (Readings, 1997) was published by Harvard University Press over fifteen years ago but continues to be read, discussed and widely cited. In the book, Readings argues that the core values of the university have been replaced by the floating signifier 'excellence'. Without specific content or reference, this term was being used by administrators to advocate market-like behaviour and manage the university as a business. According to Readings, it was necessary to found a new community of dissensus in the university, one that allowed for renewed freedom of expression, conscience and ethical attainment.

But the shift was not occurring in scholarship alone, nor only in property rights and leadership rhetoric. From 2001 to the present, American university campuses saw some of the biggest unionisation drives of any sector in the country. As Marc Bousquet (2008) would document in his book, *How the University Works: Higher Education and the Low Wage Nation*, the vast majority of these were driven by graduate students seeking to form unions because they regarded themselves more as workers than students, often for good reason, given their hours and conditions.

They also had good reason to consider themselves in need of union protection. In *Steal This University: The Rise of the Corporate University and the Academic Labour Movement* (Johnson et al., 2003), the editors had early in the last decade already gathered documentation of anti-union practices that would be the envy of some of the most notorious private corporations in the unwanted spotlight for their dubious labour practices. And in *The University against Itself: The NYU Strike and the Future of the Academic Workplace* (Krause et al., 2008), Andrew Ross and his colleagues detail a particularly vicious battle at New York University between graduate students and many full-time and adjunct faculty on the one hand and the administration and many senior faculty on the other.

Crossing picket lines at the University of Illinois, Berkeley, or NYU throughout the last decades or more, undergraduate students must surely have had pause to consider the university and its values, whatever their sympathies. Graduate students in the first decade of the new century were in little doubt they were in a workplace as surely as any other, with the added disadvantage of the inability for many to admit it.

Beyond the revelation of the university as a workplace, and one with a high degree of conflict in its labour relations, other subtle changes close to the student experience also threaten to disenchant the idea of the university (Martin, 2011; Menand, 2010). For example, the changes to the student experience promoted so fervently on more moneyed campuses, from the upgrading of cafeterias to multicultural eating stations, from the inclusion of climbing walls and skate board parks to the wining and dining of parents of both prospective and enrolled students, effectively treat students as customers. Whether or not they are called 'customers', this market-like approach to creating a consumer experience does not so much condemn the university as unethical as remove any special claim to ethics.

Students may also experience enrolment management and learning management systems that signal broader managerialist interventions in the sometimes gentile administration of traditional universities.

It matters less that some of these systems, including accounting systems or some leadership styles, borrowed from the private sector might be effective in encouraging accountability and improving life on the campus; they nonetheless can give students the impression that a university is an organisation like any other. And given that the model of the organisation today is the corporation, it is little surprise that with a little less condemnation than earlier critics who used the term *academic capitalism* or saw the university as an exploitative workplace, many recent authors speak matter-of-factly about the 'corporate university'.

Taking his inspiration from Bill Readings's book, Gary Rolfe titled his recent book *The University in Dissent: Scholarship in the Corporate University* (Rolfe, 2012). Rolfe uses the term *corporate university* to describe an institution that has drifted away from its roots in the Enlightenment and no longer pursues either of the main Enlightenment projects, neither truth nor emancipation: neither knowledge produced for itself as part of a life of the mind (and soul), nor knowledge produced to lead to more democracy and human development. Instead, argues Rolfe, it has given these tasks over to business to pursue and seeks only to serve business and be as much like a business as possible.

Other recent books are hardly more generous. Building on another important first-generation critique of the corporate university, Stanley Aronowitz's (2000) inventively prescriptive book, *The Knowledge Factory: Dismantling the Corporate University and Creating True Higher Learning*, and several other recent works propose ways out of this market-like behaviour. Aronowitz goes so far as to devote the back of his book to a new curriculum that would enact many of the values of 'true higher learning' in the way it was taught and how it was learned, but most important by re-engaging with the great classics of world civilisation.

Inspired by Aronowitz, Canada-based scholars James A. Cote and Anton L. Allahar, writing ten years later in their book *Lowering Higher Education: The Rise of the Corporate University and the Fall of Liberal Education* (Cote & Allahar, 2011), accuse the university of 'mission drift' before proposing an alternative to the return to elitism and in so doing raise the question of whether a return to classics is compatible with a more democratic mission for the university today.

Dan Clawson and Max Page (2011), also inspired by Aronowitz, take a similar prescriptive approach in their short and belligerent book on the need to invest in higher education to protect it from market forces, not integrate it with them.

The list of such works goes on and is regularly added to, most recently by a group of UK-based scholars. Stefan Collini's *What Are Universities For?* (2012) sounded an alarm after numerous warnings in his articles in the *London Review of Books* documenting first the increasing managerialist burden of auditing and ranking research 'outputs' in UK universities, then the introduction of a 'market mechanism' through trebled tuition fees and finally the introduction of favourable government preferences for private higher education in Britain.

Private providers, as they are called in the United Kingdom, are brilliantly dissected as an industry swarming with the short-term philosophy of private equity firms by another British scholar, Andrew

McGettigan, in his recent book *The Great University Gamble: Money, Markets and the Future of Higher Education* (McGettigan, 2013).

There is, incidentally, very little study of teaching and learning business ethics, or ethics at all, in this burgeoning for-profit higher-education sector, despite its size in the United States in particular. But given the way the practices of this sector have recently been roundly condemned precisely on ethical grounds by a US Congress committee report (2012), we suspect organisational ethics could perhaps be an issue for these institutions.

The clear case against private providers aside, despite this torrent of criticism beginning with the condemnation of the academic capital-ism critiques and bitter struggles over labour issues, most contemporary critics of the corporate university do not accuse the university of great crimes.

The one exception here is the relatively new exploration by scholars such as Andrew Ross (2011) of the corporate university's complicity through its overseas activities and campuses with regimes whose human rights and workplace records often amount to crimes. The long-term prospect of universities making their peace with regimes that often will not allow the term *human rights* to be written on a university home page risks not so much moral ambiguity as moral bankruptcy.

In general, the point of these critics is this: the university is no lon-ger a special place, or more exactly is no longer experienced as a place that ought to be special, or a place apart. In fact by calling it corporate, more than anything else, critics are saying it is much like the rest of the world, which is itself corporate in this sense – inspired by the best practices of the business world and attentive to customer satisfaction.

Governments, NGOs, and small businesses all seek these practices.

The phrase *corporate university* is used pejoratively not in the main because the corporation is held to be irredeemably unethical or evil, but rather because it is understood to have no special mission to be more ethical than the world around it.

To call the university corporate is to say first that it has lost whatever was special about it. Nonetheless, the ordinary business organisation is also regarded by most business ethics scholars not only as ordinary in its ethics but too often deficient even for its place in the quotidian world.

As the guest editor of AMLE's section 'Evidence, Ethics, Corruption and Value' reminds us: 'years post-Enron, we are still dealing with organ-isational corruption in the form of excessive bonuses and executive pay, sexual harassment, discrimination and bullying, to name just a few areas that are symptomatic of the absence of ethics and of control and moni-toring' (Bell, 2009, p. 253).

If the university is no longer a place apart, however contested and tentative, but a work organisation like any other, then it is also subject to the real-world failures in ethics like the ones listed earlier in reference to the corporate world, as both the labour struggles on campus and the expansion of international campuses lay bare.

To be corporate, to be just another workplace, is to be, therefore, in ethical peril. It is not to be a place where a special respite is given to allow ethics to develop and transform.

Finally, then, it seems to us that if we are to give proper credit to the work done on understanding the relationship between acting ethically and the organisational context of that ethical action – and we do think this work has merit – we must take the university as an organisational context as seriously as we have the business school itself. It may be that under further investigation these critics of the university do not tell the whole story or do not grasp the opportunities that remain in the university.

We would argue, finally, that one such missed opportunity is to engage the business school seriously. The business school is obviously no stranger to the dilemma of its context, straddling the university and the corporate world and inviting the corporate world to the table in discussions of curriculum, while at the same time being invited through consultancies and executive education into the boardroom.

But if today this is perhaps also the condition of the university more generally, at least according to its many critics, we in the business school have something to teach others about how to negotiate this new reality. In particular, it would seem our ability to distinguish good and bad corporate practice would be invaluable at a time when the word seems to be applied indiscriminately in some of the critiques.

For instance, even such piercing critiques of the corporate university, such as Christopher Newfield's *Unmaking of the Public University* (Newfield, 2011), suffer from a simple dichotomy of public sector and private sector in rhetoric that would rarely be so caricatured by good business scholars.

Tapping this discerning knowledge in business schools might mean forming more conversations across schools of business and the liberal arts, or it might entail offering practical advice to university managers and leaders beyond the walls of the business school on precisely the difference between good and bad corporate practice or the interdependence of public and private enterprise. Business students could become engaged in the debates of the corporate university and play an informed and informing role, rather than being consigned to the role of onlookers at best, or at worst those who, according to students in the arts and sciences, 'just don't get it'.

At the same time, there may be something for the business ethics scholar to learn by looking past the business school and its curriculum to the university context. The way ethics is 'taught' in the university, and especially through the liberal arts, compared to the way it is taught in the business school, may itself be worth reconsidering. In the liberal arts curriculum there was rarely a course called 'ethics', though there were usually specialty courses in philosophy with such titles. (Indeed, the relatively new phenomenon of 'moral education' in university core curricula appears a recent reaction to the threats of ethical disenchantment posed by the corporate university, as the editors of a new collection, *Debating Moral Education: Rethinking the Role of the Modern University* [Kiss & Euben, 2010], themselves imply.)

Rather, the liberal arts historically took what its proponents would understand to be a less instrumental approach to the teaching and learning of ethics. It was imagined, and still is where the traditional liberal arts curriculum holds sway, that the ethics of the student would emerge through the study of great works and that the very moral complexity and ambiguity of great works, and just as important the very act of close reading and critical interpretation of the works, would prove a kind of training ground for the development of the ethical subject.

Ethics in such courses was rarely divided into categories, applied to cases or tied to decision making. Reference might be made to philosophical schools or to contemporary social and political issues, but reading Homer or Euripides, Dickens or Zola, Ellison or Fitzgerald was primarily understood to heighten ethical sensibilities by allowing students to dwell, like the university itself, in a suspended space where decisions, applications, and categories remain at a distance.

This approach to developing the ethical subject was perhaps most famously enunciated in F. R. Leavis's withering attack on C. P. Snow, as Stefan Collini (2012) illustrates in his introduction to a new edition of Leavis's (2013) famous lecture.

This ethos of teaching ethics, however, was more often than not implicit, and even perhaps necessarily so. Incidentally, without citing this historical approach to learning ethics in the liberal arts, a recent organisational ethnography of the Harvard Business School comes to a similar conclusion about the importance of keeping ethical learning, and teaching and research, implicit. This ethnography attributes the Harvard Business School's successful organisational ethics to this implicit, non-instrumental, approach.

Today, as this 'literary culture', as Leavis called it, comes under threat from the mundane attitudes and market-like behaviour of the corporate university, this culture also becomes more visible and ironically must become more explicit to defend itself, as was the case with Leavis's outburst, itself a defence against Snow's accusation that this literary culture was Luddite in its approach to both education and the modern world. This affords us the chance to see it more clearly and to ask: in our efforts to have our colleagues in the business school accept ethics, have we been too explicit? Too quick to claim relevance? Too eager to apply ethics? Certainly our impatience is understandable given the urgencies of sustainability, workplace fairness and anti-corruption that require an ethical commitment in order to be addressed.

But perhaps the lesson of the liberal arts 'under attack' from the corporate university is to defend a space for the development of ethical maturity that does not demand immediate market-like behaviour, outcomes or decisions. This, of course, is counter-intuitive in the business school but precisely given the urgencies we face, would it not be worth trying something new?

9   Towards an African Management Education

> Our education must therefore inculcate a sense of commitment to the total community, and help the pupils accept the values appropriate to our kind of future, not those appropriate to our colonial past.
>
> Julius Nyerere, 'Education for Self-Reliance' (1967)

As one of us has noted in a series of articles together with coauthors – 'Africa: the Management Education Challenge', 'Does Africa Need an "African" Management Education Model?' and 'Management Education: Out of Africa' (Thomas, 2017; Thomas et al., 2016a, 2016b) – African businesspeople and educators repeatedly stress the need for better management education.

Such leaders, however, are less united in what kind of management education is most urgently needed. Should it emphasise theory-building as Western business scholarship does? Should it remain both close to the ground and close to students? And, most important, should it be – can it be – African, that is, continental?

Given the broad and deep history of the continent, its diverse traditions, languages and peoples, this question is at least as complex as the idea of an Asian business education or the often-unexamined idea of a universal, that is, often covertly Western, education.

Moreover, a question arises. Would we be justified in calling a distinctly African management education a liberal management education? This and other questions we will address in this chapter while at the same time leaving open the definitive responses for Africans themselves to answer.

In his *Pedagogy in Progress: Letters to Guinea-Bissau*, the Brazilian educator Paolo Freire (1978) noted he was not an expert come 'to fix a problem'. Instead, he offered what he called 'authentic help', a kind of help, he explained, where 'all who are involved help each other mutually' (p. 8), adding 'we will have nothing to teach if we do not learn from and with you' (p. 79).

This is the kind of mutual help we hope to enter into in this chapter. We are greatly aided in 'learning from and with' Africa education by

168

joining a discussion already in progress. Africans have continuously and creatively addressed just such issues, both in the past and in the present. But it is with the past that we begin.

It should by now go without saying that there are deep and varied traditions of learning in Africa, from the wisdom of Ethiopian Coptic Priests to Maxims of Ptah-Hop in Ancient Egypt. Augustine, an African, wrote *City of God* in what is now Algeria, founding Christian theology. Yoruba cosmologies are still taken up, studied and practised today not only in Nigeria but also throughout the vast African diaspora. The Dinka and Masai peoples also developed highly sophisticated cosmologies still in effect today. Perhaps better known by the word that has travelled, Bantu peoples in South Africa developed a philosophy around the concept of *Ubuntu*, a deeply humane theory of being. The Shona people have their *hunhuism*, a theory of personhood.

Indeed, the list of philosophies is as large as the myriad peoples, cultures and languages of the continent. And as the African management scholar Stella Nkomo (2011) reminds us, most famous, perhaps even among those kept ignorant of the African history of knowledge production, are the 'universities' of Timbuktu in Mali and the library of Alexandria in Egypt.

Moreover, contemporary African philosophy and theory has also developed a vibrant canon and includes scholars such as V. Y. Mudimbe, Achille Mbembe and Emmanuel Chukwudi Eze. One could add to this list contemporary feminist scholars such as Molara Ogundipe, as well as diasporic Africans such as Frantz Fanon, Aime Cesaire, C. L. R. James and Amy Jacques Garvey. One would also be compelled to include performing artists such as Fela Kuti and Miriam Makeba in any list of African thinkers.

The Negritude movement in the arts and the Pan-African movement in politics, sociology and economics provided a wealth of resources for any curriculum, inside Africa or beyond. In short, seeking African philosophy, literature, poetry, historiography, cosmology and performing arts to orient and ground a distinctly African management education would not be hard. But it has also not been done.

Several attempts have been made in earnest. *African-Centred Management Education: A New Paradigm for an Emerging Continent* by David N. Abdulai (2014) is one such attempt. He calls for an African-centred management education capable of meeting the challenge of Africa's huge reserve of natural resources. He uses the work of Gary Becker to argue that it was human capital – rather than the developmental state – that was responsible for the rise of Taiwan, Singapore and Japan and that building African-centred human capital will help

Africa ride the wave of its extractive economy. Leaving aside the historical question of whether this is an accurate understanding of those nation-states – and Robert Wade, Alice Amsden and Meredith Woo-Cumings among others would certainly not be persuaded (Amsden, 1991, 1992, 2007; Woo-Cumings, 1998, 1999) – its reliance on Becker's work undermines its premise.

In fact, the only consistent characteristic one can discover in Abdulai's concept of African-centred management is its being performed by Africans. This is so historically in his examples, which parallel Western accounts of successful management in all aspects except where they are found, and in his use of theory, which is relentlessly a Western management theory like Becker's.

Abdulai's challenge is obvious. African indigenous knowledge – where African philosophy resides – suffers the same fate as all indigenous knowledge today, only doubly so. Both in the Atlantic slave trade and its subsequent diaspora, indigeneity was permanently displaced, and in the experience of colonialism indigenous knowledge was for long regarded at best as a drag on development, or modernity, and at worse dangerous and subversive.

Honouring that indigenous knowledge and seeing how it challenges management concepts and practices rather than simply adapting or assimilating to those concepts and practices, is a challenge that requires going outside the management literature and studying these philosophies and the ways they manifest themselves in conversations, rituals, performances, art and social arrangements. But this challenge is, of course, consonant with the theme of this book. Management education is essential but not sufficient in our world today. No place is this more the case than Africa. But nowhere is it more daunting.

It is not possible to separate this awaiting project of an African (liberal) management education from the larger question of the struggles and fate of higher education on the continent, itself requiring contextualisation. There is no need to re-enact the violent fate that befell the continent of Africa by retelling it in detail, from which the scholar Saidiya Hartman (2008) famously warned us in the American context. This story is well known to anyone who dares to look, as it is to anyone who must live it.

Torn apart first by 300 years of the Atlantic slave trade, the continent then experienced 150 years of settler colonialism, more in some parts than others. After often bloody independence struggles, the continent emerged underdeveloped by this colonialism and wounded by the history of traffic in humans. Bold efforts to seize freedom and an independent path showed some successes but also many failures or reversals, these often with outside, neocolonial 'help'. Those countries that did emerge ran directly into the debt crises of the 1970s and 1980s and the growth-stifling policies of structural adjustment.

As numerous development economists have argued beyond much doubt, these early neoliberal International Monetary Fund (IMF) policies were a disaster for the continent and in direct contrast to strategies followed in Asia that would prove so successful. Only in the last couple of decades have some African countries burst through this tunnel of punishments visited on the continent. And even here, 'civil' wars, often again with foreign interests pulling strings in the background, tragically undermine the possibilities from Libya to the Congo and Somalia to Côte D'Ivoire (Escobar, 1995; Ha-Joon, 2002; Kohli, 2004; Sender & Smith, 1986).

Moreover as V. Y. Mudimbe (1988) argues in his classic book the *Invention of Africa*, Africa underwent not just a military, political and economic conquering and colonisation, but also a discursive one that took place at the epistemological level, determining the very terms through which Africa would be understood. This thorough process produced what Mudimbe called 'fabulous acculturations' (p. 207), as part of his argument that fully dividing African and imperial histories or cultures is both impossible and risks isolating, even freezing, a dynamic African history.

However, Mudimbe has not always been heeded. Even today as Africa is said to be rising, this narrative is one that the Tanzanian businessman Ali Mufuruki (2014) notes is somewhat misleading and derivative. As he reminds us, even the term *Africa rising* comes from outside, from a Western journalist, and was adopted by some classes of Africans. But in fact the growth rates of 6 per cent to 7 per cent are largely in basic commodities and mainly spurred by Chinese, Indian and Western companies exploiting these natural resources and primary products, placing Africa – even in its rise – back in a position emphasising a rich nature rather than a rich culture.

In fact, weakened by the long shadow of colonial history and recent imposition of debts, proxy and resource wars, and recalcitrant settler populations, Africa today struggles to meet this interest in its continental wealth on equal terms. Finally, we must reckon with these words from C. L. R. James in his pioneering *A History of Pan-African Revolt* (1969):

The states which the African nationalist leaders inherited were not in any sense African. With the disintegration of the political power of the imperialist states in Africa, and the rise of the militancy of the African masses, a certain political pattern took shape. Nationalist political leaders built a following, they or their opponents gained support among the African civil servants who had administered the imperialist state, and the newly independent African state was little more than the old imperialist state now administered and controlled by black nationalists. (p. 116)

James concludes devastatingly and prophetically: 'That these men, western-educated and western-oriented, had or would have little that was nationalist or African to contribute to the establishment of a truly new and truly African order was seen most clearly by the late Frantz Fanon' (p. 117). Fanon is still studied so much today in part because he represents that truly African order and in part because that order has yet to arrive. As much as one might like to have history start over again with the current phase of 'globalisation', this living legacy must be dealt with in any management education that purports to carry the values and the experiences of Africans.

Because, as with the continent so goes the whole education system in Africa. It too has laboured under this historical burden. As the historian Basil Davidson wrote: 'The racism of the colonial rulers has gripped them at every stage. All the colonial systems, as we have seen, had used the weapon of racism. They used it to keep Africans at the bottom of the ladder of development. They used it to teach Africans that the bottom of the ladder was their proper place' (1994, p. 183; Davidson, 1988, 1992, 1994). It was what Davidson called an education for inferiority.

Davidson continues: 'knowledge is a way to understanding; and understanding is the way to power. The colonial systems blocked each of these ways. The systems were there to keep power for the colonial rulers' (1994, p. 184).

But with independence, Davidson notes, 'the gates of knowledge were opened'. He adds that 'a revolution in education was therefore needed' (p. 184); this meant 'decolonising' the curriculum, including importantly the colonial legacy enforcing the inferiority of girls, typified by the lack of any educational opportunity for the vast majority of African girls under colonial rule (Susuman et al., 2015). The 2014 rates were as low as 11 per cent in Niger, 24.4 per cent in Central African Republic, 25.8 per cent in Somalia and 29.2 per cent in Mali. It was a gigantic and continent-wide task, yielding great results in quantity and literacy and some results in quality, decolonisation and sustainability.

As Ousseina Alidou, Silvia Federici and George Caffentzis noted in *A Thousand Flowers: Social Struggles against Structural Adjustment in the African Universities* (Federici et al., 2000; see also Federici & Caffentzis, 2004), the SAPs (the IMF's structural adjustment programmes of the 1980s and 1990s) and World Bank combined to halt the expansion of higher education in Africa, supposedly in favour of more primary education funding. However, ten years after their policies were implemented primary education attendance was actually down, and the universities were crumbling. The policies severely undermined local African academics and promoted international expertise.

In fact, as Federici (2012) notes, in another piece, by the 1990s Africa was receiving more foreign advice per capita than any other continent. But she also notes that despite the squeezing of African higher education, student numbers continue to expand as, despite the cost, underfunding and police and state repression in many countries, youth continue to demand higher education.

Moreover, despite all of these historical and contemporary challenges, it should be noted that African philosophy – and knowledge forms including scholarship, music, dance and the arts – are all thriving, bearing the burden yet flowering anew. As Columbia University Professor Souleymane Bachar Diagne in *African Art as Philosophy* (Diagne, 2012) makes clear, African thinking takes place through art and performance and not just through what are thought to be in the West proper forms of theorising.

It would seem to be the right time to talk about a specifically liberal management education in Africa combining the urgency of getting on top of this growth and managing and investing for Africa and all Africans *and* at a moment when African culture is at its strongest. It is the right time but this is where the challenge begins. Let us assume that the word *liberal* is to be replaced by all of the knowledge forms just mentioned. How do we talk then about a management education with what we might call for now African 'characteristics'?

To propose an answer to this question – a proposed answer that will remain partial, speculative and ultimately subject to the common will of Africans – we are going to suggest, to use a phrase from the great African leader Amilcar Cabral (1974), that we return to the source. The answers lie in the history of thought and practice on the continent. But first we must also offer a caveat.

There is a vibrant African management studies community. We have learnt from them, and we hope they will see our particular focus on global comparative curricular reform as useful. We are on their territory and offer our experiences in Asia, the United States and Europe in that spirit of contribution.

A Return to the Source

In thinking about building a management education with African characteristics, with African cultures, heritages, histories at its heart, we start from three major challenges that such a curriculum would have to address. We will speak of curriculum in the singular because there can be no doubt that the challenges faced across Africa result from a continental position. In other words, once we begin to recount the history of Africa, we see that the whole continent, far from being marginal, has been central to the making of global modernity.

We follow scholars such as Eric Williams (1994) and W. E. B. Dubois (1947) in this observation. From the Moorish empire in Southern Europe to the Atlantic slave trade, to nineteenth-century colonisation, Africa has shaped Europe and the 'New World' profoundly, culturally, and, too, it has funded it. Nonetheless, there are indeed many 'Africas', as the online journal *Africa Is a Country* (n.d.) also makes clear (Binyanvanga, 2005).

In practice, African management curricula will vary, within a common *longue duree*. Finally, such an approach, seeking a common continental curriculum from which to experiment and improvise, is in keeping with the thought of a number of African education theorists today such as Professors Yusef Waghid at Stellenbosch University in South Africa and Connie Nshemereirwe at Uganda Martyrs University (Nshemereirwe, 2016a, 2016b; Waghid, 2014; Waghid et al., 2005). And, indeed, we take inspiration from the African journal *The Chimurenga Chronic*'s July 2015 special issue on the continental integrity of Africa when it says

the Sahara has never been a boundary, real or imagined. Trade caravans, intellectuals, literatures, human resources and political ideas have long circulated from Timbuktu to Marrakesh, from Khartoum to Tunis and Cairo and beyond. Marked by an urgency to unsettle the fictitious divide, this issue continues Chimurenga's on-going quest to present alternative political, economic, historical, geographical and cultural cartographies of the continent. To imagine Africa, and to speak of it, outside the maps drawn at the Berlin Conference (1884–85). (*Chimurenga Chronic*, 2015)

We therefore identify three challenges next that result from the centrality of the continent in the modern world and apply across the continent. Moreover, for each of the challenges we name, we also propose a form of specifically African management curriculum to address these challenges.

The first of these, returning to Davidson, is the legacy of the degradation of African women and girls. The source of this disadvantage and denigration runs deeper than colonial education policies to the Atlantic slave trade. The disrespect of women of African descent continues to endure and has been aggravated by masculinist regimes, forced migration and civil war.

On the other hand, a curriculum seeking to address this first challenge can draw on a wealth of sources, especially the matrilineal heritages of many African cultures and the contemporary dominance by women of many of the marketplaces in Africa, from the great Onitsha market in southeastern Nigeria to village markets in East Africa to the souks of Morocco.

Women run Africa's markets exercising specific forms of power and sociality. Any management curriculum that neglects the importance of these markets to both African life and the African economy is negligent but any curriculum that addresses these markets has a chance to speak specifically of women, gender and empowerment on the continent.

A second challenge that we would like to identify in the spirit of Freire's mutual help is the managing of foreign direct investment. This challenge cuts across management education for both private-sector and public-sector employment, a model we know well from Singapore's successful integration of management capacity across these sectors. Whether it is in infrastructure or the extractive industries or industrial agriculture, foreign direct investment is behind the notion of Africa 'rising' – a theme questioned by some African business leaders such as Ali Mufuruki (2014).

How can such investments be managed by African polities for the benefit of local people – to capture knowledge transfer, protect the environment and ensure and improve the population's health – not just offer employment that may or may not last beyond the strategic plans of the foreign investor or the foreign government that backs them?

This is the key question and key challenge in the external-facing economies of Africa. It is a question that cannot be addressed without attention to the interface of the public and private sectors in African countries and especially the competence and commitment to national purpose in both sectors. However, a model already exists for just such a management education, as the quotation by Julius Nyerere at the opening of this chapter reminds us.

Of course, African socialism may seem an unlikely source for answering this question – after all, management studies is traditionally hostile to such philosophies in general (despite the fact that the second-biggest business economy in the world is officially socialist). But in many ways, the closest parallel exercise to thinking a management education that takes the management competence of both the state and the private sector seriously is to be found in the experience of the previous generation of Africa's most talented thinkers as they attempted to create a form of a national programme of socialism with African characteristics.

Acknowledged as the best and brightest minds of the anti-colonial and independence era on the continent, Kwame Nkrumah of Ghana, Sekou Toure of Guinea, Amilcar Cabral of Cape Verde and

Guinea-Bissau, Julius Nyere of Tanzania, Ahmed Ben Bella of Algeria, Patrice Lumumba of the Congo and Chris Hani of South Africa were, as the management scholar Nceku Nyathi (2008) shows, organisation theorists. They were also all men, another reason to foreground our first challenge.

However, they were inspired by what they saw as the wastefulness, incompetence and corruption of colonial rule to build something better in the bureaucracies of their states. James reminds us that many failed because those bureaucracies were not fully decolonised. Nonetheless, they stressed the education, commitment and technical know-how of state managers as fundamentally necessary to their national projects.

Moreover, African socialism was not only continental – understanding itself as the potential realisation of Pan-Africanism – but also an internationalism before this globalisation. As Vijay Prashad (2008) documents in *The Darker Nations* – a reference to Dubois – there was a general globalisation for a century that involved all those nations seeking decolonisation and exploring new independence. In other words, these organisational thinkers understood themselves to be facing the challenge of a global economy and needing management knowledge equal to that challenge.

They knew too that socialism was not alien to Africa but had been damaged by the long history visited on Africa. It could be recovered in a way foregrounding forms of collective life and common purpose that predated the Western ideology (indeed, as Cedric Robinson [2001] teaches us, such life in Europe also predated this ideology). In their organisational accomplishments (and failures), they also point the way in allowing us to suggest, and to teach, that organisational thinking and management thinking are also not alien, Western imports.

But most important, they recover a time when the public sector was not abandoned to its fate as perpetually inefficient, corrupt or ineffective. A curriculum that took their efforts seriously would be one that could inspire today's African management class to invest in the state, to work in the state and to work with the state.

Why is this important? The only models we have of successfully managing large flows of foreign direct investment for the broad benefit of local populations come from Asian countries, where high levels of competence exist in the public sector, where the state directs and regulates this investment and the state invests. We are speaking of course of Singapore, in our own experience, and of Taiwan, South Korea and, earlier, Japan.

It is not too much to say that the long history of state exams, the history of bureaucracy as a proud tradition of statecraft in the region, together with more contemporary nationalism and conflict, produced a management education that does not belittle or neglect the role of the state in what are nonetheless market economies.

Part of this curriculum must therefore be a sober, non-ideological, evidence-based assessment of IMF, World Bank and other donor policies in Africa over the last forty years. And part of it must also be an equally sober, non-ideological, evidence-based assessment of earlier effort in Africa, under the banner of a home-grown and recovered African socialism, to utilise the state as an effective part of the management of foreign investment, infrastructure and co-ordinated planning.

There is no question of going back to this model for management education, certainly, but nor is it possible to move forward without this grounding, this return to the source, as Amilcar Cabral puts it.

Let us now propose a third challenge and provisional approach before finally outlining a sample curriculum, presented only heuristically. This third challenge is technology. And perhaps counter-intuitively, it may be addressed by the arts.

As Professor Achille Mbembe (2016) wrote:

Mobile telephony in particular has revolutionised the ways Africans interact and the way small and medium enterprises, farmers and informal traders, operate. As a result, mobile revenue is today equivalent to 3.7% of African GDP – more than triple its share in developed economies where it was an incremental innovation. Were the internet to eventually match or exceed the level of impact mobile telephony has already achieved, it could contribute some $300 billion to Africa's GDP by 2025, according to a 2011 report by consultancy McKinsey. It is calculated that, in this leapfrog scenario, increased Internet penetration and use could propel private consumption almost 13 times higher than current levels of $12 billion, reaching some $154 billion by 2025.

But where the author goes from there is revealing and requires two lengthy quotations. He moves from this observation on technology straight to the arts in Africa.

First, he notes how Hegel did not think Africans capable of the arts and then notes, contrary to Hegel's ignorance, the contemporary explosion of the arts that is only the latest manifestation of this rich way of life in Africa:

The magic of the arts of Africa and its diaspora has always derived from its power of dematerialisation, its capacity to inhabit the commonplace and sensible, precisely with the aim of transforming it into an idea and an event. Historically it has come from an unambiguous recognition of the fact that the infinite cannot be captured in a form. The infinite exceeds every form – even if, from time to time, it passes through form, that is, through the finite. But what fundamentally characterises form is its own finitude. Form can only be ephemeral, evanescent and fugitive. 'To form' is to inhabit a space of essential fragility and vulnerability. This is the reason why caring and nurturing life are the main functions of the arts.

For Mbembe this means:

The idea of art as an attempt to capture the forces of the infinite; an attempt to put the infinite in sensible form, but a forming that consists in constantly doing, undoing and redoing; assembling, dis-assembling and reassembling – this idea is typically 'African'. It fully resonates with the digital spirit of our times. This is why there is a good chance that the art of the 21st century will be Afropolitan.

Mbembe goes on to lose the thread of his own argument, never really returning to what might distinguish African art, performance and indeed what Laura Harris (2012) calls social poesis, an aesthetic invention of social life across the continent. But we can pick it up.

As we have already mentioned, indigenous African philosophy shows its genius not only on the written page but also through practices in art, religion, social arrangement and constant innovation in the face of encounters, challenges and change. It is, as Mbembe says, a form of thinking and living that performs a forming, deforming, reforming of the infinite through the sensible.

Any sketches towards a truly African, or African-centred, management education would have to draw on this indigenous knowledge as it manifests in all these forms of expression that have as their main function 'caring and nurturing' through this radical openness. While such an education is a collective project, and an African-centred one as we have said, our interest in blending the humanities, social sciences and management education into a liberal management education encourages us to contribute some curricular sketches to conclude this chapter.

Ngugi wa Thiong'o retells the story that the Kenyan leader Jomo Kenyatta tells in *Facing Mount Kenya* (Kenyatta, 1965; wa Thiong'o, 1997). In Kenyan history there is an historic disruption and central, kingly authority is replaced by a much more effective and supported system of decentralised political management: *ituika*. This new form of management is, appropriately, reinforced by a performance, a periodic festival to confirm this shift. However, a second disruption – colonialism – prevents the six-month festival from being carried out. Gradually, knowledge of this form of management has been 'lost', though clearly both wa Thiong'o and Kenyatta believed it could be recovered in a new form.

Facing Mount Kenya is an anthropology of the Kikuyu people, and a highly accomplished one. Reading this indigenous anthropology, covering this indigenous knowledge of decentralised organisation, might be profitably incorporated into an African organisational theory and behaviour module. Indeed, it might be compared and contrasted to several Western management theories in a blended curriculum.

For example, how does *ituika* anticipate, revise and re-imagine in an African frame the Western management literature on autonomous work groups, creative teams or task groups? How might the festival accompanying this Kenyan system of decentralised work and management be read alongside Western literature on ritual at work, performance in the workplace, or patterns of authority and power at work?

And by way of a tentative pedagogy, reading *Facing Mount Kenya* alongside the Western classic *Wisdom of Teams* by John Katzenbach and Douglas Smith (2015) might reveal the long-standing philosophies of decentralised co-operation in African thought (and not only among the Kikuyu) and the contribution such thought might make both to an African management education and to management thought generally. Moving from anthropology to literature, we cannot fail to include Chinua Achebe's (1994) *Things Fall Apart*, regarded as one of the very greatest novels of the twentieth century. It is a novel saturated with organisational concepts – knowledge transfer, change and continuity, authority and leadership. But the novel is not an illustration of these concepts. It is an elaboration performed in African philosophy. It is a sourcebook for management theories, not a mirror of them. In the first instance, the novel represents a rich field of play. Dense layers and webs of myth, ritual, interpretation, and performance characterise the Igbo people about whom Achebe writes.

It is a text about organisational culture, of course, and it is understood as the coming of the colonial disturbance and often destruction of Igbo life and Igbo world views.

But its contribution to theories of organisational culture lies elsewhere. This is not a story of disruption. The organisational culture we encounter through Achebe is not a harmonious one unsettled from the outside but a deeply fractured and historical one. Anyone who uses the term *organisational culture* as if there is one culture in an organisation, or indeed one organisation, would be wise to read this book, as would anyone who believes gender relations can be addressed outside of larger power relations in an organisation. Imagine teaching this novel alongside the special section in the *Harvard Business Review* (2018), 'The Culture Factor'.

Vital and seminal as much of the ideas gathered from scholarship are in this special section, what Achebe offers us is something concretely African and concretely different. Here organisational culture is internally conflicted, between men and women, tradition and individualism, property and commons. It is historical and subject to constant re-interpretation, crisis and new performance. Organisational culture is rarely presented with such internal complexity and too often as a coherent unit of analysis in Western management theory.

Chinua Achebe's novel taught alongside this management theory would not only therefore be an instance of expanding the management curriculum but of diversifying management knowledge itself.

As we pursue the connections between the liberal management education curricula with which we have experimented in Singapore and London, something remarkable emerges. Not only can we begin to imagine a robust African-centred management education that is every match for our experiments, but we can also begin to glimpse the world-leading possibilities of an African liberal management education. Just as nowhere is more disadvantaged than Africa by the exclusion of culture, performance, art, philosophy and cosmology from management knowledge and education, no place may be more advantaged by the inclusion in management knowledge and education of what Mbembe (2016) called 'the magic of the arts' in Africa and the diaspora.

We will not rehearse here the extensive discussions about Africa and modernity, alternative modernities and alternatives to modernity, but our speculations in management education begin to point to an African future where the organisation of enterprises, networks, communities and markets is powered by the arts as much as the sciences, by participation as much as hierarchy and by enjoyment as much as necessity.[1] Indeed, as a way to illustrate this intuition, we can conclude with two global challenges in management education: the teaching of creativity or design thinking, and the future of finance, especially inclusive and sustainable financial technologies. Suggesting the blending of a study (and practice) of African arts with management and organisational thinking from the West (and remembering Mudimbe's admonishments) can only be an example here: Freire's 'authentic help'. Still, it suggests a way forward for what Thomas et al. called the need to address 'the challenges of increased growth, quality improvement, establishing an African identity, leveraging and other issues' (Thomas et al., 2016a, p. 47).

Taking up the challenge of design thinking and fostering creativity and 'disruptive' insights, those who have taught such courses realise that there is a basic problem in trying to 'separate form and content'. By this phrase we mean that without a developed imagination (the content) there cannot be an imaginative leap (the form). Students' supposed lack of creativity is actually a product of their limited exposure

---

[1] Okwui Enwezor on African modernities.

to the imagination in all its forms including even managerial creativity. Indeed the management scholar Stephen Linstead argues persuasively in a piece of the punk band, The Clash, that not just the band, but also its management, and even its roadies, formed a creative whole at their best, and that the manager was at this moment also a creative force (Linstead, 2010). But students are in effect banned from the content that would make them managers and creative. They are restricted to the narrow band of mass popular culture and social media, it is little wonder that their responses and suggestions all sound the same. They are drawn from a limited pool, and a shallow one. Without sounding overly like the Frankfurt School or forgetting the lessons of cultural studies, we can nonetheless suggest that culture for most students today is a giant groupthink.

Moreover, the vast majority of students are passive recipients of this groupthink and respond with create profiles, vines and memes within an equally narrow band of what is permitted as interaction. The sudden introduction of a novel with greater texture, nuance, depth and indeed breadth of history and geography will not likely alter this basic poverty of imagination. Design thinking runs aground in these rocks. Form cannot be separated from content, something about which we saw an intuition in the Queen Mary case study and the encounter with the arts there.

Of course, in the African arts this is precisely the point: form and content are *not* separated. (Though admittedly they may be in some commercial forms today.) The design of social life, political life, family life and urban life is achieved through the practice of the imagination. Of course, as we have rehearsed, this unity sometimes fails in the face of Africa's history and current predicaments but, nonetheless, a course where the arts, performance, and philosophy are not used as examples but as the tools to transform organisations, products, customer and employee relations, etc., would be a course that kept form and content together. For example, studying the history of the Market Theatre in South Africa at the outset of a course on design thinking would begin to deliver some imaginative content to students who could encounter some key points in writing, on video, and through lectures and discussions ('History', n.d.).

But creating African theatre to solve a management problem, see a management problem differently or make a breakthrough in management thinking not only takes the integration of the arts and management science further but also brings content and form together to bear on these problems.

This famous theatre, in fact, has long been engaged in this unity of imagination, creation and innovation in the institutions of African social, cultural and political life. The full imagination of theatre making is brought not as an example of imaginative thinking, or stimulus to the imagination, but as practice: the working out of a new way forward. In the classroom this requires African-centred theatre making to produce African-centred solutions. In the magic of the arts in Africa blended into a management curriculum we find a model for elsewhere.

Another crisis facing management education is apparent in the area of finance. Though finance professors continue to teach and research in good faith, the world of finance is far from healthy. It is crisis-prone on an ever-increasing scale. It contributes mightily to undesirable and unsustainable skewing of worldwide wealth. And decisions about the future of many countries and companies who have diverse and numerous stakeholders are often taken solely by this stakeholder. It has long been apparent that a healthy stock market and a healthy economy and society are two increasingly divergent phenomena.

One attempted answer to this management studies problem (of course, it is much bigger than management studies) is to introduce research and teach inclusive financial technologies. These tools achieve a great deal of good – regularising wage payments, allowing people with only a mobile phone account to keep money safely, for instance. But they increase the number of consumers of financial services worldwide, not the number of owners of financial capital. Thus they do nothing to deal with the democracy deficit that has beset financial capital and that reaches some of its most intractable levels in Africa. Yet once again, Africa may present a solution where we have otherwise failed.

We turn to the *Ohemma*, or 'market queens', of Ghana. According to Customer Unity and Trust Society (CUTS) Ghana, a policy think tank in the West African nation, the market queens or mothers play a key role in the overall economy but also provide vital services in food security, financing for farmers, employment for youth and diversity of diet, to name only a few (CUTS, 2016).

Students might first watch the dated but still important 'Disappearing World' series from the BBC, *Asante Market Women*. The consultant for this film was an Asante anthropologist, Charlotte Boaitey.

First, of course, the students need to learn that there was in fact no disappearance going on – in fact, the opposite. However, the film opens up a discussion on African cosmology, on the role of language, proverb, religion and music in the organisation of the massive markets that now characterise most of West Africa and that are run by women in many African nation-states, not just Ghana. However, Ghana offers a particular African-centred philosophy of organisation.

Again, this philosophy is not without its history, conflict and change, especially around gender relations. But it might very fruitfully be integrated into a management curriculum on corporate governance, including many of its key theoretical tributaries from agency theory to stakeholder theory. Eventually, larger development questions on the role of the state versus the role of the market – a rich development studies literature exists for Africa[2] – may also be incorporated.

But initially we can teach our students about the way women in these markets develop a form of governance that is economic, social, cultural, spiritual and performative. The ways in which the women create councils of elders and forms of deliberative decision making, dispute settlement and general regulation of a free market can all be learned as specifically African-centred innovations in governance.

These markets are huge and complex, featuring logistics and pricing and labour issues that go far beyond the Western image of a 'farmer's market'. The holistic nature of the governance – extending into mediating family relations, avoiding party political conflicts, religious, cosmological and spiritual settlements, tributes and inspirations, as well as ensuring fair competition, livelihoods, and growth – offers students an alternative model to corporate governance as currently practised in finance.

How could this African-centred form of governance be applied to finance in Africa? What benefits would Africa see if finance became governed in an African way – by women, by consensus, by disputed settlement, holistically, spiritually as well as materially, in harmony with cosmology, etc.? We can only speculate.

What is without doubt is that Africa's magic arts, its holistic forms of living, its cosmologies and philosophies, not only form the true riches of the continent but also the true gift to management education globally and therefore given the place of management in our world, to this world in all its urgent need.

---

[2] This development literature is a forgotten source for African management studies – from pioneers like Walter Rodney and Bill Warren, to John Sender and Sheila Smith on gender and development, to Timothy Mitchell on Egypt, and James Ferguson on Lesotho.

10   Conclusion

> Thought must be given to how to develop this more holistic and balanced model of management education with its higher purpose to nurture social responsibility and enhance students' moral and ethical compass in an increasingly uncertain world. The good news is that there is evidence that significant efforts are already being made to build models of liberal, responsible management education involving meaningful collaboration and co-creation across the three sectors of the economy – business, government and society.
>
> Della Bradshaw, *Rethinking Business Education* (2017)

On 13 December 2018 a group of business school leaders convened a 'Business Education Jam' at the University of Vienna in Austria. Conscious of the evolving 'Bologna process' gradually integrating higher education in Europe and the changes it would bring, these leaders used the occasion to ask searching questions about the future of undergraduate management education in Europe. Appropriately titled 'Bachelors, Business and Beyond', the Jam did indeed go well 'beyond' what one might expect from the ambit of management education. These leaders ambitiously imagined what it would mean to educate not just management students but just and ethical human beings capable of living in a complex societal framework. Just as boldly, they saw their mission as promoting a European Union where people traded freely and exchanged fairly because those engaged in such social intercourse are much less likely to go to war with each other. Management education has come a long way in the last ten years towards the 'co-creation across the three sectors of the economy' (Bradshaw, 2017, p. 9), and we have taken that sometimes thrilling, occasionally frustrating, journey with it.

We began thinking about this book only a few years after the worldwide financial crisis of 2007 to 2008. We had expected business schools to swiftly re-evaluate their role as producers of both business knowledge and business leaders once the scale of the ethical and professional failures became clear. We had anticipated some soul-searching in the profession and perhaps some disruptive innovation within business schools of the same magnitude management scholars tended to advocate in the wider economy. Nor were we intent on being mere bystanders to those transformations. Indeed, we saw the period of what we presumed would be introspection as a chance to rethink management education as a whole. We urged our colleagues on and tried where possible to lead by example.

Thus, for example, in 2009 one of us could write in the *Times Higher Education* that the only way for business schools to become truly professional schools, alongside medical and law schools, would be for them to develop a similar duty of care – not then, or unfortunately now, a common concept in business schools (Harney, 2009).

What did we mean by a duty of care? Business schools are largely committed to providing their students with value for money and a quality education, comprising a current curriculum and often including internships, international experience and contact with practitioners. Business schools also take seriously the well-being of students. One could consider these traits the satisfaction of a duty of care.

But such commitments are not in fact equivalent to that duty of care one finds in the legal or medical professions. In these the duty of care extends well beyond the law school, the medical school and their students. Once out of law school, a lawyer continues to have a duty of care both to those charged under the law, and to those victims of the transgressions of the law. The doctor takes a pledge to do no harm but also has a duty of care to the sick and afflicted. Such is the duty of care in these professions that it is inconceivable that a doctor would refuse to treat an injured person or a lawyer would abandon a wrongfully accused person. But what is the equivalent for the MBA graduate, the business professional or indeed the undergraduate who has completed management studies? Surely obeying rules and regulations does not rise to this level of duty we are examining. Duty of care is to people, not rules: to whom would such a duty be directed then? Several answers suggest themselves.

Because business relies on natural resources, perhaps the duty of care is to the biosphere, to life rather than just to people? Because it also relies on employees, perhaps the duty of care lies with them, to providing secure, liveable wages? Currently it would be difficult to argue that any such duties are widely recognised beyond legal compliance.

One might respond that it is customers and investors to whom MBA graduates owe responsibility. But this would appear to leave out the very idea of vulnerability underpinning the idea of care. Short of not cheating customers and investors, what exactly is the care involved?

It seems we have settled for specialising the idea of care among social entrepreneurs and those few committed to doing well by doing good, as the phrase goes. Without idealising the no doubt imperfect professions of medicine and law, it is unimaginable that they would reduce their application of duty of care to a few specialists. Of course, one complication is that undergraduate business education, now widespread, does not rise to the level of a professional degree, and this difference may be real. But it needs to be remembered that graduates of such undergraduate programmes do rise. They rise in business, and they rise in society. It is, of course, for this reason that our book puts so much emphasis on undergraduate education.

In another piece, in the *Financial Times* a couple of years later in 2012, our efforts to rally our colleagues continued: one way towards reform and towards regaining the trust of communities shaken in the financial scandals would be to emulate the clinic models of law and medical schools. Both of these professions offer pro bono clinics for those in need, such as free legal advice for tenants facing unfair treatment from landlords or free basic medical services for the indigent and those without shelter (in countries where such services are not provided by the state).

In a piece called 'It Is Time That Business Schools Learnt to Walk the Walk' (Harney & Dowling, 2012) we pointed to one such effort, referenced in our case study chapter on Queen Mary University of London. The NGO Clinic, later renamed Immeasure, was the first of its kind, a pro bono management consultancy based in a business school and designed for small not-for-profit organisations in need of organisational change and development.[1] The effort was both substantial and symbolic. Symbolically, we wanted to show that the business school did not think time was only money but understood that some time should be devoted to efforts that did not yield pecuniary results. Substantially, we wanted to give our time to strengthen not-for-profits that were struggling to skill-up society in the face of what might be called a kind of deskilling of social life, where either long hours or zero hours contracts left families unable to practise their own social skills.

But it was a third intervention that would prove sturdy enough to anchor this book. Again writing in the *Times Higher Education,* we confronted the regime of prolonged austerity that followed the global crisis (Harney, 2010). Against the impulse to cut funding to what might appear as the least economically vital part of the university – the liberal arts – we

---

[1] The NGO Clinic continues to this day as *Immeasure,* operated by Dr. Emma Dowling and Stefano Harney. The NGO Clinic was founded by Dowling, Harney, Professor Denise Ferreira da Silva, Dr. Ishani Chandrasekara and Professor Peter Fleming. See for more: www.theguardian.com/education/2010/nov/09/students-advise-charities.

argued that this curriculum would have to be 'at the heart' of management education if management education were to lead the recovery and at the same time right the imbalances that led to the crisis.

The prominent scholar of the contemporary university, Christopher Newfield, has argued – mostly recently on his website, Remaking the University – that the humanities made a 'great mistake' by retreating from defining a liberal arts education as a 'public good' and instead attempting to justify the market value of such an education. The liberal arts curriculum contains a wealth of nonpecuniary value to offer students and society alike, according to Newfield (2018).

But from our point of view, management studies did not regard itself as without non-pecuniary value. In truth, much knowledge in the liberal arts is put to work. It is pecuniary. Instead, we were interested in the robust encounter between the two spheres of value creation represented by management education and the liberal arts, the spheres of market and society. Our argument was not that these two curricula could be divided between the money-making and the good, much less that they could be seamlessly integrated; but rather that the productive discourse between them could serve to found a liberal management education. Such an education would enrich students, society and the marketplace by challenging and thereby strengthening both spheres. Students would respect the values of both, and thrive on the tensions, synergies and discords that ensued.

Thus we argued in that piece for the *Times Higher Education*, and it would of course be this third thrust that we pursued with enthusiasm throughout this subsequent book. We tried to do so without losing sight of the multiple dimensions necessary to sustain an ethical profession, and for this we needed a more 'holistic and balanced model'.

As one of us wrote a couple of years later for the Chartered Association of Business Schools in the book *Rethinking Business Education, Fit for the Future* that serves as the epigraph for this chapter:

The underlying question surely must be whether management education conducts itself with responsibility to society in its preparation of the students that will manage and lead others, make investment and fiscal decisions, source products and extract resources. But should management education today also provide an educational experience that enables students to develop a maturity in matters of ethics, spirit, society, culture and politics?

Thought must be given to how to develop this more holistic and balanced model of management education with its higher purpose to nurture social responsibility and enhance students' moral and ethical compass in an increasingly uncertain world. The good news is that there is evidence that significant efforts are already being made to build models of liberal, responsible management education involving meaningful collaboration and co-creation across the three sectors of the economy – business, government and society. (Bradshaw, 2017; Thomas, 2017, p. 000)

We were thinking of ethics as a praxis that would need to be reinvented as something much broader and deeper than simply obeying the law or the code of conduct or mere 'better' governance. We were thinking of a complete overhaul of the management curriculum to meet the scale of the crisis we had recently experienced. Ethics would not only have to come to the centre of management education, but it would have to comprise new practices, like the duty of care, and new materials, like those from the liberal arts. And management education itself would have to step up to lead in the university as a whole in the educational challenges of the new century. That a liberal management education would also have many other benefits, from promoting critical thinking skills to fostering creativity, to greater knowledge of the history and culture that our world shares – we were only then beginning to see the dazzling possibilities. We were filled with a sense of urgency and hope.

Things Have Changed

But now as we look back on this book, we notice a peculiar reversal. At the time we began to think about this project a lot of our exhortations were aimed at the business school, its faculty and leaders in particular. We were urging them to take action. We perceived that they were out of step with a society that wanted a more ethical and holistic approach to business. We could even say that they were out of step with a society that was more classically liberal than their institutions have become. By classically liberal we mean the belief in free and open markets, a fair playing field and penalties for those who discriminate or cheat.

The business leaders – emerging from business schools – who largely caused the financial crisis seemed to care little about these values. We are not saying those who do espouse classical liberal views always practise them. Nor are we saying that individuals in the business school were suspiciously illiberal. Most were not. What we are saying is that one could make the case that business schools, sated on the growth of the previous two decades, had become somewhat isolated both from other disciplines and from society and were increasingly viewed as conservative, particularly after the crisis. What is now striking is how much has changed.

Today one feels it is society itself that has taken a turn for the distressingly illiberal. What the great British sociologist Stuart Hall (1983, 1985) called 'authoritarian populism' three decades ago has made an alarming return. From Brazil to Turkey, Hungary to the United States, classical liberalism is in retreat if not under assault. Xenophobia, misogyny and racism blend with protectionism, nativism and jingoism in a bitter soup.

By contrast, business schools have slowly but steadily innovated and renewed themselves, as the gatherings at the University of Vienna attest and the case studies in this book illustrate. The ethical and social side of classical liberalism, represented in the liberal arts, meets the political and economic side of classical liberalism in today's best management education. It has never been more important to keep these two sides of university education together, indeed to insist on their inseparability while acknowledging their differences.

Authoritarian populism by contrast tends to feature monopoly industries monopolising willing governments while those governments mesmerise willing populations. It could not be further from the ideals of liberal management education. And so today in a twist, it is business schools we might look to as part of a broader front to pull our societies back from the brink of this authoritarian populism.

Universities have the potential to be authentically popular institutions as opposed to the fake populism of the current moment. We have argued throughout this book that if universities are to regain and strengthen this position both as moral authorities and as popular instruments in democratic life, revitalised business schools offering a liberal management education will be at the heart of this re-birth. At the end of this book, without being overly dramatic, we can say that the stakes are higher than ever. We offer a tentative conclusion that explores these stakes and readies us for the challenges ahead, challenges now far bigger than the university itself.

Two Curricula

What we would like to argue in this conclusion is that management education and the liberal arts need each other even more than when we began writing this book four years ago. Together they produce a durable and dynamic education for students facing the new challenges of business and confronting the new, increasingly illiberal, societies in which business is embedded.

But just as important is how the new illiberal societies threaten any attempts to offer either the liberal arts or management education in isolation from each other. It is perhaps not too much to say that these two curricula continue on their own separate ways at their own peril. Equally, when allied to each other, as in this book and its case studies, they offer a powerful defence against these illiberal times and open up a new global horizon for free exchange and sustainable growth. While our primary concern here is pedagogical, not political, it would be ignoring our own advice to always see business in its social, political, historical and cultural context if we did not explore this theme briefly here.

A closer look at what Stuart Hall meant by 'authoritarian populism' might be instructive. At the time Hall was writing, the 1970s and 1980s, he was primarily interested in how tabloid newspapers, television and movies, and other forms of popular culture were being mobilised in a new way for a kind of politics he considered manipulative. Parties of the right and left have tried always to persuade people of the benefits of a partisan position.

But Hall believed that authoritarian populism was different. It used the media, popular memory and mass culture to create what he called 'moral panics'. This might mean promoting fear of migrants, or crime, or poor parenting or any number of issues not associated necessarily with right or left politics. The point for Hall was that politicians would gain support by offering solutions to these moral panics.

But another agenda lay behind these promises, often less popular or even unknown. Thus, for instance, people who were not illiberal in their general views might end up voting for an illiberal politician or party out of fear or disillusionment.

This emerging phenomenon was Hall's understanding of how Margaret Thatcher – whose policies were never universally popular in the United Kingdom – came to dominate British politics. Today, from Jair Bolsonaro to Donald Trump to Narendra Modi, we see similar dynamics at work with moral panics regularly deployed in all these polities. One might note that each of these leaders favours a very strong state, especially around security. Yet each ran against the state, claiming the state was corrupt or too much in the lives of citizens, or wasteful and unaffordable. Hall noted that this 'anti-state statism', as Ruth Gilmore (2011) would later call it, accompanied the use of moral panics as a strategy of authoritarian populism. Thus people could even begin to vote against programmes that supported them.

Writing in the 1970s, Hall had already begun to insist that popular culture had escaped the monopoly of the corporate press and the influence of universities, religious organisations and state policymakers. The field he founded, cultural studies, is partly based on his early insights into the unruly ways people learned and shared views of the world beyond these traditional institutions – and indeed in resistance to attempts to manipulate them.

Though his insights were pioneering then, he could not have anticipated the way social media would come to amplify but also atomise this
unruly popular culture. Today authoritarian populism gathers the power
of social media to pose an ominous threat to classical liberal thought and
practice. Moreover, from our point of view, it threatens the university's
ability to fulfil its traditional mission as a place of free thought 'in but
not entirely of' the world, as we put it early in this book.

Now, despite their institutional conservatism leading up to and
following the global financial crisis – a crisis that might truly warrant the
word *meltdown* – business schools would seem to be essentially at odds
with this illiberal thought. After all, illiberal thought is suspicious of the
new, of innovation and of change. Such thought operates through existing
prejudices, not new paradigms. It establishes borders and roots itself in
one place. Its impulses would seem to be the opposite of everything we
seek in management knowledge and practice.

A good example is in fact our approach to social media. Those of us in
business schools tend to look at social media as a cutting-edge sector and
as a technological transformation. If a particular set of 'entrepreneurs'
creates a chat site for far-right extremists who have been kicked off
Twitter and Facebook – as was recently exposed in the massacre in the
synagogue in Pittsburgh, Pennsylvania, where the terrorist involved
had been posting his messages of hate on a site called Gab designed for
people like him – we in the business school consider this an excess of the
market. And most management scholars would acknowledge the need
for more government oversight of social media for cases like this one.
We nonetheless embrace social media as a classically liberal force in the
world. Moreover, if we were writing our conclusion several years ago we
may well have focussed on its power as a tool for change in the struggle
against authoritarian structures as in the Arab Spring, illustrating its
power to insist on classical liberalism.

But ultimately it is not these exceptionally grotesque users of social
media nor their unethical entrepreneurial enablers upon whom we
should be focussed. Rather, it is this conjuncture of social media and the
larger trend of authoritarian populism that needs attention. This combination produces a curious foil for our efforts. In this mix, both social
liberalism and economic liberalism are distorted. The co-operation that
is the actual basis of exchange as self-organisation is corroded by this
toxic mix. Individual expression replaces public discourse; class resentment replaces national compromise; and nativist sentiments replace a
global outlook. Or put another way, the connection between the individual and society is neglected, and the place of the nation in the world
community decays.

As Hall teaches us about authoritarian populism, citizens are driven apart by moral panics and seek cover in a populist figure. But today the way citizens form this attachment is often mediated through a platform. Those platforms aggregate people virtually but also promote forms of discourse and expression alien to the classical liberal tradition dedicated to a civic sphere, respect for individual rights and free commerce.

Opinions without facts, rumours without basis, dogma without religious piety and all forms of resentment and division flourish when social media becomes the catalyst for this populist figure. Such a confluence is a threat to any stand-alone liberal arts curriculum. At the same time, these platforms in conjunction with such leaders also promote anti-statism as a way to state power. And this stance undermines any stand-alone management studies curriculum. Let us briefly elaborate these dangers.

The problem for the liberal arts has long been how it comes to encompass a liberal society rather than simply a liberal class. Traditionally, the study of the liberal arts was indeed restricted to elite universities. Think of the 'PPE' degree at the United Kingdom's Oxford University. Given that they appear a luxury to many, the liberal arts continue to struggle towards a more democratic form that would allow everyone to participate in the formal study of the liberal arts. Moreover, the tabloid newspaper ridicule in the United Kingdom that met the expansion of liberal arts study – mocking subjects such as media and cultural studies – suggests the class structure underpinning the liberal arts will not easily be dislodged. A similar backlash against black and gender studies in the United States indicates today that illiberal forces would prefer the liberal arts to remain signifiers of elite tradition.

But the class marker of the liberal arts can also be manipulated into class conflict, as we know too well today. In the United Kingdom, for instance, those who voted for Brexit were said also to be voting against a certain professional, financial and creative class of London and the south-east. Thus does class shade rather than form illiberal politics: this was also undoubtedly a vote against 'foreign' populations. Stoking a resentment against the educated is a common feature of authoritarian populism, and the liberal arts end up on the demonised side of this rhetoric. New reports suggest the liberal arts in universities in Brazil are already under siege with the new election of an authoritarian populist, Jair Bolsonaro.

At the same time, the problem for management education is that the drift towards specialisation and away from the rest of the university comes at a time when a particular ideology of business is being promoted through anti-state statism. There has, of course, been a well-recognised and justified phase shift in management education over the past thirty years away from an emphasis on the stewardship and strategy of large firms and competent management within the hierarchy of those firms – in short, away from the MBA curriculum. In its place specialty master's programmes have arisen with a focus on entrepreneurship, innovation and financial management. Undergraduate management education reflects these shifts, perhaps too automatically.

In any case, today's business schools emphasise individual initiative and accomplishment over organisational loyalty and longevity. The lone entrepreneur who follows his or her dream, the leader who can come into any kind of organisation and inspire, the sole innovator who disrupts an industry, the investor who does not run with the herd – these are today's models for both postgraduate and undergraduate students.

And fair enough. At its commanding end, the global economy values and rewards this kind of thinking and these kinds of skills. However, there is the risk of a mythic individualism lurking behind some of the ways entrepreneurship, innovation and investing are presented to students.

The economies of the world still run on industries and government services that require integration, co-ordination, planning and investment. In short, they require a sense of balance between individual initiative and social co-operation. Such co-operation might take place in the firm, in civil society, or between the state and the economy. The balance of such relationships is the stuff of politics, of course, and not our primary concern. But let us interject into this scenario the illiberal but populist leader.

If we look closely at such leaders, we see repeatedly how they play upon, and distort, a mythic role of the individual in business, whose putative defence of the nation against its alleged internal and external enemies also coincidentally enriches him or her. It is difficult to choose a more apt example then Donald Trump. Although he inherited in some estimates up to $40 million, his myth of being a self-made success is crucial to his sense of self and perhaps to his political success as well. We also have no clear idea how much he is making in emoluments, but many investigative journalists and legal experts believe it is significant. The global promiscuity of his business deals is in sharp contrast to his nationalist and protectionist message to supporters ('Thanks, Pop', 2018).

But he is far from alone. Indeed, the myth of the self-made man is a *mise en abyme* among such populists even if there is a spectrum of their own personal styles of authoritarianism. No one would accuse Trump of personal austerity as a trait of self-sufficient, self-made character.

But Bolsonaro, despite living on the beach in Rio de Janeiro, presents morality as core to his independent self. Narendra Modi, prime minister of India, despite claiming to own almost no assets, will not declare his wife's wealth. He too presents himself as an authoritarian version of Gandhi, living frugally, except for his Saville Row suits and gold rings. Russian president Vladimir Putin's individualism is always on display through his infamous machismo (Arab News, 2018; Mishra, 2015; Reid, 2018). Needless to add, this heroic individualism is a stealth form for implementing statist hostility to economic liberalism. But it is equally destructive of any sense of economic history because it is theological not historical.

The very real risk is that the contemporary management curriculum – against its own inclinations and interests – will be pulled into this mythology. And, specifically, the risk is that management students will come to believe these myths, come to share this faith in the heroic individual, and where faith predominates, education is in peril. This is why management education cannot be left alone to face this fate. The liberal arts insist on the social basis of the relationship between the individual and society. They open up the subjects of history, sociology and politics through which individuals develop interdependently and are produced relationally while at the same time in the disciplines of art, performing arts and literature, the liberal arts also address our responsibilities to each other and our mutual commitments to continue these arrangements.

But this is not a matter of the liberal arts coming to the rescue. Throughout this book we have argued that the two curricula must be partners. Now with the rise of illiberal societies we can see how much the liberal arts need management education too. The liberal arts are a target of authoritarian populism because they can be associated with an 'elite' and because they can be singled out with fabricated accusations of disloyalty, immorality or even foreignness.

But management education can blunt these attacks. For example, management education achieves the universality that often eludes the liberal arts. Not only is it a popular university subject, but it is also, in a sense, populist. Business is practised by everyone and held as the prime form of social exchange by most. Everyone is understood to be capable of learning and practising business at some level. Moreover, as we have argued, today's management studies can protect the liberal arts by deploying the discursive library from which populist leaders so often draw – hard work, thrift, entrepreneurial spirit and leadership. Of course, we have noted the dangers of this coincidence, but those dangers emerge when the two curricula are isolated, do not bolster each other and each becomes vulnerable to illiberal societies.

When they are entwined the two curricula can withstand both the attacks and the appropriations of authoritarian populism. Here, to conclude, we mention only two such recent examples from a projected liberal management education, one from an economist and another from a novelist. They will suffice to make our point about the power of combining these curricula in the face of mis-characterisation and misuse of their traditions.

Mariana Mazzucato's (2011) *The Entrepreneurial State: Debunking Public vs. Private Sector Myths* was published in 2013. Mazzucato is Director of the UCL Institute for Innovation and Public Purpose in London and Chair in The Economics of Innovation and Public Value. As the title announces, her work is dedicated to puncturing the inflated claims of authoritarian populists. She uses economic history to give us a picture of the risks that states have taken in the last fifty years to invest in emerging sectors and new technologies and to renovate older industries.

'Common sense' declares that 'states cannot pick winners' – a common sense distorted by anti-state populists to malign the general competence of the state in all areas. In fact, state investment decisions have again and again paid off handsomely for many of the sectors we regard as the most innovative and complex. From platform technologies, pharmaceuticals, automobiles and others what we learn is that smart, targeted investment by the state, either directly or through universities, or protective tariffs, or created markets won the day. From Google to Amazon to Uber, today's giants are the beneficiaries of public-private co-operation. For any leader of such behemoths to downplay this business history – much less to avoid paying taxes to the state that contributed to their success – is, according to Mazzucato, hypocritical.

But from our point of view, it is also dangerous, allowing less scrupulous authoritarian leaders to mimic this position by pushing the fantasy that they got rich without the infrastructure and investment of their state. Such leadership posturing by today's CEOs, when it occurs, only provides fuel to the anti-statism of illiberal forces. As Mazzucato proves, creativity and innovation are not divided by the state/private sector but emerge in the interaction of the two.

Arundhati Roy is a renowned author of two contemporary classic novels, *The God of Small Things* and *The Ministry of Utmost Happiness* – both of which are texts taught on the Capstone at Singapore Management University (SMU) for their lessons in history and imagination. But she is equally famous for her stand against India's drift towards illiberalism. No doubt it is for this cause that she penned the 2014 extended essay introducing B. R. Ambedkar's republished

1936 classic, *The Annihilation of Caste*. Her essay is titled 'The Doctor and the Saint: Caste, Race, and Annihilation of Caste, the Debate between B. R. Ambedkar and M. K. Gandhi' (Roy, 2017). Although this debate took place in 1937, it resonates and continues in contemporary India.

Reading her essay for the potential pedagogical contribution it might make to our students, we note two things. First, as a novelist and essayist, Roy is a beautiful and persuasive writer. There is much to learn from her prose and the flow of her argument. But it is what she argues that gives us our teaching moment.

The debate between Mahatma Gandhi and Dr. Ambedkar revolves around whether Hinduism can be reformed or must be reorganised. Ambedkar argues in *The Annihilation of Caste* that the support of the *sastras* – sacred texts – for the caste system means any reform will still leave the caste system in place, and this condemns millions to a life outside democracy, understood by Ambedkar as 'liberty, fraternity, equality'.

Gandhi counters that the cultural ruling class in Hinduism, the Brahmins, need only reform – they must act with the virtue and selflessness taught in those same *sastras*.

This is precisely the argument that has been adopted in illiberal form by Hindu nationalists today, and they accuse anyone, such as Ambedkar, who advocates equality for Dalits or liberty for Muslims or fraternity for women, of attacking the religion and worse. Thus we have the chance to show students the depths of these challenges, which inevitably rebound on their education, especially the classical social liberalism necessary for globalising markets.

Our teaching can also turn to Gandhi's position on the Brahmins. Parallels can easily be drawn to calls for self-regulation and voluntary commitments to the environment that one often hears from today's business roundtables. In other words, there is a liberal echo in Gandhi's argument too. Roy notes that Ambedkar realised people's attachment to religion and that forcing them to abandon it was indeed illiberalism, even in the cause of liberalism. So, too, business groups do not want to be forced through regulation. But where does this leave the environment or the majority of castes in India? These are the question to be put to students. But the main lesson is that blending our materials deepens and strengths the perspectives we have to offer and the questions we can pose.

Finally, given the urgencies of the moment, we feel compelled to offer a negative example too. If we have argued that the power of liberal management education is that it can withstand and combat the authoritarian populism threatening the role of the university, we have also implied that liberal management scholarship would be an ally in this effort.

Harvard Business Review recently published a lengthy study by Professors Lisa Gehl and Michael Porter (2017). The authors are rightly concerned about politics in the United States, and particularly its capital, Washington, DC. They perceive that the two dominant political parties, Democrats and Republicans, have ceased to be competitors and instead have tacitly agreed to share the spoils of connections and consultancies, enriching themselves. While the authors do not say so directly, such obvious dysfunction makes it all too easy for a populist to run against the state.

Theirs is a fine portrait of monopoly rather than competition in the US political system. Unfortunately, Gehl and Porter describe this well-known gridlock, but they do not explain it. It is only too obvious to most American voters that the two main parties divide up the spoils of government and are more alike than different on most issues. We know this because Americans do not vote, despite the recent hype around higher turn-out. But why is it like this? Why is there no competition?

Gehl and Porter offer very sensible suggestions for change. But what they cannot answer is why these reasonable suggestions will be ignored. This is because Gehl and Porter have handicapped themselves at the outset by announcing they will remain solely within management scholarship. They thereby miss opportunities to incorporate decades of scholarship from development studies on state capture, for example. They use the term *political-industrial complex*, but they do not seek the scholarship that originates with this term in history and political theory. The term is derivative, of course, of the concept of the military-industrial complex. Studies of this complex, like studies around state capture in developing countries, would have yielded valuable insights into why there is no competition among the main political parties and so much collusion.

In other words, incorporation of this scholarship would have led to liberal management research with the power to examine the underlying structures of class, of accumulation, of empire, indeed of historic disenfranchisement going back to the origins of the country. In short, they might have had an answer as to why their suggestions will be ignored, and in turn this may have emboldened them towards different suggestions.

Forward with Foundations

In the twentieth century, Michel Foucault was the most cited scholar in all of the humanities. Foucault infamously 'chose' the free market over a planned economy because he believed the 'truck trade and barter' of the market made it impossible for any political leader – any authoritarian figure, populist or otherwise – to claim he understood how the whole economy worked and thus to claim the kind of knowledge that gave him full authority to rule. The market made people equal by making them equally unable to see how the whole thing works.

Social interdependence increased: people needed to co-operate with each other to buy and sell on ever-grander and deeper scales. Foucault is one of the few humanities scholars to have been read regularly in management studies, largely because he noted that specialisation and expertise could also lead to 'the mortification of perpetual submission'. In other words, many could be subject to the rule of those who managed society's organisations, replacing the rule of the sovereign with a much closer tyranny. Management scholars have used his work to raise questions about workplaces where extreme divisions of labour leave employees not just unable to see the entire market economy but even to see the point of their own labours.

'Truck trade and barter' is, of course, Smith's phrase. And the phrase about mortification comes from the forefather of sociology, Adam Ferguson. Smith and Ferguson were contemporaries, and friends, in the Scottish Enlightenment. They were chroniclers of the emerging commercial economy and especially shared an interest in the growing division of labour. Unlike Foucault their primary interest was in the way this division of labour and increased specialisation were leading to previously unknown levels of accumulation of wealth, both for individuals and for nations. But Foucault would inherit their concerns about the effects of this division of labour on the mass of people who were doing unskilled work in this emerging system.

Indeed, Smith believed that workshops, factories and mass clerking tasks were degenerative for workers – his famous fifth chapter in the *Wealth of Nations* on the division of labour is often cited as a corrective to those who use him just as a celebrant of the free market. In this chapter Smith suggests that those subject to such work lose creativity, intelligence, the ability to act civically – indeed, their physical or what he called 'martial' strength. But for all his willingness to examine these externalities of the division of labour, it remains the case that, as political theorist Lisa Hill (2007) puts it, Smith saw these problems as 'entirely ameliorable consequences for public order and personal comportment'. He recommended education programmes for workers, including lessons in civics. He added that educated workers tended to be more likely to defer to and copy their superiors, and thus to have more upright behaviour.

Smith's work is, of course, the legacy claimed by business schools. In many instances, our modest proposal of a curriculum resonates in management education as the commitment to creating leaders in society. But as we have argued throughout this book, the rhetoric of citizenship needs more than ever to be matched by an education much broader than the amelioration Smith bequeathed us, or its modern equivalent in management education programmes that offer only the bare equivalent of Smith's civics classes.

Adam Ferguson was also writing and speaking in Edinburgh at this time on the division of labour. He too saw that commercial society offered a bright future of material abundance. Unlike Smith, he saw this division of labour stemming not from the innate desire of people to exchange but because of a natural order of talents and abilities. However, he agreed with Smith that this new commercial market would transform the world. Whereas Smith was primarily interested in how to keep order in this new world, Ferguson was more concerned with how to preserve civil virtue. Thus they fell out over whether commercial society should be protected by a professional, standing army, as Smith wanted, or by a militia, about which Ferguson wrote at least one unsigned pamphlet.

Ferguson's argument against a standing army was consistent with his generally darker view of the division of labour – he thought specialised soldiers would become as degraded as any specialised worker and open to manipulation. Indeed, Ferguson's views on the division of labour are generally bleak. 'We make good work, but educate men gross, sordid, void of sentiments and manners' (Hill, 2007, p. 349), he wrote. Ferguson's emphasis was on the dangers to public life, to civic participation and holistic personality. He feared that with the rise of commerce 'society is made to consist of parts, of which none of them is animated by the spirit of society itself' (Hill, 2007, p. 350). Hence he thought that to separate those who rule from those who go to war – the arts of policy and war as he called them – was 'an attempt to dismember the human spirit' (Hill, 2007, p. 353).

Ferguson nonetheless shared Smith's belief that such adverse consequences of the division of labour could be addressed, especially given the growing wealth to which states would have access to create this education. Ferguson simply believed that the task was more urgent and more comprehensive, requiring extensive education on virtue for aristocrats and workers alike. Only a robust programme in the art of citizenship could replace what mighty commerce now made into parts. Before Smith's death, the two reconciled their friendship, as we must do today, in liberal management education.

Postscript

After writing this book over the last four to five years anchored in the environment of Singapore Management University (SMU), each of us has gained a deep and personal understanding of the interaction between the liberal arts and management education. Indeed, we both feel privileged to have been faculty members at SMU, which from its outset has tried to differentiate itself in terms of its philosophy, teaching pedagogy and mission from the more focussed national universities in Singapore, namely the National University of Singapore (NUS) and Nanyang Technological University (NTU), which to some extent, have tended to adopt British academic traditions and models.

As we have noted in our short case study of SMU in Chapter 3, SMU adapted and modified over time a liberal management education model inherited from its partnership with the Wharton School at the University of Pennsylvania. This experience of taking part in the process of producing a more Asian, and Singaporean, liberal education model provided us with insights in addressing the interactions between liberal arts and management education both about teaching and research opportunities.

As we follow our different future pathways, Stefano will continue with his co-teaching experiments through his collective School for Study in Asia, the United Kingdom, the United States, and Latin America. He is also carrying the lessons of liberal management education into research, where he is engaged in curatorial investigations of management themes.

Howard, on the other hand, will continue with his studies of business school diversity in Africa, Asia, Europe, North America and the United Kingdom. He and his coauthors have already used a social constructionist model (see Thomas et al., 2013) as the framework to research the evolution and delivery of management education in a legitimate and identifiable fashion across the contemporary world in terms of a number of articles and books, cited in the body of the text. This research as Pettigrew et al. (2014) point out has provided many valuable insights about convergence and divergence of business models

200

across continents, countries and cultural contexts. What is needed now is detailed, comparative international research using in-depth case studies to chart, analyse and interpret carefully similarity and variance in global business school models and their development. Indeed, this is the research avenue that Howard will follow in his future work.

In following this pathway Howard has been influenced by his friendships and involvement with the research published by Henry Mintzberg (McGill), Andrew Pettigrew (Said, Oxford) and Joe Porac (NYU). The characteristic that binds these three scholars together is their interest in researching and understanding organisational, and individual, strategic decision-making processes from a wide range of perspectives and contexts (e.g. universities, the National Health Service in the United Kingdom and the Scottish knitwear industry, respectively).

Therefore, Howard intends to use these perspectives as part of the theoretical framework involved in carrying out a small number of detailed case studies of innovative business schools globally. SMU, in the Asian context, is likely to be the first example, given Howard's experience as a dean, researcher and faculty member over almost a decade during SMU's dynamic and fast-paced development. Other possible examples might include Gordon Institute of Business Science (GIBS) in South Africa, Judge Business School in the United Kingdom and the Kozminski School in Poland.

In undertaking the framework, Howard will also follow an approach suggested by another friend and colleague, namely Barbara Schachermayer-Sporn (2001) to characterise the evolution of adaptive schools and universities in an evolving, knowledge-based society. She identifies seven characteristics: a responsiveness to change; an entrepreneurial mission; an innovative campus culture; evidence of cross-disciplinary collaboration; entrepreneurial, innovative management; improved, flexible governance structures and leaders who encourage innovation, flexibility, agility and willingness to change. Howard hopes to report the preliminary results of his first study by the mid-2020 time horizon.

In the meantime, both of us hope that we have inspired you, or at least some of our readers, to generate research about new, fine-grained, different models of management education particularly involving the use of liberal arts alongside core management skills. We wish you the best of luck in your endeavours.

Bibliography

Books

Abdulai, David (2014). *African-Centred Management Education: A New Paradigm for an Emerging Continent*. London: Routledge.

Adorno, Theodor (1950). *The Authoritarian Personality*. New York: Harper.

Amsden, Alice (2007). *Escape from Empire: The Developing World's Journey through Heaven and Hell*. Cambridge, MA: MIT Press.

Angus, Ian (2009). *Love the Questions: University Education and Enlightenment*. Winnipeg: Arbeiter/Ring.

Arnold, Matthew (2009 [1869]). *Culture and Anarchy*. Oxford, UK: Oxford University Press.

Arondekar, Anjali (2009). *For the Record: On Sexuality and the Colonial Archive in India*. Durham, NC: Duke University Press.

Aronowitz, Stanley (2000). *The Knowledge Factory: Dismantling the Corporate University and Creating True Higher Learning*. Boston: Beacon Press.

Augier, Mie and March, James (2011). *The Roots, Rituals, and Rhetorics of Change: North American Business Schools after the Second World War*. Stanford, CA: Stanford Business Books.

Baldwin, James (1995). *The Fire Next Time*. New York: Modern Library.
  (1998). *Collected Essays*. New York: Library of America.

Bataille, Georges (1988). *The Accursed Share: An Essay on General Economy*. New York: Zone Books.

Berardi, Franco (2009). *The Soul at Work: From Alienation to Autonomy*. Cambridge, MA: MIT Press.

Bousquet, Marc (2008). *How the University Works: Higher Education and the Low-Wage Nation*. New York: New York University Press.

Busch, Annett and Annas, Max, eds. (2008). *Sembene Ousmane: Interviews*. Jackson: University of Mississippi Press.

Cabral, Amilcar (1974). *Return to the Source: Selected Speeches of Amilcar Cabral*. New York: Monthly Review Press.

Carnegie Foundation for the Advancement of Teaching (2011). *Rethinking Undergraduate Management Education: Liberal Learning for the Profession*. San Francisco, CA: Jossey-Bass.

Chomsky, Noam, Katznelson, Ira, Lewontin, Richard C., Montgomery, David, Nader, Laura, Ohmann, Richard, Siever, Ray, Wallerstein, Immanuel, and Zinn, Howard (1997). *The Cold War and the University: Toward an Intellectual History of the Postwar Years*. New York: New Press.

Christensen, Clayton and Eyring, Henry (2012). *The Innovative University*. San Francisco, CA: Jossey-Bass.

Clawson, Dan and Page, Max (2011). *The Future of Higher Education*. New York: Routledge.

Cohn, Bernard (1997). *Colonialism and Its Forms of Knowledge: The British in India*. Princeton, NJ: Princeton University Press.

Colby, Anne, Ehrlich, Thomas, Sullivan, William M. and Dolle, Jonathan R. (2011). *Rethinking Undergraduate Business Education: Liberal Learning for the Profession*. San Francisco, CA: Jossey-Bass.

Cole, Jonathan (2010). *The Great American University*. New York: Perseus Books.

Collini, Stefan (2012). *What Are Universities For?* London: Penguin.

Conde, Maryse (1994). *I, Tituba: The Black Witch of Salem*. New York: Ballantine Books.

Cote, James and Allahar, Anton (2011). *Lowering Higher Education: The Rise of the Corporate University and the Fall of Liberal Education*. Toronto: University of Toronto Press.

Davidson, Basil (1988). *The African Slave Trade*. Revised ed. New York: Back Bay Books.

(1992). *The Black Man's Burden*. New York: Three Rivers Press.

(1994). *Modern Africa: A Social and Political History*. 3rd ed. London: Longman.

Dewey, John (1977). *Education Today*. New York: Greenwood Press.

Diagne, Souleymane Bachir (2012). *African Art as Philosophy*. Chicago: University of Chicago Press.

Drucker, Peter (1964). *Managing for Results*. Oxford, UK: Heinemann.

(1989). *The New Realities*. Reprint ed. New Brunswick, NJ: Transaction Publications.

DuBois, William Edward Burghardt (1947). *The World and Africa: An Inquiry into the Part Which Africa Has Played in World History*. New York: Viking.

Eliot, T. S. (1997 [1920]). *The Sacred Wood and Major Early Essays*. New York: Dover Publications.

Englis, Fred (1992). *The Cruel Peace: Living through the Cold War*. London: Aurum Press.

Erickson, Paul, Klein, Judy L., Daston, Lorraine, Lemov, Rebecca, Sturm, Thomas, and Gordin, Michael D. (2013). *How Reason Almost Lost Its Mind: The Strange Career of Cold War Rationality*. Chicago: University of Chicago Press.

Escobar, Arturo (1995). *Encountering Development: The Making and Unmaking of the Third World*. Princeton, NJ: Princeton University Press.

Fayol, Henri (1930). *Industrial and General Administration*. London: Pitman & Sons.

Federici, Silvia (2004). *Caliban and the Witch: Women, the Body and Primitive Accumulation*. New York: Autonomedia.

Federici, Silvia, Caffentzis, George, and Alidou, Ousseina eds. (Committee for Academic Freedom in Africa) (2000). *A Thousand Flowers: Social Struggles against Structural Adjustment in African Universities*. Trenton, NJ: Africa World Press.

Fleming, Peter (2009). *Authenticity and the Cultural Politics of Work*. Oxford, UK: Oxford University Press.

(2015). *Resisting Work*. Philadelphia, PA: Temple University Press.

(2015). *The Mythology of Work*. London: Pluto Press.

(2017). *The Death of Homo Economicus*. London: Pluto Press.

(2018). *Sugar Daddy Capitalism*. Medford, MA: Polity Press.

Foucault, Michel (1979). *Power, Truth, Strategy*. Sydney: Feral Publications.

(2002). *The Archaeology of Knowledge*. London: Routledge.

(2007). *The Politics of Truth*. Los Angeles, CA: Semiotext(e)/MIT Press.

Fragueiro, Fernando and Thomas, Howard (2011). *Strategic Leadership in the Business School, Keeping One Step Ahead*. Cambridge, UK: Cambridge University Press.

Freire, Paulo (1978). *Pedagogy in Progress: Letters to Guinea-Bissau*. New York: The Seabury Press.

French, Robert and Grey, Christopher (1996). *Rethinking Management Education*. London: Sage.

Gabor, Andrea (2002). *The Capitalist Philosophers: The Geniuses of Modern Business*. New York: Three Rivers Press.

Geertz, Clifford (1963). *Peddlers and Princes: Social Change and Economic Modernization in Two Indonesian Towns*. Chicago: University of Chicago Press.

(1971). *Agricultural Involution: The Process of Ecological Change in Indonesia*. Berkeley: University of California Press.

(1973). *The Interpretation of Cultures*. New York: Basic Books.

Gilligan, Carol (1982). *In a Different Voice: Psychological Theory and Women's Development*. Cambridge, MA: Harvard University Press.

Gilligan, Carol, Ward, Janie, McLean Taylor, Jill, and Bardige, Betty, eds. (1989). *Mapping the Moral Domain: A Contribution of Women's Thinking to Psychological Theory and Education*. Cambridge, MA: Harvard University Press.

Goodman, Paul (1960). *Growing Up Absurd: Problems of Youth in the Organized System*. New York: Random House.

Grey, Christopher (2005). *A Very Short, Fairly Interesting and Reasonably Cheap Book about Studying Organisations*. London: Sage.

Hanlon, Gerard (2016). *The Dark Side of Management: A Secret History of Management Theory*. New York: Routledge.

Harney, Stefano and Moten, Fred (2013). *The Undercommons: Fugitive Planning and Black Study*. Chico, CA: AK Press.

Hartman, Saidiya (2008). *Lose Your Mother: A Journey along the Atlantic Slave Route*. New York: Farrar, Straus, and Giroux.

Hofstede, Geert (2001 [1980]). *Culture's Consequences*. 2nd ed. Thousand Oaks, CA: Sage.

Hofstede, Geert and Hofstede, Gert Jan (2005). *Cultures and Organizations: Software of the Mind*. 2nd ed. New York: McGraw-Hill.

Isaac, Joel (2012). *Working Knowledge: Making the Human Sciences from Parsons to Kuhn*. Cambridge, MA: Harvard University Press.

James, C. L. R. (2012). *A History of Pan-African Revolt*. Reissue. San Francisco: PM Press.

Johnson, Benjamin, Kavanagh, Patrick, and Wattson, Kevin, eds. (2003). *Steal This University: The Rise of the Corporate University and the Academic Labour Movement*. New York: Routledge.

Kant, Immanuel (1992). *The Conflict of the Faculties*. Lincoln: University of Nebraska Press.

Katzenbach, John and Smith, Douglas (2015). *Wisdom of Teams. Reprint.* Boston, MA: Harvard Business Review Press.

Kenyatta, Jomo (1965). *Facing Mount Kenya*. 3rd ed. London: Mercury Books.

Kerr, Clark (2001). *The Uses of the Universities*. 5th ed. Cambridge, MA: Harvard University Press.

Khurana, Rajesh (2007). *From Higher Aims to Hired Hands: The Social Transformation of American Business Schools and the Unfulfilled Promise of Management as a Profession*. Princeton, NJ: Princeton University Press.

Kirp, David (2009). *Shakespeare, Einstein and the Bottom Line: The Marketing of Higher Education*. Cambridge, MA: Harvard University Press.

Kiss, Elizabeth and Euben, J. Peter, eds. (2010). *Debating Moral Education: Rethinking the Role of the Modern University*. Durham, NC: Duke University Press.

Kolsky, Elizabeth (2010). *Colonial Justice in British India*. Cambridge, UK: Cambridge University Press.

Krause, Monika, Nolan, Mary, Palm, Michael, and Ross, Andrew, eds. (2008). *The University against Itself: The NYU Strike and the Future of the Academic Workplace*. Philadelphia, PA: Temple University Press.

Lang, Cecil ed. (1998). *The Letters of Matthew Arnold. Vol. II: 1860–65*. Virginia: Virginia University Press.

Leavis, F. R. (2013). *Two Cultures? The Significance of C. P. Snow*. Cambridge, UK: Cambridge University Press.

Levinas, Emmanuel (1969). *Totality and Infinity: An Essay on Exteriority*. Pittsburgh, PA: Duquesne University Press.

(1985). *Ethics and Infinity: Conversations with Phillipe Nemo*. Pittsburgh, PA: Duquesne University Press.

Lippman, Walter (2007). *Liberty and the News*. Princeton, NJ: Princeton University Press.

Lowen, Rebecca (1997). *Creating the Cold War University: The Transformation of Stanford*. Berkeley: University of California Press.

Ludden, David, ed. (2001). *Reading Subaltern Studies*. New Delhi: Permanent Black.

Macaulay, Thomas Babington. Minute of 2 February 1835 on Indian Education. In Young, G. M. ed. (1957). *Macaulay, Prose and Poetry*. Cambridge: Harvard University Press, pp. 721–2.

Martin, Randy (2011). *Under New Management: Universities, Administrative Labour and the Professional Turn*. Philadelphia, PA: Temple University Press.

Marx, Karl (2002[1848]). *The Communist Manifesto*. London: Penguin.

Marx, Karl and Engels, Friedrich (2012). *The Communist Manifesto*. London: Verso.

Mazzucato, Mariana (2011). *The Entrepreneurial State*. London: Anthem Press.

McGettigan, Andrew (2013). *The Great University Gamble: Money, Markets and the Future of Higher Education*. London: Pluto Press.

Meltzer, Allan (2012). *Why Capitalism?* New York: Oxford University Press.

Melvin, Jess (2018). *The Army and the Indonesian Genocide: Mechanics of Mass Murder*. London: Routledge.

Menand, Louis (2010). *The Marketplace of Ideas, Reform and Resilience in the American University.* New York: W. W. Norton.

Miller, Toby (2012). *Blow Up the Humanities.* Philadelphia, PA: Temple University Press.

Mills, C. Wright (1957). *The Power Elite.* New York: Oxford University Press.

Mintzberg, Henry (2005). *Managers Not MBAs.* San Francisco, CA: Berret-Kochler.

Mitropoulos, Angela (2012). *Contract & Contagion; From Biopolitics to Oikonomia.* Chico, CA: AK Press.

Mouffe, Chantal (1999). *The Challenge of Carl Schmitt.* London: Verso.

Mudimbe, V. Y. (1988). *The Invention of Africa: Gnosis, Philosophy, and the Order of Knowledge.* Bloomington: Indiana University Press.

Negri, Antonio (2003). *Time for Revolution.* trans. Mandarini, Matteo. London: Continuum.

   (2015). *Factory of Strategy: Thirty-Three Lessons on Lenin.* trans. Arianna Bove. New York: Columbia University Press.

Newfield, Christopher (2011). *Unmaking of the Public University.* Cambridge, MA: Harvard University Press.

Newman, Carol, Page John, Rand, John, Shimeles, Abebe, Soderbom, Mans, and Tarp, Finn, eds. (2016). *Manufacturing Transformation: Comparative Studies of Industrial Development in Africa and Emerging Asia.* Oxford, UK: Oxford University Press.

Newman, John Henry (1852). *The Idea of the University.* London: Longman Green.

Noble, David (2002). *Digital Diploma Mills: The Automation of Higher Education.* New York: Monthly Review Press.

Oguibe, Olu, and Enwezor, Okui (1999). *Reading the Contemporary: African Art from Theory to the Marketplace.* London: Institute of International Visual Arts.

Parker, M. (2018). *Shut Down the Business School: What's Wrong with Management Education.* London: Pluto Press.

Pasquinelli, Matteo (2008). *Animal Spirits: A Bestiary of the Commons.* Rotterdam: NAi Publishers.

Peters, K., Smith, R. R. and Thomas, H. (2018). *Rethinking the Business Models of Business Schools.* Bingley, UK: Emerald Publishing.

Pettigrew, Andrew, Cornuel, Eric and Hommel, Ulrich, eds. (2014). *The Institutional Development of Business Schools.* Oxford: Oxford University Press.

Prakash, Gyan (1999). *Another Reason: Science and the Imagination of Modern India.* Princeton, NJ: Princeton University Press.

Prashad, Vijay (2008). *The Darker Nations: A People's History of the Third World.* New York: New Press.

Readings, Bill (1997). *The University in Ruins.* Cambridge, MA: Harvard University Press.

Richards, Ivor (2004 [1929]). *Practical Criticism.* London: Routledge.

Robinson, Cedric (2001). *An Anthropology of Marxism.* London: Ashgate.

Rodney, Walter (1972). *How Europe Underdeveloped Africa.* London: Bogle-L'Ouverture Publications.

Roethlisberger, Fritz Jules and Dickson, William John (1939). *Management and the Worker.* Cambridge, MA: Harvard University Press.

Rolfe. Gary (2012). *The University in Dissent: Scholarship in the Corporate University*. New York: Routledge.

Roy, Arundhati (2017). *The Doctor and the Saint: Caste, Race, and the Annihilation of Caste*. Chicago, IL: Haymarket Books.

Schrecker, Ellen (1998). *No Ivory Tower: McCarthyism and the Universities*. Oxford, UK: Oxford University Press.

Shrecker, Ellen (1986). *No Ivory Tower: McCarthyism and the Universities*. Oxford, UK: Oxford University Press.

Shukaitis, Stevphen (2015). *The Composition of Movements to Come: Aesthetics and Cultural Labour After the Avant-Garde*. London: Rowman & Littlefield.

Slaughter, Sheila and Rhoades, Gary (1999). *Academic Capitalism: Politics, Policies and the Entrepreneurial University*. Baltimore, MD: Johns Hopkins University Press.

Sloan, Alfred (1972). *My Years with General Motors*. New York: Doubleday.

Starkey, K. and Tiratsoo, N. (2007). *The Business School and the Bottom Line*. Cambridge, UK: Cambridge University Press.

Symonds, Richard (1993). *Oxford and Empire: The Last Lost Cause*. Oxford, UK: Oxford University Press.

The Nanopolitics Group (2014). *Nanopolitics Handbook*. Chico, CA: AK Press.

Thomas, H., Lee, M., Thomas, L. and Wilson, A. (2014). *Securing the Future of Management Education: Competitive Destruction or Constructive Innovation?* Bingley, UK: Emerald Publishing.

(2016a). *Africa: The Management Education Challenge, Volume 1*. Bingley, UK: Emerald Publishing.

Thomas, H., Lee, M., Thomas, L. & Wilson, A. (2017). *Africa: The Management Education Challenge Vol 2*. Bingley, UK: Emerald Publishing.

Thomas, H., Lorange, P. & Sheth, J. (2013a). *The Business School in the 21st Century: Emergent Challenges and New Business Models*. Cambridge, UK: Cambridge University Press.

Thomas, Howard, Thomas, Lynne, and Wilson, Alex (2013b). *Promises Fulfilled and Unfulfilled in Management Education*. Bingley, UK: Emerald Publishing.

Trumphour, John (1989). *How Harvard Rules: Reason in the Service of Empire*. Boston, MA: South End Press.

United States Senate Health, Education, Labor and Pensions Committee (2012). *For Profit Higher Education: The Failure to Safeguard the Federal Investment and Ensure Student Success*. Washington, DC: US G.P.O.

Veblen, Thorsten (1918). *The Higher Learning in America*. New York: Huebsch.

Vincent, Joan (2002). *The Anthropology of Politics*. Oxford, UK: Blackwell.

Wade, Robert (2004). *Governing the Market: Economic Theory and the Role of Government in East Asian Industrialization*. Princeton, NJ: Princeton University Press.

Waghid, Yusef (2014). *African Philosophy of Education Reconsidered: On Being Human*. London: Routledge.

Waghid, Yusef, Van Wyk, Berte, Adams, Faried, and November, Ivan eds. (2005). *African(a) Philosophy of Education: Reconstructions and Deconstructions*. Stellenbosch: Stellenbosch University Printers.

Werbner, Richard and Ranger, Terence (1996). *Post-colonial Identities in Africa*. London: Zed Books.

Wilder, Craig (2013). *Ebony and Ivy: Race, Slavery and the Troubled History of America's Universities*. London: Bloomsbury Press.
Williams, Eric (1994). *Capitalism and Slavery*. Chapel Hill: University of North Carolina Press.
Williams, Raymond (1960). *Culture and Society*. New York: Anchor.
Woo-Cumings, Meredith (1999). *The Developmental State*. Ithaca, NY: Cornell University Press.
Young-Bruehl, Elizabeth (2009). *Why Arendt Matters*. New Haven, CT: Yale University Press.
Zingales, Luigi (2012). *A Capitalism for the People: Recapturing the Lost Genius of American Prosperity*. New York: Basic Books.

Book Chapters

Amsden, Alice (1992). A Theory of Government Intervention in Late Industrialization. In Putterman, Louis and Rueschemeyer, Dietrich, eds., *State and Market in Development*. Boulder, CO: Lynne Rienner Publishers, 53–84.
Chang, Ha-Joon (2002). Institutions and Economic Development: 'Good Governance' in Historical Perspective. In *Kicking Away the Ladder: Development Strategy in Historical Perspective*. London: Anthem Press, 69–122.
Ferguson, James (1990). Conceptual Apparatus. In *The Anti-politics Machine: 'Development,' Depoliticization, and Bureaucratic Power in Lesotho*. Cambridge, UK: Cambridge University Press, 26–75.
Gilman, Nils (2002). Involution and Modernization: The Case of Clifford Geertz. In Cohen, Jeffrey and Dannhaeuser, Norbert. *Economic Development: An Anthropological Approach*. Walnut Creek, CA: Rowman & Littlefield, 3–22.
Hall, Stuart (1983). The Great Moving Right Show. In Hall, Jacques ed. *The Politics of Thatcherism*. London: Lawrence and Wishart, 19–39.
Kohli, Atul (2004). The Colonial Origins of a Modern Political Economy: The Japanese Lineage of Korea's Cohesive-Capitalist State. In *State-Directed Development: Political Power and Industrialization in the Global Periphery*. Cambridge, UK: Cambridge University Press, 27–61.
Kropotkin, Peter (1912). Brain Work and Manual Work. In *Fields, Factories, and Workshops*. 2nd ed. London: Thomas Nelson and Sons, 199–224.
Kirp, David (2003). *Shakespeare, Einstein, and the Bottom Line: The Marketing of Higher Education*. Cambridge, MA: Harvard University Press.
Linstead, S. (2010). Turning Rebellion into Money: The Clash, Creativity and Resistance to Commodification. In Townley, Barbara, ed. *Managing Creativity: Exploring the Paradox*. Cambridge, UK: Cambridge University Press.
Macaulay, Thomas Babington. (2 February 1835). Minute of 2 February 1835 on Indian Education. In Young, G. M., ed. *Macaulay, Prose and Poetry*. Cambridge, MA: Harvard University Press, 721–9.
Miller, Toby. (2009.) A Future for Media Studies. In Beaty, Bart, Briton, Derek, Filex, Gloria, and Sullivan, Rebecca, eds. *How Canadians Communicate III*. Athabasca: Athabasca University Press, 35–53.

Mitchell, Timothy (2002). Introduction. In *Rule of Experts: Egypt, Techno-Politics, Modernity*. Berkeley: The University of California Press, 1–15.

Nader, Laura (1972). Up the Anthropologist – Perspectives Gained from Studying Up. In Hymes, Dell ed. *Reinventing Anthropology*. New York: Pantheon, 284–311.

Sender, John and Smith, Sheila (1986). Trade, Industrialization and the State in the Post-colonial Period. In *The Development of Capitalism in Africa*. London: Routledge, 67–109.

Simon, Herbert (1976). The Business School: A Problem in Organisational Design. In *Administrative Behaviour*. 3rd ed. New York: Free Press.

Simon, Herbert (1991). *Models of My Life*. New York: Basic Books.

Taylor, Frederick (1967 [1911]). Shop Management. In *Scientific Management*. New York: Norton, 17–54.

Thomas, H. (2017). Rethinking and Re-evaluating the Purpose of the Business School. In Bradshaw, D., ed. *Rethinking Business Education: Fit for the Future*. London: Chartered Association of Business Schools (CABS), 8–9.

Warren, Bill (1980). Colonialism: Dr Jekyll and Mr Hyde. In *Imperialism: Pioneer of Capitalism*. London: Verso, 125–156.

Williams, Raymond (2005). *Culture and Materialism: Selected Essays*. New York: Verso.

Woo-Cumings, Meredith (1998). The Political Economy of Growth in East Asia: A Perspective on the State, Market, and Ideology. In *The Role of Government in East Asian Economic Development*. Oxford, UK: Clarendon Press, 323–334.

Journal Articles

Abend, Gabriel (2013). The Origins of Business Ethics in American Universities, 1902–1936. *Business Ethics Quarterly* 23, 71–205.

Amsden, Alice (1991). Diffusion of Development: The Late-Industrializing Model and Greater East Asia. *American Economic Review* 81(2), 282–286.

Arenella, Lynn, Davi, Angelique, Veeser, Cyrus, and Wiggins, Roy (2009). The Best of Both Worlds: Infusing Liberal Learning into a Business Curriculum. *Liberal Education* 95(1), 50–55.

Bell, Myrtle (2009). Introduction: On Evidence, Ethics, Corruption, and Values. *Academy of Management Learning and Education* 8(2), 252–254.

Bennis, Warren and O'Toole, James (2005). How Business Schools Lost Their Way. *Harvard Business Review* 83(5), 96–104.

Birtch, Thomas and Chiang, Flora (2013). The Influence of Business School's Ethical Climate on Students' Unethical Behavior. *Journal of Business Ethics* 123(2), 283–294.

Brooks, Cleanth (1983). I. A. Richards and 'Practical Criticism.' *The Sewanee Review* 89(4), 586–595.

Chakrabarty, Dipesh (2015). Subaltern Studies in Retrospect and Reminiscence. *South Asia: Journal of South Asian Studies* 38(1), 10–18.

Chew, Bryon and McInnis-Bowers, Cecilia (2004). Blending Liberal Arts and Business Education *Liberal Education* 90(1), 56–63.

Cot, Annie (2011). A 1930s North American Creative Community: The Harvard 'Pareto Circle'. *History of Political Economy* 43(1), 131–159.

Dalton, Craig and Mason-Deese, Liz (2012). Counter(Mapping) Actions: Mapping as Militant Research. *ACME* 11(3), 439–466.

Derrida, Jacques et al. (1996). Of the Humanities and Philosophical Disciplines. *Surfaces* 108(1).

Dunne, Stephen and Harney, Stefano (2013). More Than Nothing? Accounting, Business, and Management Studies, and the Research Audit. *Critical Perspectives on Accounting* 24(4–5), 338–349.

Egri, Carolyn (2013). Introduction: Challenging Times for Business Ethics Education. *Academy of Management Learning and Education* 12(1), 70.

Enwezor, Okwui (2003). The Postcolonial Constellation: Contemporary Art in a State of Permanent Transition. *Research in African Literatures* 34(4), 57–32.

Epstein, Edwin (2010). BEQ at Twenty: The State of the Journal, the State of the Academic Field, and the State of Business Ethics: Some Reflections. *Business Ethics Quarterly* 20(4), 733–736.

Federici, Silvia and Caffentzis, George (2004). Globalization and Professionalization in Africa. *Social Text* 22(2), 81–99.

Floyd, Larry, Xu, Feng, Atkins, Ryan and Caldwell, Cam (2013). Ethical Outcomes and Business Ethics: Toward Improving Business Ethics Education *Journal of Business Ethics* 117(4), 753–776.

Ghoshal, S. (2005). Bad Management Theories Are Destroying Good Management Practices. *Academy of Management Learning and Education* 4(1), 75–79.

Giacalone, Robert and Promislo, Mark (2013). Broken When Entering: The Stigmatization of Goodness and Business Ethics Education. *Academy of Management Learning and Education* 12, 96–101.

Giacalone, Robert and Thompson, Kenneth (2006). Business Ethics and Social Responsibility Education: Shifting the Worldview. *Academy of Management Learning and Education* 5, 266–277.

Gilligan, Carol (1990). Joining the Resistance: Psychology, Politics, Girls and Women. *Michigan Quarterly Review* 29(4), 501–536. http://hdl.handle.net/2027/spo.act2080.0029.004:06.

Hall, Stuart (1985). Authoritarian Populism: A Reply to Jessop et al. *New Left Review* 151.

Harney, Stefano. (2010). In the Business School. *Edu-Factory Journal* 2, 1.

Harris, Laura (2012). What Happened to the Motley Crew?: C. L. R. James, Hélio Oiticica, and the Aesthetic Sociality of Blackness. *Social Text* 112, 49–75.

Harvey, David (2002). The Art of Rent. *Socialist Register* 38, 93–110.

Hill, Lisa (2007). Adam Smith, Adam Ferguson and Karl Marx on the Division of Labour. *Journal of Classical Sociology* 7(3), 339–366.

Gilmore, Ruth (2011). What Is to Be Done? *American Quarterly* 63(2), 245–64.

Kavanagh, Donncha (2013). Making, Breaking and Following Rules: The Irvine Case. *Research in the Sociology of Organizations* 37, 27–54.

Kenworthy, Amy (2013). Introduction: Entrepreneurship, Economics, Ethics, Morality, and War. *Academy of Management Learning and Education* 12(1), 142–144.

Kong, Lily (2015). Education in Management and the Liberal Arts: Never the Twain Shall Meet? *The Business Times*, 17.

Livingston, Sterling (1971). The Myth of the Well-Educated Manager. *Harvard Business Review* 49(1), 79–89.

March, James (1972). A Garbage Can Model of Organizational Choice. *Administrative Science Quarterly* 17(1), 1–25

Mbembe, Achille (2016). Africa in the New Century. *The Massachusetts Review* 57(1), 91–104. DOI 10.1353/mar.2016.0031.

Nkomo, Stella (2011). A Postcolonial and Anti-colonial Reading of 'African' Leadership and Management in Organization Studies. *Organization* 18(3), 365–386.

Nyerere, Julius K. (1967). Education for Self-Reliance. *The Ecumenical Review* 19(4), 382–403. (Originally booklet, March 1967, government printer, Dar es Salaam.) Also available at www.julius.org/resources/view/education_for_self_reliance and www.swaraj.org/shikshantar/resources_nyerere.html.

Pettigrew, A. and Starkey, K. (2016). The Legitimacy and Impact of Business Schools: Key Issues and a Research Agenda. *Academy of Management Learning and Education* 15(4), 649–64.

Pfeffer, Jeffrey and Fong, Christina (2002). The End of the Business Schools? Less Success Than Meets the Eye. *Academy of Management Learning and Education* 1(1), 78–95.

Schachermayer-Sporn, Barbara (2001). Building Adaptive Universities: Emerging Organizational Forms Based on Experiences of European and US Universities. *Tertiary Education and Management* 7(2), 121–134.

Schoemaker, Paul (2008). The Future Challenges of Business: Rethinking Management Education. *California Management Review* 50(3), 119–139.

Spender, J. C. (2008). Book Review of Khurana's (2007) Book. *Academy of Management Review* 33(4), 1022–26.

Spivak, Gayatri (2005). Use and Abuse of Human Rights. *boundary 2*: 32(1), 131–89.

Starik, Mark, Rands, Gordon, Marcus, Alfred, and Clark, Timothy (2010). From the Guest Editors: In Search of Sustainability in Management Education. *Academy of Management Learning and Education* 9(3), 377–383.

Susuman, A Sathiya, Chialepeh, Wilson, Bado, Aristide and Lailulo, Yishak (2015). High Infant Mortality Rate, High Total Fertility Rate and Very Low Female Literacy in Selected African Countries. *Scandinavian Journal of Public Health* 44(1), 2–5.

Thomas, Howard (2017). Management Education Out of Africa. *Asian Management Insights* 4(1), 68–75.

Thomas, Howard and Harney, Stefano (2013). Towards a Liberal Management Education. *Journal of Management Development* 32(5), 508–524.

Thomas, Howard, Lee, Michelle, Thomas, Lynne, and Wilson, Alexander (2016b). Does Africa Need an 'African' Management Education Model? *Global Focus* 10(2), 58–63.

Thomas, Howard and Wilson, Alexander (2011). Physics Envy, Cognitive Legitimacy or Practical Relevance: Dilemmas in the Evolution of Management Research in the U.K. *British Journal of Management* 22(3), 443–456.

Valentine, Sean, Nam, Seung-Hyun, Hollingworth, David, and Hall, Callie (2013). Ethical Context and Ethical Decision Making: Examination of an Alternative Statistical Approach for Identifying Variable Relationships. *Journal of Business Ethics* 124(3), 509–526.

wa Thiong'o, Ngugi (1997). Enactments of Power: The Politics of Performance Space. *The Drama Review (TDR)* 41(3), 11.30.

Waddock, Sandra and Lozano, Josep (2013). Developing More Holistic Management Education: Lessons Learned from Two Programs. *Academy of Management Learning and Education* 12(2), 265–284.

Williams, Raymond (1983). Cambridge English and Beyond. *London Review of Books* 5(12), 3–8.

Working Papers

Bradshaw, Della ed. (2017). *Rethinking Business Education*. Chartered Association of Business Schools. https://charteredabs.org/wp-content/uploads/2017/11/Rethinking-Business-Education-Chartered-ABS.pdf.

Colby, Anne, Ehrlich, Thomas, Sullivan, William, and Dolle, Jonathan (2011). *Rethinking Undergraduate Business Education: Liberal Learning for the Profession*. San Francisco, CA: Jossey-Bass.

Cooke, Bill (2002). *The Denial of Slavery in Management Studies*. Management in Development Group Working Paper Series. Manchester, UK: Institute for Development Policy and Management, University of Manchester.

CUTS (2016). *Understanding the Role of Maize Market Queens in Ghana*. Jaipur: CUTS.

Gehl, Lisa and Porter, Michael (2017). Why Competition in the Politics Industry Is Failing America. Harvard Business School. www.hbs.edu/competitiveness/Documents/why-competition-in-the-politics-industry-is-failing-america.pdf.

Nyathi, Nceku (2008). The Organisational Imagination in African Anti-Colonial Thought, unpublished PhD thesis, University of Leicester. Accessible at https://lra.le.ac.uk/bitstream/2381/4381/1/2008nyathinphd.pdf.

Media: Film

I Am Not Your Negro (2016). Raoul Peck dir. Velvet Film.

La Noire de… (1966). Ousmane Sembène dir. New Yorker Video.

North by Northwest (1959). Alfred Hitchcock dir. Metro-Goldwyn-Mayer.

Our Man in Havana (1959). Carol Reed dir. Columbia Pictures.

Silkwood (1983). Mike Nichols dir. 20th Century Fox.

Soylent Green (1983). Richard Fleischer dir. Metro-Goldwyn-Mayer.

The Century of the Self (2002). Adam Curtis. BBC Four.

The Fog of War (2003). Errol Morris dir. Sony Pictures Classics.

The Manchurian Candidate (1962). John Frankenheimer dir. United Artists.

Media: Novels

Achebe, Chinua (1994). *Things Fall Apart*. New York: Anchor.

Bulawayo, No Violet (2013). *We Need New Names*. New York: Back Bay Books.

Dick, Philip (1969). *Ubik*. Garden City: Doubleday.
Doctorow, E. L. (1991). *The Book of Daniel*. New York: Continuum.
Greene, Graham (1981 [1958]). *Our Man in Havana*. New York: Viking Press.
Mailer, Norman (1997). *The Fight*. New York: Vintage.
Miller, Arthur (1952). *The Crucible*. London: Penguin.
Zamyatin, Yevgeny (1972). *We*. New York: HarperCollins.

Events

Bove, Arianna (April 2010). 'Work and Labour: The Labour of Translation'.
Composition & Commons Co-research Project. (May 2008). 'Future Promises –
  The Life and Work of Stanley Aronowitz'.
Measure for Measure: A Workshop on Value from Below. (September 2007).
  Goodenough College, London.
Queen Mary School of Business and Management Events. Histories &
  Cartographies of Global Capitalism. http://busman.qmul.ac.uk/research/
  research-centres/centreforethicsandpolitics/events/.

Web

Africa Is a Country. https://africasacountry.com/about.
Arab News. Erdogan Appoints Himself Head of Turkey's Wealth Fund.
  Arab News. 12 September 2018.   www.arabnews.com/node/1371121/
  business-economy.
Bove, Arianna. *Generation Online*. http://generation-online.org/other/discussion.htm
Chimurenga Chronic (July 2015). *Muzmin/The Sahara Is Not a Boundary*.
Counter/Mapping QMary. https://countermappingqmary.blogspot.com/.
Federici, Silvia (2012). African Roots of United States University Struggles
  from the Occupy Movement to the Anti-Student-Debt Campaign. *eipcp*.
  http://eipcp.net/transversal/0112/federici/en.
Giacalone, Robert (2013). Virtual Editor, Business Ethics and Management
  Education. *Academy of Management Learning and Education*. http://aom.org/
  BusinessEthics/.
Harney, Stefano (18 November 2010). The Heart of Good Business. *Times
  Higher Education*.   www.timeshighereducation.com/news/the-heart-of-
  good-business/414296.article.
Harney, Stefano (24 March 2011). Touches of Evil. *Times Higher Education*.
Harney, Stefano (30 July 2009). Experience Is Not Enough. *Times Higher
  Education*. www.timeshighereducation.com/news/experience-is-not-enough/
  407552.article.
Harney, Stefano (17 November 2011). Occupied by Fear. *Times Higher Education*.
Harney, Stefano and Dowling, Emma (27 May 2012). It Is Time That
  Business Schools Learnt to Walk the Walk. *Financial Times*. www.ft.com/
  content/0057e972-5e38-11e1-85f6-00144feabdc0.
Harvard Business Review (January–February 2018). *The Culture Factor*. https://
  hbr.org/2018/01/the-culture-factor.
History. *Market Theatre*. https://markettheatre.co.za/history.

Human Resources. Equality Data. *Queen Mary.* http://hr.qmul.ac.uk/equality/
data/.

Kavanagh, Donncha (2010). Reviewing March's Vision. *28th Standing Conference
on Organisational Symbolism.* Lille.

Mbembe, Achille (29 June 2016). Africa in the New Century. *Africa Is a
Country.* https://africasacountry.com/2016/06/africa-in-the-new-century.

Menon, Nivedita (15 July 2016). It Isn't about Women. *The Hindu.*
www.thehindu.com/opinion/lead/It-isn%E2%80%99t-about-women/
article14488767.ece.

Minor Compositions. http://minorcompositions.info/.

Mishra, Pankaj. Narehdra Modi: The Devisive Manipulator Who Charmed the
World. *The Guardian.* 9 November 2015. www.theguardian.com/world/2015/
nov/09/narendra-modi-the-divisive-manipulator-who-charmed-the-world.

Mufuruki, Ali (2014). *Is Africa Really 'Rising'?* TEDxEUston. www.youtube.com/
watch?v=OjgJ2KpyJ5w.

Newfield, Christopher (13 September 2018). Remaking the Humanities Story: A
Piece of Missing Theory. *Remaking the University.*
http://utotherescue.blogspot.com/2018/09/rewriting-humanities-story-
piece-of.html.

Newfield, Christopher (16 December 2015). The Humanities as Service
Departments: Facing the Budget Logic. *Profession (MLA Humanities
Commons).* https://profession.mla.hcommons.org/2015/12/16/the-
humanities-as-service-departments-facing-the-budget-logic/.

Nshemereirwe, Connie (2016b). How a Theory Born in the 1930s Could Transform
African Education Systems. *The Conversation.* https://theconversation.com/
how-a-theory-born-in-the-1930s-could-transform-african-education-
systems-62201.

Nshemereirwe, Connie (27 June 2016a). An Education That Liberates – Paulo
Freire. https://learngrowrepeat.wordpress.com/2016/06/27/discovering-
freire/.

Pasquinelli, Matteo. The Sabotage of Rent. *Cesura Acceso.* http://cesura-
acceso.org/issues/the-sabotage-of-rent-matteo-pasquinelli/.

Queen Mary Countermapping Collective and the Counter-Cartographies
Collective (2012). Countermap of the University. *Countermap Collection.*
http://countermapcollection.org/collection/countermap-university/.

Queen Mary Countermapping Collective. Countermapping the University.
Lateral. http://csalateral.org/issue1/content/countermapping.html.

Reid, Michael. Jair Bolsonaro and the Perversion of Liberalism. *The Economist.* 27
October 2018. www.economist.com/the-americas/2018/10/27/jair-bolsonaro-
and-the-perversion-of-liberalism.

Ross, Andrew (11 May 2011). Middle East: Rights, Freedom and Offshore
Academics. *University World News.* www.universityworldnews.com/
article.php?story=20110429165843773.

Singapore Management University (2019). www.smu.edu.sg/programmes/
core-curriculum

Thanks, Pop. Donald Trump's Inheritance. *The Economist.* 6 October 2018.
www.economist.com/united-states/2018/10/06/donald-trumps-inheritance.

The Art of Rent. *Generation Online.* http://generation-online.org/other/
    artofrent.htm.
University of California Irvine (1966). *1966–67 Catalogue.*
Wainaina, Binyanvanga (2005). How to Write about Africa. *Granta.* https://
    granta.com/How-to-Write-about-Africa/.
We are the Paper. http://wearethepaper.org/.
Wolfe, Audra (28 August 2013). Defending Cold War Science. *Berfrois.*
    www.berfrois.com/2013/08/cold-war-social-science-by-audra-j-wolfe/.
Zingales, Luigi (2013). Do Business Schools Incubate Criminals? *Bloomberg.*
    www.bloomberg.com/news/2012-07-16/do-business-schools-incubate-
    criminals-.html.

Index